Random House
Bad Speller's
Dictionary

Random House
Bad Speller's
Dictionary

Second Edition

Joseph Krevisky
and Jordan L. Linfield

RANDOM HOUSE
NEW YORK

ISBN: 0-679-76433-X

Manufactured in the United States of America
9 8 7 6 5 4 3 2

New York   Toronto   London   Sydney   Auckland

Introduction

It has been thirty years since we wrote the first book that answered the Catch-22 of spelling: *How do I find a word in the dictionary if I don't know how to spell it?* Our answer was simple: *Look it up by its wrong spelling.* So we compiled the first dictionary for bad spellers—which so many of us are (some of us even flaunt it as a badge of pride). The nearly two million copies of the *Bad Speller's Dictionary* that have been sold confirm the persistence of the spelling problem. In fact, our vast new collection of actual examples of misspellings from many sources—television, newspapers, magazines, advertisements, correspondence, essays, memos—suggests that the phenomenon has become much worse. That deterioration has been accelerated by our educational system, too much television, excessive reliance on electronic spell checkers, and the emergence of so many new words.

That's why we have prepared this new revised and enlarged edition for the 1990's. We have added thousands of current words from business, computers, entertainment, medicine, psychology, religion, science, and the law.

It's Our English Language

The main source of our problems with spelling is the irregular crazy pattern of English spelling. A late-night TV talk show displayed an ad for a bug killer that kills your *aunts* [ants]. A leading newspaper ran a headline about a boat race that read: "Neither knew who *one*" [won]. Another paper called a tough cop a *psyhco* [psycho]. The American Library Association, a model of correctness, passed out a flyer that read: "Information pollution: *whose* fouling our system?" [who's] And the diplomas for one year's graduates of the U.S. Naval Academy read, "U.S. *Navel* Academy."

The other source of our spelling problems is the fact that spelling and pronunciation often simply don't match. In other languages, such as Spanish, letters always have the same pronunciation. Spanish *i* is always pronounced like the *ee* in *feet*, the *a* like the *a* in *father*, the *u* like the *oo* in *fool*. English vowels, on the other hand, have many varied pronunciations. *A* is one sound in *hat*, another in *hate*, still another in *all*, in *care*, in *father*. *E* is *ee* in *cede*, *eh* in *sell*, *u* in *berth*, a little like the *ai* of *air* in the word *where*, and so on. Consonants are a bit easier to handle, but you still have the *c* of *cell* and the *s* of *sell*, the *c* of *coffee* and the *k* of *kernel*.

Turn it around and start with sounds, and it's just as confusing. The long *a* sound of *hate* is *ei* in *weight* or *feign* and *ai* in *wait*. The long *e* sound, as in *feet*, shows up as *feat, mien, believe, receive,* and *recede.*

While Spanish vowels are all pronounced distinctly, regardless of their location in the word, this is not so in English. In multisyllabic words we often pronounce only the vowel in the stressed syllable clearly and slur the other syllables. The other vowels often tend to have the same buried sound—something like "uh" or "ih," regardless of whether the vowel is *a, e, i, o,* or *u. Vacation* becomes "vuhcation," *innocent* is "insent," *probably* is "probibly" or (running the two *b*'s together) "probly." We strongly urge you to rely on your dictionary to check the pronunciation of words, as this will often help you to spell correctly.

Words that look or sound alike create special difficulties. Confusion of words that seem as simple as *to, too,* and *two* and *there, their,* and *they're* are commonplace. We certainly can't rely on our computer spell checkers, which lack the capacity to spot look-alikes or sound-alikes. This popular poem describes the dilemma well:

Spellbound

I have a spelling checker,
It came with my PC;
It plainly marks four my revue
Mistakes I cannot sea.
I've run this poem threw it,
I'm sure your please too no,
Its letter perfect in it's weigh,
My checker tolled me sew.

How to Use This Dictionary

The **Bad Speller's Dictionary** has three sections—a list of incorrect and correct spellings, a list of words that look or sound alike, and a quick list of correct spellings.

Incorrect/Correct List

This section is a collection of thousands of commonly misspelled words arranged alphabetically by their misspellings so that you can find the word by looking for it either as you think it's spelled or by the way it sounds. The phonetic misspelling is a common source of error. Looking for this type of misspelling is the easiest way to find a word when you're not sure how to spell it.

You will find the incorrect spelling in the left-hand column of this section, and the correct spelling in the right-hand column. Thus, if you have an "addiction" to "CD-ROMs" for your "computer" and you're not sure of the spellings, you will find:

Incorrect	Correct
adiktion	addiction
ceedee rom	CD-ROM
seedy rom	CD ROM
cumputer	computer

It's important that you check the *complete* correct spelling in the right-hand column, for while we focus on initial errors, we have also included additional misspellings in other parts of the word. Thus, we show "innsomia" for "insomnia" to emphasize, at the beginning of the word, the common error of doubling a consonant; but we add the omission of the "n" near the end to underscore the tendency to drop consonants when they have a difficult sound like "mn."

Look/Sound Alikes Section

This section provides a carefully selected list of some of the most common and important words that are confused because they look or sound alike. A brief definition or key word enables you to distinguish the meanings of the pairs (or triplets, or quadruplets). Examples:

abject (spiritless), **object** (a material thing; to oppose)
infect (contaminate), **infest** (swarm), **invest** (to put in money)

Quick List of Correct Spellings

The Quick List of Correct Spellings includes all the words from the "Correct" part of the Incorrect/Correct list, plus all the main entries in the Look/Sound Alikes section. Thus, if you are reasonably confident about the spelling of a word, you can check this list first.

Double Asterisk (**)

A double asterisk after a correct spelling on the Incorrect/Correct List or on the Quick List means that the word also appears in the Look/Sound Alike section. Take the word "piece," meaning a portion. This is often misspelled "*peice*." But it is also sometimes confused with its homonym "peace," meaning absence of conflict.

We would welcome your sending us examples—clippings, memos, etc., for our future editions. Send them to us at Innovation Press, c/o Random House. Many thanks, and have some fun, too.

Incorrect	Correct	Incorrect	Correct
abait	**abate**	abuze	**abuse**
abaration	**aberration****	abzurd	**absurd**
abarent	**aberrant****	accademic	**academic**
abarigine	**aborigine**	acceed	**accede****
abawtion	**abortion**	accerasy	**accuracy**
abbandon	**abandon**	accidently	**accidentally**
abbatement	**abatement**	acclame	**acclaim**
abbet	**abet**	accnowledge	
abblaze	**ablaze**		**acknowledge**
abbolition	**abolition**	accoustics	**acoustics**
abborshun	**abortion**	accownt	**account**
abbort	**abort****	accrew	**accrue**
abbout	**about**	accrobat	**acrobat**
abbrasive	**abrasive**	accross	**across**
abbsorb	**absorb**	accrostic	**acrostic**
abbstinence	**abstinence**	accumen	**acumen**
abbstrak	**abstract****	accur	**occur****
abbuze	**abuse**	accurit	**accurate**
abby	**abbey**	accurred	**occurred**
abdeman	**abdomen**	accute	**acute**
abduck	**abduct**	acennd	**ascend**
abel	**able**	acertain	**ascertain**
abeld	**abled**	acheive	**achieve**
abelism	**ableism**	Ackilles heel	**Achilles heel**
aberation	**abrasion****	acktivist	**activist**
abharant	**abhorrent****	ackustics	**acoustics**
abhoar	**abhor**	ackwire	**acquire**
abillity	**ability**	aclame	**acclaim**
abiss	**abyss**	aclimate	**acclimate**
abjeck	**abject****	acnowledgement	
abley	**ably**		**acknowledgment**
abnoxious	**obnoxious**	acommodate	
abragate	**abrogate****		**accommodate**
abraid	**abrade**	acompany	**accompany**
abreviate	**abbreviate**	acompanyment	
abrup	**abrupt**		**accompaniment**
absalutuly	**absolutely**	acomplice	**accomplice****
abscence	**absence**	acomplish	**accomplish****
abserd	**absurd**	acord	**accord**
absess	**abscess****	acordion	**accordion**
absint	**absent**	acost	**accost**
abstanance	**abstinence**	acount	**account**
abstetrician	**obstetrician**	acountent	**accountant**
abt	**apt**		

Incorrect	Correct	Incorrect	Correct
acquantence		adenda	**addenda**
	acquaintance	adequatly	**adequately**
acquasition	**acquisition**	adged	**aged**
acquitle	**acquittal**	adict	**addict**
acrabat	**acrobat**	adige	**adage**
acredidation		adiktion	**addiction**
	accreditation	adinoma	**adenoma**
acredit	**accredit**	adishon	**edition****
acrege	**acreage**	adition	**addition****
acros	**across**	adjatent	**adjutant**
acrue	**accrue**	adjustible	**adjustable**
acselerate	**accelerate**	admanition	**admonition**
acsesery	**accessory**	admendment	**amendment**
acshual	**actual**	admerable	**admirable**
acsident	**accident****	adminnistrater	
actavist	**activist**		**administrator**
acter	**actor**	admisable	**admissible**
actualy	**actually****	admitance	**admittance**
acuire	**acquire**	admition	**admission**
acumenacal	**ecumenical**	adolesent	**adolescent**
acumulate	**accumulate**	adoor	**adore**
acurecy	**accuracy**	adop	**adopt****
acuse	**accuse**	adress	**address**
acustom	**accustom**	aduce	**adduce****
acwitt	**acquit**	advanse	**advance**
adam	**atom**	advantige	**advantage**
adaquete	**adequate**	advizable	**advisable**
addams apple		advizer	**adviser**
	Adam's apple	advisery	**advisory**
addement	**adamant**	advurtize	**advertise**
addhere	**adhere**	adyou	**adieu****
addhesion	**adhesion**	afair	**affair****
addick	**addict**	afect	**affect****
addmanition	**admonition**	affire	**afire**
addministeration		affraid	**afraid**
	administration	Africca	**Africa**
addmiral	**admiral**	afgan	**Afghan**
addmit	**admit**	afible	**affable**
addorible	**adorable**	afidavit	**affidavit**
addrenal	**adrenal**	afiliate	**affiliate**
addult	**adult**	afinity	**affinity**
addvantagous		afirm	**affirm**
	advantageous	afirmative	**affirmative**
addvertisement		afix	**affix**
	advertisement	aflict	**afflict**
adelesense	**adolescence**	afluence	**affluence**

Incorrect	Correct	Incorrect	Correct
aford	**afford**	airea	**area****
aforizm	**aphorism**	aireel	**aerial**
afrade	**afraid**	Aireh	**Eire****
afront	**affront**	airis	**heiress**
afrontry	**effrontery**	airlume	**heirloom**
aftakare	**aftercare**	airobic	**aerobic**
aftanoon	**afternoon**	airoplane	**airplane**
aftawerds	**afterwards**	Aisha	**Asia**
afthalmologist		aithe	**eighth**
	ophthalmologist	ajacent	**adjacent**
afurmative	**affirmative**	ajed	**aged**
agany	**agony**	ajeism	**ageism**
agast	**aghast**	ajenda	**agenda**
ageing	**aging**	ajile	**agile**
agenst	**against**	ajudication	**adjudication**
agensy	**agency**	ajurn	**adjourn****
agern	**adjourn****	ajustable	**adjustable**
agervate	**aggravate**	ajutent	**adjutant**
aggrarian	**agrarian**	akademy	**academy**
aggree	**agree**	ake	**ache**
aggreshun	**aggression****	aker	**acre**
aggriculture	**agriculture**	aklaim	**acclaim**
agground	**aground**	akne	**acne****
aggue	**ague**	aknolege	**acknowledge**
agillity	**agility**	akolite	**acolyte**
agincys	**agencies**	akording	**according**
aginise	**agonize**	aks	**axe****
agism	**ageism**	akseed	**accede****
agoe	**ago**	aksel	**axle****
agrafobia	**agoraphobia**	akselerate	**accelerate**
agrandize	**aggrandize**	aksent	**accent****
agreable	**agreeable**	akses	**axis****
agread	**agreed**	aksess	**access****
agregate	**aggregate**	aksidents	**accidents****
agreing	**agreeing**	aktiv	**active**
agressive	**aggressive**	akute	**acute**
agrieved	**aggrieved**	akward	**awkward**
ahmond	**almond**	akyupunkcher	
ahmz	**alms****		**acupuncture**
ahnroot	**en route**	alagy	**allergy****
ahntray	**entrée**	albyumin	**albumin**
ahnwee	**ennui**	alcahole	**alcohol**
ahts	**arts**	aleby	**alibi**
aile	**aisle****	aleet	**elite**
ainshent	**ancient**	alege	**allege****
air aparent	**heir apparent**	alegiance	**allegiance**

Incorrect	Correct	Incorrect	Correct
alegro	**allegro**	altoe	**alto**
alergy	**allergy****	altrueizm	**altruism**
aleveate	**alleviate**	alturnit	**alternate****
alfabet	**alphabet**	alude	**allude****
alfanoomeric		alure	**allure**
	alphanumeric	alurgic	**allergic**
alfer	**alpha**	alyanation	**alienation**
alian	**alien**	amallgamated	
aliance	**alliance**		**amalgamated**
aline	**align**	amature	**amateur****
aljee	**algae**	amaty	**amity****
alkamy	**alchemy**	ambbasador	**ambassador**
alkohol	**alcohol**	ambbiguous	**ambiguous**
alkoholic	**alcoholic**	ambeance	**ambiance** or
alla kart	**à la carte**		**ambience**
allanon	**Al-anon**	ambolism	**embolism**
allbino	**albino**	ambyalance	**ambulance**
alldenty	**al dente**	amealiorate	**ameliorate**
allee	**alley****	ameeba	**amoeba**
allert	**alert**	ameritus	**emeritus**
allgorythm	**algorithm**	amerous	**amorous**
allie	**ally****	amfetamine	**amphetamine**
allimoney	**alimony**	aminable	**amenable**
allkoholism	**alcoholism**	amiosentesis	
allmanac	**almanac**		**amniocentesis**
allmighty	**almighty**	ammalgam	**amalgam**
allmost	**almost**	ammbition	**ambition**
allone	**alone**	ammend	**amend****
alloof	**aloof**	Ammerican	**American**
allottment	**allotment**	ammex	**AMEX**
allowence	**allowance**	ammity	**amity****
allready	**already****	ammount	**amount**
allso	**also**	ammplafacation	
although	**although**		**amplification**
alltogether	**altogether****	ammtrack	**Amtrak**
alluminum	**aluminum**	amneezha	**amnesia**
always	**always****	amonia	**ammonia**
almer matter	**alma mater**	amoor	**amour****
alocate	**allocate**	amoung	**among**
alot	**allot**	ampeer	**ampere**
alow	**allow****	amplafy	**amplify**
alowed	**allowed****	ampp	**amp**
alright	**all right**	ampythitter	**amphitheater**
alsoeran	**also ran**	ampyutate	**amputate**
altar ego	**alter ego**	amuk	**amok**
altenate	**alternate****	amunition	**ammunition**

Incorrect	Correct	Incorrect	Correct
amusment	**amusement**	annew	**anew**
amuze	**amuse**	annger	**anger**
amyable	**amiable****	anngora	**angora**
analise	**analyze****	annima	**anima****
analitic	**analytic**	annimal	**animal****
anamal	**animal****	annimus	**animus**
anamoly	**anomaly**	annoint	**anoint**
anbolic	**anabolic**	annomaly	**anomaly**
anceint	**ancient**	annomy	**anomie****
ancologist	**oncologist**	anntartika	**Antarctica**
aneemic	**anemic**	anntasid	**antacid**
anend	**anent**	anntena	**antenna**
anereksia nervous		anntrax	**anthrax**
	anorexia nervosa	annuel	**annual****
anewity	**annuity**	annull	**annul****
anewrism	**aneurism or**	anologous	**analogous**
	aneurysm	anonimus	**anonymous**
anex	**annex**	anotate	**annotate**
anfetamine	**amphetamine**	anouncement	
angery	**angry**		**announcement**
angwish	**anguish**	anoyence	**annoyance**
angziety	**anxiety**	anplifier	**amplifier**
anihilate	**annihilate**	anpule	**ampule****
anilgesic	**analgesic**	anputation	**amputation**
anilist	**analyst****	anputee	**amputee**
anjina	**angina**	anpyatate	**amputate**
anjioma	**angioma**	anser	**answer**
anjycardeogram		ansester	**ancestor**
	angiocardeogram	ansestree	**ancestry**
ank	**ankh**	anshent	**ancient**
ankaman	**anchorman**	antabody	**antibody**
ankel	**ankle**	antaganist	**antagonist**
anker	**anchor**	antartic	**antarctic**
ankshus	**anxious**	antaseptic	**antiseptic**
ankst	**angst**	antatoksin	**antitoxin**
annalasis	**analysis**	antchovy	**anchovy**
annaljesic	**analgesic**	ante-American	
annalog	**analog****		**anti-American**
annalogy	**analogy**	antebiotic	**antibiotic**
annatomy	**anatomy**	antedepresent	
anndroyd	**android**		**antidepressant**
annecdotal	**anecdotal**	anteek	**antique****
annecdote	**anecdote**	antehistomin	
annerexia	**anorexia**		**antihistamine**
annesthetic	**anesthetic**	antisapate	**anticipate**
		antisedent	**antecedent**

Incorrect	Correct	Incorrect	Correct
antiseed	**antecede**	appauled	**appalled**
antybody	**antibody**	appeel	**appeal**
anual	**annual****	appeerence	**appearance**
anualee	**annually**	appellete	**appellate**
anuity	**annuity**	appenndisitis	**appendicitis**
anull	**annul****	appere	**appear**
anulled	**annulled**	apperence	**appearance**
anurism	**aneurism or**	applys	**applies**
	aneurysm	apnia	**apnea**
anuther	**another**	appointy	**appointee**
anwee	**ennui**	appologize	**apologize**
any where	**anywhere**	appology	**apology****
apagee	**apogee**	appostrophe	**apostrophe**
aparatus	**apparatus**	appraisel	**appraisal**
aparel	**apparel**	apprenntise	**apprentice**
aparent	**apparent**	appreshible	**appreciable**
apartide	**apartheid**	appropo	**apropos**
apathesis	**apotheosis**	appptitude	**aptitude**
apaul	**appall**	apraise	**appraise****
apeal	**appeal**	apreciate	**appreciate**
apear	**appear**	aprecot	**apricot**
apease	**appease**	aprehend	**apprehend**
apeks	**apex**	aprentice	**apprentice**
apell	**apple**	aprin	**apron**
apellate	**appellate**	aproach	**approach**
apend	**append**	apropriate	**appropriate**
apendectomy		aprove	**approve**
	appendectomy	aproximate	**approximate**
apendix	**appendix**	aquaintance	**acquaintance**
apetite	**appetite****	aquire	**acquire**
aphrocentric	**Afrocentric**	aquisition	**acquisition**
aplacater	**applicator**	aquittal	**acquittal**
aplaud	**applaud**	aquitted	**acquitted**
apliance	**appliance**	aragant	**arrogant**
aplicant	**applicant**	araign	**arraign****
aplication	**application**	arange	**arrange****
aplum	**aplomb**	aray	**array**
aply	**apply**	arbatrate	**arbitrate**
apoinment	**appointment**	arber	**arbor**
apoint	**appoint**	arbitery	**arbitrary**
apokriful	**apocryphal**	ardeco	**art deco**
apologize	**apologize**	aready	**already****
apologys	**apologies**	arears	**arrears**
aposle	**apostle****	arebag	**airbag**
apparentally	**apparently**	areena	**arena**
appartment	**apartment**	arest	**arrest**

Incorrect	Correct	Incorrect	Correct
arewaves	**airwaves**	artical	**article**
argo	**argot**	artilery	**artillery**
arguement	**argument**	artisticly	**artistically**
argyue	**argue**	artry	**artery**
arial	**aerial**	artwear	**artware**
ariola	**areola**	arye	**awry**
ariseing	**arising**	arythimia	**arrhythmia**
arithmatic	**arithmetic**	asadosis	**acidosis**
arithmia	**arrhythmia**	asalt	**assault**
arive	**arrive**	asanine	**asinine**
arkade	**arcade**	asasinate	**assassinate**
arkaic	**archaic**	asassin	**assassin**
arkangel	**archangel**	asault	**assault**
arkatipe	**archetype**	asay	**assay****
arkeology	**archeology**	asaylent	**assailant**
Arkinsaw	**Arkansas**	ascance	**askance**
arkitect	**architect**	asemble	**assemble**
arkives	**archives**	asent	**assent****
armastice	**armistice**	aserb	**acerb**
armfull	**armful**	asert	**assert****
arodynamics		asess	**assess**
	aerodynamics	aset	**asset**
arogance	**arrogance**	asetone	**acetone**
arogant	**arrogant**	asfalt	**asphalt**
aronautics	**aeronautics**	asfixia	**asphyxia**
aroogala	**arugula**	ashaimed	**ashamed**
arosol	**aerosol**	ashawr	**ashore**
arow	**arrow**	ashin	**ashen**
arrabesk	**arabesque**	ashure	**assure**
arraingment	**arrangement**	asid	**acid**
arrane	**arraign****	asign	**assign**
arrcive	**archive**	asimilationist	
arressted	**arrested**		**assimilationist**
arrise	**arise**	asist	**assist**
arristocrat	**aristocrat**	asistent	**assistant**
arrivel	**arrival**	askee	**ASCII**
arround	**around**	asma	**asthma**
arrouse	**arouse****	asociate	**associate**
arrsenic	**arsenic**	asorbtion	**absorption**
artafakt	**artifact**	asparation	**aspiration**
artaficial	**artificial**	aspirent	**aspirant****
arte	**art**	asprin	**aspirin****
artee	**arty**	assale	**assail**
arterosklerosis		assalt	**assault**
	arteriosclerosis	assesed	**assessed**
artic	**arctic**	assimilateable	**assimilable**

Incorrect	Correct	Incorrect	Correct
assinement	**assignment****	atrosity	**atrocity**
assinine	**asinine**	attavism	**atavism**
assistence	**assistance****	attom	**atom**
assoshiation	**association**	attone	**atone**
asspargis	**asparagus**	aturney	**attorney**
assperin	**aspirin****	audable	**audible**
asspire	**aspire**	audeofile	**audiophile**
asstigmatizm	**astigmatism**	audiance	**audience**
asstonish	**astonish**	Augest	**August**
asstrigent	**astringent**	augziliary	**auxiliary****
asstronimy	**astronomy**	aukward	**awkward**
assylum	**asylum**	auntitoksin	**antitoxin**
ast	**asked**	aunuled	**annulled**
astablish	**establish**	autabigraphy	**autobiography**
asternot	**astronaut**		
astoot	**astute**	autaimunity	**autoimmunity**
astrangement			
	estrangement	autamatic	**automatic**
asume	**assume**	autamobile	**automobile**
asurence	**assurance****	autapilot	**autopilot**
asurtive	**assertive**	auther	**author**
atach	**attach****	authority	**authority**
atack	**attack****	autoefocus	**autofocus**
atact	**attacked**	automashun	
atain	**attain**		**automation****
atashay	**attaché****	auxilary	**auxiliary****
atemt	**attempt**	avalable	**available**
atend	**attend**	avan-guard	**avant-garde**
atendence	**attendance****	avantage	**advantage**
atendent	**attendant**	aveary	**aviary**
atenshun	**attention**	aveater	**aviator**
atenyuate	**attenuate**	aved	**avid**
atest	**attest**	aventitious	**adventitious**
athalete	**athlete**	avilanch	**avalanche**
athaletic	**athletic**	avocate	**advocate**
athritis	**arthritis**	avoidible	**avoidable**
athyist	**atheist**	avrage	**average**
atic	**attic**	avursion	**aversion**
atire	**attire**	avvenue	**avenue**
atitude	**attitude****	avvokado	**avocado**
atmisfere	**atmosphere**	aw	**awe****
atract	**attract**	awdacious	**audacious**
atrafy	**atrophy**	awdiance	**audience**
atreum	**atrium**	awdio	**audio**
atribute	**attribute**	awdit	**audit**
atrition	**attrition**	awditoriem	**auditorium**

Incorrect	Correct	Incorrect	Correct
awear	**aware**	ayclair	**éclair**
awefel	**awful****	ayelash	**eyelash**
aweight	**await**	ayeth	**eighth**
awktion	**auction**	ayker	**acre**
awkwid	**awkward**	ayleet	**élite**
awra	**aura**	ayleus	**alias**
aw revoir	**au revoir**	aymanorea	**amenorrhea**
awrgee	**orgy**	aymen	**amen**
awsome	**awesome**	aynus	**anus****
awsteer	**austere**	ayorta	**aorta**
awt	**ought****	aypron	**apron**
awthentick	**authentic**	ayress	**heiress**
awthorety	**authority**	ayrobics	**aerobics**
awtimaticly	**acentric****	aysentric	**acentric****
	automatically	aysian	**Asian**
awtism	**autism**	aytheist	**atheist**
awtum	**autumn**	azbestus	**asbestos**
axident	**accident**	Azher	**Asia**
axxed	**asked**	azma	**asthma**

Incorrect	Correct	Incorrect	Correct
babeesit	**babysit**	balence	**balance**
bachler	**bachelor**	balerina	**ballerina**
backinal	**bacchanal**	baleywick	**bailiwick**
backround	**background**	balistics	**ballistics**
backwerd	**backward**	balital	**belittle**
bagage	**baggage**	balkany	**balcony**
bagd	**bagged**	ballid	**ballad****
bage	**badge**	ballit	**ballot****
baggs	**bags**	baloon	**balloon**
bagin	**begin**	balpoint	**ballpoint**
baheemoth	**behemoth**	bambu	**bamboo**
bahn	**barn**	bamitsvah	**Bar Mitzvah**
baige	**beige**	bamy	**balmy**
baist	**baste**	bananna	**banana**
bakbone	**backbone**	bancwet	**banquet****
bakkstabber	**backstabber**	bandige	**bandage**
baklog	**backlog**	baner	**banner**
bakon	**bacon**	bangoes	**banjos**
bakteria	**bacteria**	banista	**banister**
baktrack	**backtrack**	bankrup	**bankrupt**
balay	**ballet****	bankrupcy	**bankruptcy**
bale out	**bailout**	bannana	**banana**

Incorrect	Correct	Incorrect	Correct
banndana	**bandana**	batton	**baton**
banndit	**bandit**	battry	**battery**
bannish	**banish**	baught	**bought****
banwaggen	**bandwagon**	bawd rait	**baud rate**
bapptise	**baptize**	bawk	**balk**
baptiss	**Baptist**	bawsht	**borscht**
baracks	**barracks**	baybe	**baby**
barage	**barrage**	baye	**bey**
barate	**berate**	baygel	**bagel**
barbacue	**barbecue**	baysball	**baseball**
barbeturate	**barbiturate**	bayshing	**Beijing**
bareeved	**bereaved**	baysment	**basement**
barell	**barrel**	bazzoka	**bazooka**
bargin	**bargain**	beap	**beep**
baricuda	**barracuda**	bearfaced	**barefaced**
barier	**barrier**	beatle	**beetle**
barikade	**barricade**	beautyful	**beautiful**
barish	**bearish**	becomeing	**becoming**
barly	**barley**	becon	**beacon**
barmshell	**bombshell**	becum	**become**
barnfire	**bonfire**	becuz	**because**
barrberian	**barbarian**	beddbug	**bedbug**
barrometer	**barometer**	bedder	**better****
basall	**basal**	beddmate	**bedmate**
bashe	**bash**	bedspred	**bedspread**
basicly	**basically**	beealy	**bialy**
basik	**basic**	bee-bee-ess	**BBS**
basitracin	**bacitracin**	beefor	**before**
basiz	**basis****	beegan	**began**
bassin	**basin**	beehaf	**behalf**
bassk	**bask**	beenball	**beanball**
bassketbawl	**basketball**	beeoh	**B.O.**
bassmitzve	**Bas Mitzvah**	beeref	**bereft**
bassque	**Basque**	beest	**beast**
bastid	**bastard****	beestial	**bestial**
bata	**beta**	beestro	**bistro**
batallian	**battalion**	beever	**beaver**
batared baby		beeware	**beware**
	battered baby	beewilder	**bewilder**
batchler	**bachelor**	befor	**before**
baten	**batten**	befrend	**befriend**
baterd wimmen		begel	**bagel**
	battered women	beger	**beggar**
batered wife	**battered wife**	beginer	**beginner**
batery	**battery**	begining	**beginning**
batray	**betray**	behavier	**behavior**

Incorrect	Correct	Incorrect	Correct
beir	**bier****	bestyal	**bestial**
beladona	**belladonna**	beuty	**beauty**
beleaf	**belief**	bevrage	**beverage**
beleive	**believe**	biakemistry	**biochemistry**
belicose	**bellicose**	Bibel	**Bible**
beligerant	**belligerent**	biche	**bitch**
belitel	**belittle**	bied	**bide****
bellfree	**belfry**	bigest	**biggest**
beltweigh	**Beltway**	biggamy	**bigamy**
belweather	**bellwether**	biggot	**bigot**
bely	**belie****	biggshot	**big shot**
benafit	**benefit**	biggwig	**bigwig**
bended	**bent**	bilbord	**billboard**
benefishal	**beneficial**	bild	**build****
benefishery	**beneficiary**	bilet	**billet**
beneith	**beneath**	biliard	**billiard**
benifited	**benefited**	biline	**byline**
benine	**benign**	bilion	**billion**
bennevelent	**benevolent**	bilionnaire	**billionaire**
bennzacane	**benzocaine**	billyus	**bilious**
benshmark	**benchmark**	bilofair	**bill of fare**
benz	**bends**	bilt	**built**
beogrephy	**biography**	bilyus	**bilious**
beond	**beyond**	bimmbo	**bimbo**
beopsy	**biopsy**	binay brith	**B'nai B'rith**
bequethe	**bequeath**	binery	**binary**
beray	**beret**	binnoculars	**binoculars**
berbin	**bourbon**	biosentrism	**biocentrism**
berden	**burden**	bipass	**bypass**
berger	**burger**	birdy	**birdie**
bergler	**burglar**	bisek	**bisect**
berglery	**burglary**	biseps	**biceps**
berial	**burial**	bisk	**bisque**
berieved	**bereaved**	biskit	**biscuit**
berlap	**burlap**	bisy	**busy**
berlesk	**burlesque**	biten	**bitten**
bernout	**burnout**	biter	**bitter**
bernt	**burnt**	bivawhacked	**bivouacked**
berryberry	**beriberi**	bivwak	**bivouac**
berser	**bursar****	biyou	**bayou**
bersitis	**bursitis**	bizness	**business**
berst	**burst**	bizz	**biz**
berthmother	**birthmother**	blader	**bladder**
berthstone	**birthstone**	blair	**blare**
beseige	**besiege****	blakbord	**blackboard**
beserk	**berserk**	blakgard	**blackguard**

Incorrect	Correct	Incorrect	Correct
blakhed	**blackhead**	boch	**botch****
blakmale	**blackmail**	bodd	**bod**
blamless	**blameless**	boddy	**body**
blanche	**blanch**	boddygard	**bodyguard**
blankit	**blanket**	bodiss-ripper	**bodice-ripper**
blasay	**blasé**	boggocity	**bogosity**
blasfemy	**blasphemy**	bogin	**bogon**
blasst	**blast**	bogis	**bogus**
blasster	**blaster**	boicot	**boycott**
blaytant	**blatant**	boid	**bird**
blead	**bleed**	boistrous	**boisterous**
bleap	**bleep****	bokay	**bouquet**
bledd	**bled**	bolester	**bolster**
bleech	**bleach**	bom	**bomb****
bleek	**bleak**	bombox	**boombox**
blerb	**blurb**	bonde	**boned**
blest	**blessed**	bondfire	**bonfire**
bleve	**believe**	bone vivante	**bon vivant**
blined	**blind**	bonet	**bonnet**
blisster	**blister**	boney	**bony****
blite	**blight**	bonion	**bunion**
blith	**blithe**	bonis	**bonus**
blits	**blitz**	bon swar	**bon soir**
blizard	**blizzard**	bonz	**bones**
blobb	**blob**	boobu	**bubo**
blockaid	**blockade**	boodwar	**boudoir**
blodbathe	**bloodbath**	booey	**buoy****
blok	**block****	bookay	**bouquet**
blonnd	**blond**	bookeeping	**bookkeeping**
blosom	**blossom**	boorzhwa	**bourgeois**
blote	**bloat****	boose	**booze**
bloted	**bloated**	boosom	**bosom**
bloter	**blotter**	booteek	**boutique**
blowse	**blouse**	bord	**board****
blubaby	**blue baby**	bordaline	**borderline**
blubery	**blueberry**	borow	**borrow**
blublud	**blueblood**	bosa noeva	**bossa nova**
blud	**blood**	bost	**boast**
bluf	**bluff**	bosy	**bossy**
blugen	**bludgeon**	botelneck	**bottleneck**
blunnder	**blunder**	botes	**boats**
blunnt	**blunt**	botom	**bottom**
bluprint	**blueprint**	botsun	**boatswain**
blurr	**blur**	bottel	**bottle**
boan	**bone**	bottimless	**bottomless**

Incorrect	Correct	Incorrect	Correct
botyalism	**botulism**	brokin	**broken**
boundry	**boundary**	brokrage	**brokerage**
bouyant	**buoyant**	bronkiel	**bronchial**
boykot	**boycott**	broshure	**brochure**
boyler plait	**boiler plate**	brounstone	**brownstone**
bozzo	**bozo**	browz	**browse****
brade	**braid****	brue	**brew**
bragart	**braggart**	bruk	**brook**
brah	**bra**	brunkitis	**bronchitis**
brail	**Braille**	brusk	**brusque**
brakeven	**break-even**	bruthers	**brothers**
brakout	**breakout**	bruz	**bruise****
brakup	**breakup**	brybe	**bribe**
brandee	**brandy**	buckel	**buckle**
brane	**brain**	Buda	**Buddha**
branestorm	**brainstorm**	budee	**buddy****
bran-new	**brand-new**	buety	**beauty**
braselet	**bracelet**	bufalo	**buffalo**
braul	**brawl**	bufer	**buffer**
bravry	**bravery**	buffay	**buffet**
bravvado	**bravado**	bufoon	**buffoon**
brawdway	**Broadway**	bugd	**bugged**
brayces	**braces**	buge	**budge**
braysen	**brazen**	bugel	**bugle**
brazere	**brassiere**	bugg	**bug**
breakible	**breakable**	bujet	**budget**
breakthru	**breakthrough**	buk	**buck**
bredth	**breadth****	buke	**book**
breefkase	**briefcase**	buket	**bucket**
breif	**brief**	buksom	**buxom**
brekfast	**breakfast**	buldje	**bulge**
brest	**breast**	buldozer	**bulldozer**
brethern	**brethren**	bulean	**Boolean**
breze	**breeze**	bulit	**bullet**
bridgroom	**bridegroom**	bulitin	**bulletin**
brige	**bridge**	bullemia	**bulemia**
briggader	**brigadier**	bullivard	**boulevard**
briliant	**brilliant**	bullwork	**bulwark**
brissel	**bristle**	bullyon	**bouillon****
Britanica	**Britannica**	buly	**bully**
brite	**bright**	bumbelbee	**bumblebee**
Britin	**Britain****	bumer	**bummer**
britle	**brittle**	bumfog	**BOMFOG**
broak	**broke**	bummper	**bumper**
brocalli	**broccoli**	bundel	**bundle**
broe	**bro'**	bunglow	**bungalow**

Incorrect	Correct	Incorrect	Correct
bunz	**buns**	buyproduct	**byproduct**
burbin	**bourbon**	buz	**buzz**
burch	**birch**	buze	**booze**
burglery	**burglary**	buzwords	**buzzwords**
buriel	**burial**	byass	**bias**
buro	**bureau**	bycultural	**bicultural**
burth mark	**birthmark**	bycuspid	**bicuspid**
burthrite	**birthright**	bycycle	**bicycle**
busibody	**busybody**	byenial	**biennial****
busness	**business**	byeout	**buy-out**
busom	**bosom**	bye-sink	**bissync**
bussel	**bustle**	byfokal	**bifocal**
bussted	**busted**	byin	**buy-in**
busteeay	**bustier**	byle	**bile**
busyly	**busily**	bylingwal	**bilingual**
bute	**boot****	bynary	**binary**
butician	**beautician**	byofeedback	**biofeedback**
butiful	**beautiful**	byology	**biology**
butsher	**butcher**	byonics	**bionics**
butten	**button**	byopsy	**biopsy**
bux	**bucks**	bypolar	**bipolar**

		C	
cabage	**cabbage**	calipso	**calypso**
cabanet	**cabinet**	calizhun	**collision****
cabel	**cable****	calkulus	**calculus**
cach	**catch**	callamity	**calamity**
caddenza	**cadenza**	callender	**calendar****
cafateria	**cafeteria**	callisthenics	**calisthenics**
cafay olay	**café au lait**	calocwiel	**colloquial**
cafeine	**caffeine**	calry	**calorie**
caffay	**café**	calsium	**calcium**
caffs	**calves**	camafloge	**camouflage**
cafkaesk	**Kafkaesque**	camalot	**Camelot**
caigy	**cagey**	camara	**camera**
cairtaker	**caretaker**	camelia	**camellia**
cakafony	**cacophony**	cameradery	**camaraderie**
caktus	**cactus**	camfer	**camphor**
calaco	**calico**	cammcorda	**camcorder**
Calafornia	**California**	canalony	**canneloni**
calcalate	**calculate**	canibis	**cannabis**
caleber	**caliber**	cansel	**cancel**
calidiscope	**kaleidoscope**	canser	**cancer**

Incorrect	Correct	Incorrect	Correct
canvis	**canvas****	carnul	**carnal****
canyen	**canyon**	caroner	**coroner****
caos	**chaos**	carot	**carrot****
capachino	**cappucino**	carowse	**carouse**
capashus	**capacious**	carravan	**caravan**
capcher	**capture**	carrbon dyoxide	
capible	**capable**		**carbon dioxide**
capilary	**capillary**	carrbuncle	**carbuncle**
capitchulate	**capitulate**	carredboard	**cardboard**
capitil	**capital****	carrees	**carries****
caposies sarkoma		carress	**caress**
	Kaposi's Sarcoma	carriage	**carriage**
capp	**cap**	carrjack	**carjack**
cappacity	**capacity**	carrnadge	**carnage**
caprese	**caprice**	carrotid	**carotid**
caprishous	**capricious**	carrpal	**carpal**
capsel	**capsule**	carsinogen	**carcinogen**
capshun	**caption**	cart blansh	**carte blanche**
capt	**capped**	cartalige	**cartilage**
captan	**captain**	cartell	**cartel**
captation fee		cartin	**carton**
	capitation fee	cartune	**cartoon**
carabean	**Caribbean**	carworn	**careworn**
caracter	**character**	carying	**carrying**
caratea	**karate**	casarole	**casserole**
carateen	**carotene**	cascaid	**cascade**
carbahidrate		caset	**cassette**
	carbohydrate	casheer	**cashier**
carben	**carbon**	cashmear	**cashmere**
carberater	**carburetor**	cashoe	**cashew**
carbin monoxide		caskit	**casket**
	carbon monoxide	casmint	**casement**
cardiak	**cardiac**	casock	**cassock**
cardnil	**cardinal**	cassel	**castle**
carear	**career**	cassenova	**Casanova**
carees	**caries****	cassino	**casino**
carefull	**careful**	casstrait	**castrate**
careing	**caring**	castagate	**castigate**
caricatour	**caricature**	castinet	**castanet**
caried	**carried**	casulty	**casualty**
carit	**carat****	cataclism	**cataclysm****
carkass	**carcass**	catagory	**category**
carm	**calm****	catapiller	**caterpillar**
carma	**karma**	catar	**catarrh**
carmel	**caramel**	catastrofy	**catastrophe**
carnivul	**carnival**	catelogue	**catalog**

Incorrect	Correct	Incorrect	Correct
cateract	**cataract**	cemicle	**chemical**
cathater	**catheter**	cenchury	**century**
catheedral	**cathedral**	cencus	**census**∗∗
Cathlic	**Catholic**	cennter	**center**
caticomb	**catacomb**	cenotta	**sonata**
catilyon	**cotillion**	censitivity	**sensitivity**
catipult	**catapult**	centegrade	**centigrade**
catotonic	**catatonic**	centrel	**central**
catridge	**cartridge**	centrifigle	**centrifugal**
CATT skan	**CAT scan**	cerabelum	**cerebellum**
cattfish	**catfish**	cereberal	**cerebral**
cattlike	**catlike**	cerfue	**curfew**
cauff	**cough**∗∗	ceriff	**serif**
cavelcaid	**cavalcade**	cerimony	**ceremony**
caveleir	**cavalier**	certin	**certain**
cavernus	**cavernous**	chace	**chase**
caviatt	**caveat**	chagrinned	**chagrined**
cavvity	**cavity**	chaif	**chafe**
cawcashon	**Caucasian**	chaist	**chaste**∗∗
cawcus	**caucus**	chalenge	**challenge**
cawk	**caulk**	champeen	**champion**
cawleflower	**cauliflower**	champoo	**shampoo**
cawny	**corny**	chane	**chain**
caws sayleb	**cause célèbre**	chanel	**channel**∗∗
cawshun	**caution**	changable	**changeable**
cawz	**cause**∗∗	chanoocah	**Chanukah** or
cayjin	**Cajan or Cajun**		**Hanukah**
caynsian	**Keynesian**	chaplin	**chaplain**
cazm	**chasm**	chapple	**chapel**
cazoo	**kazoo**	charaty	**charity**
ceder	**cedar**	chare	**chair**
cee e oh	**CEO**	chariet	**chariot**
ceedee rom	**CD-ROM**	charrter	**charter**
ceese	**cease**∗∗	chartible	**charitable**
celabacy	**celibacy**	chastaty	**chastity**
celalite	**cellulite**	chater	**chatter**
celebrait	**celebrate**∗∗	chatt	**chat**
cellebrity	**celebrity**	chauffuer	**chauffeur**∗∗
celophane	**cellophane**	chawk	**chalk**
celtser	**seltzer**	chawk tawk	**chalk talk**
celulitis	**cellulitis**	chawtle	**chortle**
celuloid	**celluloid**	cheder	**cheddar**
celulose	**cellulose**	cheep	**cheap**∗∗
celyaler	**cellular**	cheet	**cheat**
cemantics	**semantics**	cheez	**cheese**
cematary	**cemetery**∗∗	cheif	**chief**

Incorrect	Correct	Incorrect	Correct
cheiftin	**chieftain**	cigret	**cigarette**
chelo	**cello**	cilynder	**cylinder**
chemest	**chemist**	ciment	**cement**
cherbert	**sherbet**	cinagog	**synagogue**
cherch	**church**	cinamon	**cinnamon**
cherib	**cherub**	Cinncinatti	**Cincinnati**
cherning	**churning**	cinoshure	**cynosure**
cherrish	**cherish**	circal	**circle**
chesnut	**chestnut**	circomstance	
chestity	**chastity**		**circumstance**
chieftin	**chieftain**	circuler	**circular**
chikkenpoks	**chicken pox**	circumfrence	
children	**children**		**circumference**
chimny	**chimney**	cirkit	**circuit**
chints	**chintz**	cirkumsize	**circumcise**
chipendale	**Chippendale**	cirrcumvent	**circumvent**
chipp	**chip**	cirviks	**cervix**
chivelrus	**chivalrous**	cist	**cyst**
chivelry	**chivalry**	cisterhood	**sisterhood**
chizel	**chisel**	cistitis	**cystitis**
choclit	**chocolate**	cistoscopy	**cystoscopy**
choper	**chopper**	citazen	**citizen**
chorkole	**charcoal**	citris	**citrus**
chossen	**chosen**	cival	**civil**
chouder	**chowder**	civlisation	**civilization**
chow main	**chow mein**	clamer	**clamor**
choyce	**choice**	clamidia	**chlamydia**
chrisanthemun		clanish	**clannish**
	chrysanthemum	clarevoiant	**clairvoyant**
chrisen	**christen****	clarvoiance	**clairvoyance**
Christyan	**Christian****	clasify	**classify**
chuby	**chubby**	clauz	**clause****
chuk	**chuck**	cleanex	**kleenex**
chumy	**chummy**	clearinse	**clearance**
chunel	**Chunnel**	cleek	**clique****
chynatown	**Chinatown**	cleeshay	**cliché**
cibercrud	**cybercrud**	clense	**cleanse**
cibernetics	**cybernetics**	cleptamania	**kleptomania**
ciberspace	**cyberspace**	cleracle	**clerical**
ciborg	**cyborg**	clere	**clear**
ciclamate	**cyclamate**	clevige	**cleavage**
cicle	**cycle**	clientell	**clientele**
ciclone	**cyclone**	climit	**climate**
cicofant	**sycophant**	clincker	**clinker**
cieling	**ceiling****	clinnic	**clinic**
ci-fi	**sci-fi**	cliper	**clipper**

Incorrect	Correct	Incorrect	Correct
clitteris	**clitoris**	cokpit	**cockpit**
cloan	**clone****	cokroch	**cockroach**
clober	**clobber**	coktale	**cocktail**
clok	**clock**	colaborate	**collaborate**
cloke	**cloak**	colapse	**collapse**
cloraform	**chloroform**	colar	**collar****
cloral hidrate		colateral	**collateral**
	chloral hydrate	coldslaw	**coleslaw**
closh	**cloche**	colebluded	**cold-blooded**
closit	**closet**	colect	**collect**
cloun	**clown****	colecter	**collector**
cloyster	**cloister**	coled	**cold**
cloz	**clothes****	coleegue	**colleague**
clozing	**closing**	colege	**college****
clozout	**closeout**	colegiate	**collegiate**
clozure	**closure**	colen	**colon****
clubb	**club**	coler	**color****
cluby	**clubby**	colera	**cholera**
cluch	**clutch**	colerachura	**coloratura**
cludge	**kludge**	Coleseum	**Colosseum**
clumzy	**clumsy**	colestral	**cholesterol**
clyent	**client**	colick	**colic**
clymax	**climax**	collander	**colander**
cnish	**knish**	collapsable	**collapsible**
coad	**code**	colleck	**collect**
coak	**coke**	collegit	**collegiate**
coam	**comb**	collition	**coalition**
coar	**core****	collitis	**colitis**
coardump	**core dump**	collonic	**colonic**
cobawl	**cobol**	collosal	**colossal**
cobler	**cobbler**	colloseum	**coliseum**
cocane	**cocaine**	collostomy	**colostomy**
coch	**coach**	colonaid	**colonnade**
codeen	**codeine**	colone	**cologne****
coersion	**coercion**	colslaw	**coleslaw**
cofee	**coffee**	colum	**column**
coff	**cough****	colusion	**collusion****
coffeklotsh	**kaffeeklatsch**	colyumist	**columnist**
cofin	**coffin**	comemorate	
cognative	**cognitive**		**commemorate**
cogulate	**coagulate**	comendable	
cohearint	**coherent**		**commendable**
coherce	**coerce**	comenshurite	
coinsidence	**coincidence**		**commensurate**
cojitait	**cogitate**	comercial	**commercial**
cokanut	**coconut**	comftable	**comfortable**

Incorrect	Correct	Incorrect	Correct
comikazi	**kamikazi**	comunicate	**communicate**
comission	**commission**	comunity	**community**
comit	**commit****	comurce	**commerce**
comited	**committed**	comute	**commute**
comittee	**committee****	conasseur	**connoisseur**
commedian	**comedian**	conceed	**concede**
commedy	**comedy****	concensus	**consensus**
commen	**common**	concequence	**consequence**
commet	**comet****	concer	**concur****
commic	**comic**	concientious	
comming	**coming**		**conscientious****
comminism	**communism**	concieve	**conceive**
commoon	**commune**	conclaive	**conclave**
commpendum		concock	**concoct**
	compendium	concorse	**concourse**
commplementry		concreet	**concrete**
	complementary**	concurense	**concurrence**
commpression		concushin	**concussion**
	compression	condaminimum	
commyuter	**commuter**		**condominium**
comodity	**commodity**	condamint	**condiment**
comotion	**commotion**	condem	**condemn****
companyon	**companion**	condesend	**condescend**
comparitive	**comparative**	condinsashun	
compatable	**compatible**		**condensation**
compatense	**competence**	condishun	**condition**
compeet	**compete**	condoe	**condo**
compeled	**compelled**	condrum	**condom**
compell	**compel**	conduck	**conduct**
compermize	**compromise**	conect	**connect**
competant	**competent**	conection	**connection**
compinsashun		confadense	**confidence**
	compensation	confascate	**confiscate**
compis	**compass**	confederit	**confederate**
compitition	**competition**	confekshinery	
complacate	**complicate**		**confectionary**
complexshun	**complexion**	confered	**conferred**
complience	**compliance**	conferm	**confirm**
composishun	**composition**	confes	**confess**
compoze	**compose**	confinment	**confinement**
comprahend	**comprehend**	configrashun	
comprible	**comparable**		**conflagration**
compulsery	**compulsory**	confortable	**comfortable**
compyuter	**computer**	confrence	**conference**
comred	**comrade**	Confushus	**Confucius**
comtroller	**comptroller**	congagate	**conjugate**

Incorrect	Correct	Incorrect	Correct
congell	**congeal**	conseed	**concede**
congenyal	**congenial****	conseive	**conceive**
congradulate		consentrait	**concentrate**
	congratulate	consentrick	**concentric**
congrigashun		consept	**concept**
	congregation	consert	**concert**
congrous	**congruous**	conservitory	**conservatory**
conjer	**conjure**	consession	**concession**
conjeture	**conjecture**	conshunse	**conscience****
conjugle	**conjugal**	conshuss	**conscious****
conker	**conquer****	consil	**consul****
conncentrate	**concentrate**	consiliate	**conciliate**
Connecticut	**Connecticut**	consinement	**consignment**
connglomerate		consintration	
	conglomerate		**concentration**
conngres	**congress**	consise	**concise**
connisseur	**connoisseur**	consistant	**consistent**
connjunction	**conjunction**	consitter	**consider**
connjunctivitis		consoladate	**consolidate**
	conjunctivitis	consomate	**consummate**
connosewer	**connoisseur**	consoul	**console**
connsidrable	**considerable**	constible	**constable**
connspicuous		constilashun	**constellation**
	conspicuous	constint	**constant**
connstitution	**constitution**	consumtion	**consumption**
connstruck	**construct**	consynment	**consignment**
connsultent	**consultant**	consyurge	**concierge**
conntest	**contest**	contajus	**contagious**
conntraseptive		contane	**contain**
	contraceptive	contanent	**continent**
conntrast	**contrast**	contempry	**contemporary**
connvalecent		contemtable	**contemptible**
	convalescent	conterary	**contrary**
connvent	**convent**	conterception	
connvention	**convention**		**contraception**
connvertable	**convertible**	contimplate	**contemplate**
connvick	**convict**	continense	**countenance****
connviktion	**conviction****	continnualy	**continually**
conotashun	**connotation**	continuous	**continuous****
conote	**connote**	contore	**contour**
conpute	**compute**	contractural	**contractual**
consanent	**consonant**	contrarywise	**contrariwise**
consavation		contratan	**contretemps**
	conservation**	contravershil	
conseal	**conceal**		**controversial**
conseat	**conceit**	contraversy	**controversy**

Incorrect	Correct	Incorrect	Correct
contribeaut	**contribute**	coridor	**corridor**
controled	**controlled**	corigated	**corrugated**
controll	**control**	coril	**coral****
contry	**country**	corn-beef	**corned beef**
conture	**contour**	cornise	**cornice**
conubeal	**connubial**	cornor	**corner****
conviless	**convalesce**	coroborate	**corroborate**
convilute	**convolute**	corperal	**corporal****
convinient	**convenient**	corpisle	**corpuscle**
convirge	**converge**	corpration	**corporation**
convirse	**converse**	corraled	**corralled**
convirtable	**convertible**	corrona	**corona**
convolse	**convulse**	corronary	**coronary**
conyak	**cognac**	corsarge	**corsage**
coo daytah	**coup d'état**	corse	**course****
coo di gra	**coup de grâce**	corsit	**corset**
cood	**could**	cort	**court****
coodent	**couldn't**	cortazone	**cortisone****
cookee cutter		cortison	**courtesan****
	cookie cutter	cortmarshal	**courtmartial**
cookoo	**cuckoo**	cortroom	**courtroom**
cookry	**cookery**	corz	**corps****
cooky jar	**cookie jar**	cosher	**kosher**
cooly	**coolly****	costic	**caustic**
coopay	**coupé**	cosy	**cozy**
coopon	**coupon**	cotage	**cottage**
cooprate	**cooperate**	cotin	**cotton**
cootour	**couture**	counsler	**counselor****
coper	**copper**	counterseptive	
copeus	**copious**		**contraceptive**
cople	**couple**	courticy	**courtesy****
copyriter	**copywriter**	covrage	**coverage**
copywright	**copyright**	cowch potatoe	
cor	**corps****		**couch potato**
coral	**corral****	cowerd	**coward****
coralation	**correlation**	cowhyde	**cowhide**
corderoy	**corduroy**	cowndown	**countdown**
cordnation	**coordination**	cownterfit	**counterfeit**
coreandar	**coriander**	cowntes	**countess**
corect	**correct**	cowwboy	**cowboy**
corectness	**correctness**	coytus	**coitus**
coredless	**cordless**	Cozak	**Cossack**
corelate	**correlate**	cozmanaut	**cosmonaut**
corenia	**cornea**	cozmapolitan	
coreografy	**choreography**		**cosmopolitan**
corespond	**correspond**	cozmic	**cosmic**

Incorrect	Correct	Incorrect	Correct
cozzin	**cousin****	critisise	**criticize**
craby	**crabby**	crittic	**critic****
cradenchle	**credential**	crokadile	**crocodile**
craffty	**crafty**	crokay	**croquet****
crain	**crane**	crokete	**croquette****
craion	**crayon**	crome	**chrome**
crak	**crack**	cronic	**chronic**
crakel	**crackle**	cronology	**chronology**
cramberry	**cranberry**	croocial	**crucial**
cramm	**cram**	crood	**crude**
crashendo	**crescendo**	crool	**cruel**
craul	**crawl**	croop	**croup**
craws-egsamine		croopya	**croupier**
	cross-examine	crooze	**cruise****
crawssrode	**crossroad**	crosection	**cross section**
craydal	**cradle**	crosepurposes	
craynium	**cranium**		**cross-purposes**
craypes	**crepes****	crosreference	
cream de la cream			**cross-reference**
	creme de la creme	croud	**crowd**
creap	**creep**	cround	**crowned**
creashun	**creation**	crowch	**crouch**
credable	**credible**	crowen	**crone**
creddit	**credit**	crowshay	**crochet****
credeter	**creditor**	crsanthemun	
credlus	**credulous**		**chrysanthemum**
creedence	**credence**	cruch	**crutch**
creem	**cream****	crue	**crew**
creese	**crease****	cruely	**cruelly**
cresh	**crèche**	cruesade	**crusade**
cressent	**crescent**	crulty	**cruelty**
creture	**creature**	crum	**crumb**
crewelty free	**cruelty free**	crussty	**crusty**
criket	**cricket**	crute	**cruet**
crimnal	**criminal**	cruzer	**cruiser**
crimsin	**crimson**	cryed	**cried**
criple	**cripple**	cubbard	**cupboard**
cripptografer		cubbicle	**cubicle**
	cryptographer	Cuber	**Cuba**
cript	**crypt**	cuepay	**coupé**
criptic	**cryptic**	cuhoots	**cahoots**
Crismas	**Christmas**	cukie	**cookie**
Cristian	**Christian****	culcher	**culture**
cristilize	**crystallize**	culd	**culled****
critacal	**critical**	cule	**cool**
criteek	**critique****	culer	**color****

Incorrect	Correct	Incorrect	Correct
cullesterole	**cholesterol**	cupon	**coupon**
cullinary	**culinary**	curancy	**currency**
cultavate	**cultivate**	curchef	**kerchief**
cumand	**command****	curent	**current****
cumense	**commence**	curiculum	**curriculum**
cumfortable	**comfortable**	curige	**courage**
cuming	**coming**	curios	**curious**
cumpound	**compound**	curiousity	**curiosity**
cumprehension		curley	**curly**
	comprehension	curnel	**kernel****
cumputer	**computer**	curonel	**colonel****
cunclude	**conclude**	currare	**curare**
cundemm	**condemn****	curree	**curry**
cundone	**condone**	curretage	**curettage**
cundum	**condom**	cursere	**cursor**
cunferr	**confer**	curst	**cursed**
cungressional		curteous	**courteous**
	congressional	curtesy	**courtesy****
cuning	**cunning**	custid	**custard**
cunjugale	**conjugal**	custidy	**custody**
cunservative	**conservative**	custimor	**customer****
cunspiracy	**conspiracy**	cuting edge	**cutting edge**
cunstitoot	**constitute**	cuttup	**cutup**
cunstruktion	**construction**	cuver	**cover**
cunsult	**consult**	cuvinant	**covenant**
cunsume	**consume**	cwafeur	**coiffure**
cuntaminate	**contaminate**	cyder	**cider**
cuntralto	**contralto**	cynecure	**sinecure**
cuntraption	**contraption**	cypher	**cipher**
cuntrive	**contrive**	cyropracter	**chiropractor**
cuntry	**country**	cyubic	**cubic**
cunvention	**convention**	cyumin	**cumin**

D

Incorrect	Correct	Incorrect	Correct
dabate	**debate**	dakiri	**daiquiri**
dable	**dabble**	dakron	**dacron**
dabochery	**debauchery**	dakshound	**dachshund**
dacolté	**décolleté**	dalapadate	**dilapidate**
dadda	**Dada**	dalia	**dahlia**
dafodile	**daffodil**	dalinkwent	**delinquent**
dager	**dagger**	daluge	**deluge**
dait rape	**date rape**	damenshin	**dimension**
daity	**deity**	damige	**damage**

Incorrect	Correct	Incorrect	Correct
danderuf	**dandruff**	deefensive	**defensive**
dandylion	**dandelion**	deeflate	**deflate**
dane	**deign**	deel	**deal**
danjros	**dangerous**	deelete	**delete**
dary	**dairy****	deelusion	**delusion**
dassiay	**dossier**	deepression	**depression**
daterbass	**data base**	deesel	**diesel**
datta	**data**	deesensitize	**desensitize**
dauter	**daughter**	deestruck	**destruct**
davelop	**develop**	deetached	**detached**
dawg	**dog**	deetoxification	
dawk	**dork**		**detoxification**
dawne	**dawn**	deeture	**detour**
daybu	**debut**	deeva	**diva**
daycore	**decor**	deeviant	**deviant**
dayly	**daily****	deeviation	**deviation**
dayne	**deign**	deevower	**devour**
daysy-	**daisy-wheel**	def	**deaf**
daytabase	**data base**	defakate	**defecate**
dazel	**dazzle**	defalt	**default**
debaner	**debonair**	defanitely	**definitely**
debry	**debris**	defanition	**definition**
debths	**depths**	defeet	**defeat**
decarate	**decorate**	defence	**defense**
deceive	**deceive**	defendent	**defendant**
decend	**descend**	defensable	**defensible**
decese	**decease**	defered	**deferred**
deciet	**deceit**	defficit	**deficit**
decleration	**declaration**	deffinit	**definite****
decmal	**decimal**	defie	**defy**
decon	**deacon****	definitly	**definitely**
decreese	**decrease**	defishent	**deficient**
decription	**decryption**	defiunce	**defiance**
ded	**dead****	deflaytion	**deflation**
deddline	**deadline**	defrence	**deference**
dedecate	**dedicate**	defyed	**defied**
dedlock	**deadlock**	dehidrate	**dehydrate**
deduse	**deduce****	dekaid	**decade**
deebug	**debug**	dekonjestant	
deeception	**deception**		**decongestant**
deecompression		delagate	**delegate**
	decompression	deleetion	**deletion**
deeconstruck	**deconstruct**	delemma	**dilemma**
deecumposed		delite	**delight**
	decomposed	delivry	**delivery**
deeductable	**deductible**	dellhuge	**deluge**

Incorrect	Correct	Incorrect	Correct
delliberate	**deliberate**	derje	**dirge**
dellicacy	**delicacy**	derrivative	**derivative**
dellicatessan	**delicatessen**	desabl	**decibel**
dellicious	**delicious**	desastrous	**disastrous**
dellv	**delve**	descover	**discover**
delly	**deli**	descrepancy	**discrepancy**
delt	**dealt**	descriminate	**discriminate**
delux	**deluxe**	desease	**disease**
demacrat	**democrat**	desecant	**desiccant**
demeening	**demeaning**	Desember	**December**
deminish	**diminish**	desency	**decency**
deminstrate	**demonstrate**	desent	**decent****
demmented	**demented**	desicion	**decision**
demmocrasy	**democracy**	desicrate	**desecrate****
demmography		desided	**decided**
	demography	desifer	**decipher**
demogogue	**demagogue**	desine	**design**
demonstratable		desireable	**desirable**
	demonstrable	desolit	**desolate****
demytass	**demi-tasse**	desparate	**desperate**
dence	**dense**	despare	**despair**
denie	**deny**	desprit	**desperate**
dentafrice	**dentifrice**	dessertion	**desertion**
denteen	**dentine**	dessicate	**desiccate****
dentel	**dental**	dessmal	**decimal**
dentice	**dentist**	desstop	**desktop**
dentle damn	**dental dam**	desstructive	**destructive**
denyal	**denial**	destenation	**destination**
deodarant	**deodorant**	destribute	**distribute**
depature	**departure**	det	**debt**
dependant	**dependent****	detale	**detail**
dependible	**dependable**	deteck	**detect**
depervation	**deprivation**	deteriate	**deteriorate**
depo	**depot**	detestible	**detestable**
depot-prevera		deth	**death**
	depo-provera	detocks	**detox**
deppillitary	**depilatory**	detter	**debtor**
depresent	**depressant**	detterent	**deterrent**
depreshiation		dettergent	**detergent**
	depreciation	dettermine	**determine**
depricate	**deprecate****	dettour	**detour**
deprieve	**deprive**	deveant	**deviant**
deps	**depths**	deveate	**deviate**
depudy	**deputy**	devel	**devil**
derick	**derrick**	devellop	**develop**
derileck	**derelict**	deversity	**diversity**

Incorrect	Correct	Incorrect	Correct
devert	**divert**	dilligent	**diligent**
devest	**divest**	dillute	**dilute**
devide	**divide**	dilog	**dialogue**
devine	**divine**	dilusion	**delusion**
devistate	**devastate**	dimeen	**demean**
devius	**devious**	dimensha precox	
devorce	**divorce**		**dementia praecox**
devulge	**divulge**	dimminative	**diminutive**
dewoe	**duo**	dimmwit	**dimwit**
dexterous	**dextrous**	dimolish	**demolish**
dezign	**design**	dimond	**diamond**
dezil	**diesel**	dinamic	**dynamic**
diacese	**diocese**	dinate	**dinette**
diafram	**diaphragm****	dingee	**dingy****
diatishn	**dietitian**	dinomite	**dynamite**
dicesion	**decision**	dint	**didn't**
dich	**dish**	diper	**diaper**
dichwasher	**dishwasher**	dipleat	**deplete**
dicksie	**Dixie**	diplomer	**diploma**
dicline	**decline**	diposit	**deposit**
didjital	**digital**	dipprived	**deprived****
diebetes	**diabetes**	dirdy	**dirty**
dieing	**dying****	direcshon	**direction**
dielaprare	**dial-a-prayer**	dirive	**derive**
dielation	**dilation****	dirogatory	**derogatory**
dier	**dire**	dirth	**dearth**
dierea	**diarrhea**	diry	**diary****
difakto	**de facto**	dis	**diss**
diference	**difference**	disadent	**dissident**
diftheria	**diphtheria**	disagrement	**disagreement**
difibralate	**defibrillate**	disallusion	**disillusion**
dificult	**difficult**	disalow	**disallow**
difrenshal	**differential**	disanent	**dissonant**
difuse	**diffuse**	disapate	**dissipate**
digestable	**digestible**	disaprobashon	
diggnity	**dignity**		**disapprobation**
diggress	**digress**	disaray	**disarray**
diggs	**digs**	disasterous	**disastrous**
diging	**digging**	disatisfy	**dissatisfy**
dihard	**diehard**	disavantaged	
dijest	**digest**		**disadvantaged**
dijitallus	**digitalis**	disaybled	**disabled**
diktionery	**dictionary**	disbersment	**disbursement**
dilect	**dialect**	discod	**discard**
dillema	**dilemma**	disconsilite	**disconsolate**
dilletant	**dilettante**	disconsurt	**disconcert**

Incorrect	Correct	Incorrect	Correct
discribe	**describe**	disqualafy	**disqualify**
discrimanate	**discriminate**	disrepitible	**disreputable**
discription	**description**	disrup	**disrupt**
discurtius	**discourteous**	dissability	**disability**
discwalafy	**disqualify**	dissagree	**disagree**
disdane	**disdain**	dissapoint	**disappoint**
disect	**dissect**	dissappear	**disappear**
disegragate	**desegregate**	dissastrous	**disastrous**
disembowl	**disembowel**	dissc	**disc or disk**
disemenate	**disseminate**	disscharge	**discharge**
disenfermation		disscorse	**discourse**
	disinformation	disscount	**discount**
disent	**dissent****	disscover	**discover**
disentery	**dysentery**	disscretion	**discretion**
disertion	**desertion**	disscusion	**discussion**
disfunctional		dissern	**discern**
	dysfunctional	disheveled	**disheveled**
disgize	**disguise**	dissinfect	**disinfect**
disiduos	**deciduous**	dissinflation	**disinflation**
disign	**design**	dissinter	**disinter**
disimalar	**dissimilar**	dissipline	**discipline**
disipline	**discipline**	dissk	**disc or disk**
disklosher	**disclosure**	disskette	**diskette**
disko	**disco**	dissmis	**dismiss**
diskretionery		dissmount	**dismount**
	discretionary	dissplay	**display**
disleksia	**dyslexia**	dissposil	**disposal**
dismantel	**dismantle**	disspute	**dispute**
dismissel	**dismissal**	dissrespect	**disrespect**
disociate	**dissociate**	disstemper	**distemper**
disolution	**dissolution**	distracation	**distraction**
disolve	**dissolve**	distaf	**distaff**
disonest	**dishonest**	distastful	**distasteful**
dispair	**despair**	distence	**distance**
disparije	**disparage**	disterb	**disturb**
dispasition	**disposition****	distilation	**distillation**
dispensery	**dispensary**	distingwish	**distinguish**
dispeptic	**dyspeptic**	distint	**distinct**
disperporshin		distraut	**distraught**
	disproportion	distres	**distress**
dispicible	**despicable**	districk	**district**
displacment	**displacement**	distrofy	**dystrophy**
disposess	**dispossess**	distroy	**destroy**
disposible	**disposable**	distruction	**destruction**
dispurse	**disperse****	disuade	**dissuade**
		disy	**dicey**

Incorrect	Correct	Incorrect	Correct
disy	**dizzy**	dont	**don't**
dito	**ditto**	donut	**doughnut**
ditretis	**detritus**	doosh	**douche**
divaden	**dividend**	dooty	**duty**
divice	**device****	dopomine	**dopamine**
divied	**divide**	dorible	**durable**
divise	**devise****	dormatory	**dormitory**
divoid	**devoid**	dormint	**dormant**
divoshin	**devotion**	dosege	**dosage**
divurje	**diverge**	dosile	**docile**
divver	**diver**	dosseay	**dossier**
divvertikulosis		dott	**dot**
	diverticulosis	doubble dipper	
divvestiture	**divestiture**		**double-dipper**
divvine	**divine**	doubel diget	**double-digit**
divvision	**division**	doudy	**dowdy**
dizaster	**disaster**	douner	**downer**
dizease	**disease**	dounfall	**downfall**
diznee	**Disney**	doungrade	**downgrade**
do process	**due process**	dounside	**downside**
doal	**dole**	dounsize	**downsize**
doam	**dome**	dountime	**downtime**
dockudramer	**docudrama**	dourger	**dowager**
docter	**doctor**	dout	**doubt**
doctrinare	**doctrinaire**	dovtale	**dovetail**
docuementery		dowe	**Dow**
	documentary	dowenpour	**downpour**
dodel	**dawdle**	dowery	**dowry**
doenate	**donate**	downsoning	**downzoning**
doge	**dodge**	downtoun	**downtown**
doged	**dogged**	dragen	**dragon**
dogeral	**doggerel**	dramer	**drama**
dohmed	**domed**	dranege	**drainage**
dokument	**document**	draun	**drawn**
doledrums	**doldrums**	drawwback	**drawback**
dolfin	**dolphin**	dred	**dread**
doller	**dollar**	dreem	**dream**
domanere	**domineer**	drege	**dredge**
domasile	**domicile**	drery	**dreary**
dominent	**dominant**	drifwood	**driftwood**
dominyon	**dominion**	drivin	**drive-in**
domono	**domino**	drivven	**driven**
doner	**donor**	drivway	**driveway**
dongaree	**dungaree**	drizel	**drizzle**
donky	**donkey**	drol	**droll**
donstairs	**downstairs**	droping	**dropping**

Incorrect	Correct	Incorrect	Correct
droup	**droop**	dupplicate	**duplicate**
drouze	**drowse**	durby	**derby**
drownded	**drowned**	durma	**derma**
droyd	**droid**	durmatitis	**dermatitis**
drugery	**drudgery**	durration	**duration**
druggstore	**drugstore**	durres	**duress**
drugist	**druggist**	durring	**during**
drummstick	**drumstick**	duse	**deuce**
drunkeness	**drunkenness**	dussedup	**dust-up**
dryd	**dried**	dustee	**dusty**
dryvbuy	**drive-by**	dutyful	**dutiful**
dryve	**drive**	duve	**dove**
dubb	**dub**	duz	**does****
dubbel	**double**	duzen	**dozen**
dubbius	**dubious**	duzzens	**dozens**
duce	**deuce**	dwarve	**dwarf**
Duch	**Dutch**	dweam	**DWEM**
dudenum	**duodenum**	dwebe	**dweeb**
dueable	**doable**	dyagnose	**diagnose**
duely	**duly****	dyagonal	**diagonal**
dule	**dual****	dyal	**dial**
dulsit	**dulcet**	dyaretic	**diuretic**
dum	**dumb**	dyaspera	**diaspora**
dumby	**dummy**	dyce	**dice****
dume	**doom**	dycotomy	**dichotomy**
dumean	**demean**	dyet	**diet****
dumestic	**domestic**	dyitery	**dietary**
dumfound	**dumbfound**	dynasor	**dinosaur**
dumpee	**dumpy**	dyner	**diner****
dumpp	**dump**	dyning	**dining**
dungin	**dungeon****	dyoxen	**dioxin**
dunse	**dunce**	dyulog	**dialogue**
dupleks	**duplex**	dyve	**dive**
duplisity	**duplicity**	dyvon	**divan**

	E		
earing	**earring**	ebulient	**ebullient**
earlyer	**earlier**	eccise	**excise**
earwacks	**earwax**	ecconomic	**economic**
easly	**easily**	ech	**etch****
easment	**easement**	eckwity	**equity**
eavoke	**evoke**	eclesiestical	**ecclesiastical**
ebiny	**ebony**	eclips	**eclipse**

Incorrect	Correct	Incorrect	Correct
eco	**echo**	efishent	**efficient**
economacal	**economical**	efnocentric	**ethnocentric**
edable	**edible****	ege	**edge****
edatorial	**editorial**	eggs party	**ex parte**
eddit	**edit**	eggsecutive	**executive**
edima	**edema**	egoe	**ego**
edipiss complex		egplant	**eggplant**
	Oedipus complex	egsack	**exact**
edipus	**Oedipus**	egschange	**exchange**
editer	**editor**	egsit	**exit**
educatable	**educable**	egsplore	**explore**
edyucate	**educate**	egstempiraneus	
ee male	**E-mail**		**extemporaneous**
eeclampsia	**eclampsia**	egstink	**extinct**
eeger	**eager**	egstract	**extract**
eegle	**eagle**	egsume	**exhume**
eegocentric	**egocentric**	egzalt	**exalt****
eejaculate	**ejaculate**	egzert	**exert**
eelastic	**elastic**	egzist	**exist**
eelation	**elation**	egzotic	**exotic**
eele	**eel**	eibrow	**eyebrow**
eelection	**election**	eightteen	**eighteen**
eelectron	**electron**	eithernet	**Ethernet**
eeliptikal	**elliptical**	ejeck	**eject**
eemerging	**emerging**	ejiss	**aegis**
eemetic	**emetic**	ekcite	**excite**
eerake	**earache**	eklectic	**eclectic**
eerode	**erode**	ekology	**ecology**
eesop	**ESOP**	ekonomy	**economy**
eest	**east**	eks	**ex**
eether	**either****	eksalt	**exalt****
eethus	**ethos**	eksamorf	**exomorph**
eevakuate	**evacuate**	ekschange	**exchange**
eevaluate	**evaluate**	eksclude	**exclude**
eevent	**event**	eksclusive	**exclusive**
eeventially	**eventually**	ekscrewshiate	**excruciate**
eeviction	**eviction**	eksec	**exec**
eevocative	**evocative**	ekseed	**exceed****
eface	**efface**	eksillerate	**exhilarate**
efect	**effect****	eksist	**exist**
efedrin	**ephedrine**	eksistence	**existence**
efemminate	**effeminate**	eksize	**excise**
efervesent	**effervescent**	eksort	**exhort**
effert	**effort**	ekspadite	**expedite**
eficashus	**efficacious**	ekspansion	**expansion**
efishency	**efficiency**	ekspier	**expire**

Incorrect	Correct	Incorrect	Correct
eksploit	**exploit**	ellusadate	**elucidate**
ekspossure	**exposure**	elum	**elm**
ekspressway	**expressway**	elve	**elf**
ekspurt	**expert**	emagrint	**emigrant****
ekstacy	**ecstasy**	emale	**E-mail**
ekstend	**extend**	emanense	**eminence**
ekstermination		emarald	**emerald**
	extermination	embalism	**embolism**
ekstirpate	**extirpate**	embarassed	**embarrassed**
ekstole	**extol or extoll**	embasador	**ambassador**
ekstortion	**extortion**	embelish	**embellish**
ekstra	**extra**	embezle	**embezzle**
ekwater	**equator**	emblim	**emblem**
ekzonerate	**exonerate**	embomb	**embalm**
elafantisis	**elephantiasis**	embos	**emboss**
elagent	**elegant**	embrase	**embrace**
elagie	**elegy****	embrio	**embryo**
elament	**element****	embroyder	**embroider**
elavate	**elevate**	emfasis	**emphasis**
elbo	**elbow**	emfizema	**emphysema**
eleck	**elect**	eminate	**emanate**
eleet	**elite**	emisary	**emissary**
elefent	**elephant**	emity	**enmity****
elegable	**eligible**	emmaskulatin	
elegants	**elegance**		**emasculation**
elektristy	**electricity**	emmbedded	**embedded**
elfs	**elves**	emmergancy	**emergency**
elikser	**elixir**	emmployee	**employee**
elipse	**ellipse**	emolient	**emollient****
elipsis	**ellipsis**	emoshun	**emotion**
elisit	**elicit****	emperialism	**imperialism**
ellaberate	**elaborate**	empethy	**empathy**
ellaquent	**eloquent**	empier	**empire****
ellavation	**elevation**	emporer	**emperor**
elldoper	**L-dopa**	empotence	**impotence**
ellectercardagram		empressionism	
	electrocardiogram		**impressionism**
ellectorate	**electorate**	emptyness	**emptiness**
ellectronics	**electronics**	emty	**empty**
ellementary	**elementary****	emurge	**emerge****
ellevator	**elevator**	enamerd	**enamored**
elliminate	**eliminate****	enamy	**enemy****
ellisit	**elicit****	enchellada	**enchilada**
ellnino	**el Niño**	encite	**incite****
ellude	**elude****	encoed	**encode**
elluminate	**illuminate****	encompes	**encompass**

Incorrect	Correct	Incorrect	Correct
encorporate	**incorporate**	enterprenoor	
encript	**encrypt**		**entrepreneur**
endamorf	**endomorph**	enterview	**interview**
endere	**endear**	entier	**entire**
endever	**endeavor**	entimasy	**intimacy**
endoctrinate	**indoctrinate**	entise	**entice**
endorsment	**endorsement**	entolerance	**intolerance**
endouw	**endow**	entreet	**entreat**
enertia	**inertia**	entreprise	**enterprise**
enfarction	**infarction**	enuf	**enough**
enferior	**inferior**	enunsiate	**enunciate**
enfidell	**infidel**	envade	**invade**
enfiltrate	**infiltrate**	envaygle	**inveigle**
enfinite	**infinite**	envelup	**envelop****
enfisema	**emphysema**	envestigate	**investigate**
enflation	**inflation**	envie	**envy**
enfluence	**influence**	envirement	**environment**
enforcible	**enforceable**	envius	**envious**
enformercial	**informercial**	envoke	**invoke**
engeneer	**engineer**	envyable	**enviable**
Englind	**England**	enyuresis	**enuresis**
enhabit	**inhabit**	epacure	**epicure**
enhale	**inhale**	epademic	**epidemic**
enherit	**inherit**	epasod	**episode**
enigetic	**energetic**	epataf	**epitaph****
enitial	**initial**	epedermis	**epidermis**
enitiate	**initiate**	episcene	**epicine**
enivate	**enervate****	eplepsy	**epilepsy**
enncounter	**encounter**	eppick	**epic****
ennthoosiastic		eppok	**epoch****
	enthusiastic	equalibrium	**equilibrium**
enntry	**entry**	equaly	**equally**
enny	**any**	equanocks	**equinox**
enoble	**ennoble**	equidy	**equity**
enraige	**enrage**	equipt	**equipped**
enrap	**enwrap****	equivilent	**equivalent**
enrole	**enroll****	erace	**erase**
ensefalitis	**encephalitis**	eratic	**erratic****
ensime	**enzyme**	erb	**herb**
ensin	**ensign**	erban	**urban****
enstill	**instill**	erbs	**urbs**
entale	**entail**	erchin	**urchin**
entamology		eredrum	**eardrum**
	entomology**	erektion	**erection**
entatain	**entertain**	eresa	**ERISA**
enterance	**entrance**	ergency	**urgency**

Incorrect	Correct	Incorrect	Correct
erind	**errand****	ethacal	**ethical**
erithromicin		etikete	**etiquette**
	erythromycin	etsetra	**et cetera**
erje	**urge**	eufology	**ufology**
erk	**irk**	eunicorn	**unicorn**
erl	**earl**	euniform	**uniform**
erly	**early**	eunilatoral	**unilateral**
ermin	**ermine**	eutopia	**utopia**
ernest	**earnest**	evalushun	**evolution**
eroneus	**erroneous**	evapperate	**evaporate**
eror	**error****	evedence	**evidence**
erray	**array**	evenshul	**eventual**
errgo	**ergo**	evesdrop	**eavesdrop**
errgonomics	**ergonomics**	evick	**evict**
errosion	**erosion**	eviserate	**eviscerate**
errsatz	**ersatz**	evning	**evening**
erth	**earth**	evry	**every**
Ery	**Erie****	evrywear	**everywhere**
eryudite	**erudite**	evul	**evil**
esay	**essay****	evulve	**evolve**
escoriate	**excoriate**	evvaluate	**evaluate**
escourt	**escort**	evvaluation	**evaluation**
esculator	**escalator**	exackly	**exactly**
esence	**essence**	exacute	**execute**
esential	**essential**	exagarate	**exaggerate**
Eskamo	**Eskimo**	examanation	
eskeroll	**escarole**		**examination**
eskwisite	**exquisite**	exaust	**exhaust**
esofagus	**esophagus**	excape	**escape**
espianoge	**espionage**	excede	**exceed****
esscape	**escape**	excell	**excel****
esskwire	**esquire**	excentric	**eccentric****
essoteric	**esoteric**	excercise	**exercise****
esspousal	**espousal**	excitment	**excitement**
esstate	**estate**	exembank	**Eximbank**
essteemed	**esteemed**	exemt	**exempt**
esstimation	**estimation**	exessive	**excessive**
esstragin	**estrogen**	exgurshin	**excursion**
estamate	**estimate**	exhail	**exhale**
esteme	**esteem**	exhorbitant	**exorbitant**
Ester	**Easter**	exibit	**exhibit**
estract	**extract**	existance	**existence**
et	**ate****	exitus	**exodus**
etealogy	**etiology**	exkreet	**excrete**
eternaty	**eternity**	exort	**exhort**

Incorrect	Correct	Incorrect	Correct
expeled	**expelled**	extraordinary	
expell	**expel**		**extraordinary**
expence	**expense**	extravert	**extrovert**
expendible	**expendable**	extravigent	**extravagant**
experashun	**expiration****	extreem	**extreme**
experiance	**experience**	exurpt	**excerpt**
explaination	**explanation**	exxpedition	**expedition**
explative	**expletive**	exxperement	**experiment**
explisit	**explicit**	exxploit	**exploit**
expres	**express**	exxport	**export**
expresso	**espresso**	exxtent	**extent****
expurteez	**expertise**	exxterminate	**exterminate**
exray	**x-ray**	exxternal	**external**
exsecutive	**executive**	exxtort	**extort**
exseed	**exceed****	exxtract	**extract**
exsellent	**excellent**	exxtrapolate	**extrapolate**
exsept	**except****	exzema	**eczema**
exseptional	**exceptional****	exzile	**exile**
exsessive	**excessive**	exzilirate	**exhilarate**
exsist	**exist**	ey	**eye****
exsiteable	**excitable**	eyekon	**icon**
exsize	**excise**	eyesite	**eyesight**
exsperience	**experience**	eyesometric	**isometric**
exstacy	**ecstasy**	eyestrane	**eyestrain**
exstol	**extol or extoll**	Eyetalian	**Italian**
extateretorial		eyether	**either****
	extraterritorial	eyris	**iris**
extention	**extension**	eyudee	**IUD**
extersensery	**extrasensory**	ezein	**ezine**
extracate	**extricate**	ezy	**easy**
extracuricular		ezzampel	**example**
	extracurricular		

F

Incorrect	Correct	Incorrect	Correct
fabel	**fable**	facshun	**faction**
fabrakate	**fabricate**	facter	**factor**
fabrik	**fabric**	factery	**factory**
fabulus	**fabulous**	factsimile	**facsimile**
facalty	**faculty**	fadd	**fad**
faceing	**facing**	fadelity	**fidelity**
fachewal	**factual**	faery	**fairy****
fachuos	**fatuous**	faim	**fame**
facinate	**fascinate**	fain	**feign****

Incorrect	Correct	Incorrect	Correct
faiseoff	**face-off**	farse	**farce**
fakshus	**factious**	farsited	**farsighted**
faksimile	**facsimile**	fasaving	**facesaving**
fakt	**fact**	fase	**face**
faktual	**factual**	faseless	**faceless**
fakulty	**faculty**	fasen	**fasten**
falback	**fallback**	faseshus	**facetious**
fale	**fail**	fashial	**facial**
falibel	**fallible**	fashinable	**fashionable**
falicitate	**felicitate**	fashist	**fascist**
falicy	**fallacy**	fashon	**fashion**
falkin	**falcon**	fasilitate	**facilitate**
fallocrasy	**phallocracy**	fasility	**facility****
fallsafe	**failsafe**	fasill	**facile**
fallse	**false**	fasinate	**fascinate**
fallsees	**falsies**	fasithia	**forsythia**
fallshud	**falsehood**	fasodd	**façade**
fallter	**falter**	fassen	**fasten**
fallus	**phallus**	fassion	**fashion**
falopian tube		fasstidious	**fastidious**
	fallopian tube	fateeg	**fatigue**
falsafy	**falsify**	fatel	**fatal****
falseto	**falsetto**	faten	**fatten**
falt	**fault**	fatful	**fateful****
faluble	**fallible**	fathim	**fathom**
familiar	**familiar**	fationable	**fashionable**
familyarize	**familiarize**	fattality	**fatality**
famin	**famine**	faty	**fatty**
famly	**family**	faught	**fought**
fammer	**farmer**	fauster	**foster**
fammished	**famished**	faverible	**favorable**
famus	**famous**	favrit	**favorite**
fanagle	**finagle**	fawce	**force**
fancyful	**fanciful**	fawceps	**forceps**
fane	**feign****	fawcet	**faucet****
fanntasise	**fantasize**	fawd	**ford**
fansy	**fancy**	fawklift	**forklift**
fanticy	**fantasy****	fawl	**fall**
fantom	**phantom**	fawmat	**format**
farely	**fairly**	fayed	**fade**
farenheit	**Fahrenheit**	faylure	**failure**
farfecht	**farfetched**	fayselift	**face-lift**
faringitis	**pharyngitis**	fayth	**faith**
farmacy	**pharmacy**	fayze	**faze****
faroe	**faro**	fead	**feed**
farrenheight	**Fahrenheit**	feadback	**feedback**

Incorrect	Correct	Incorrect	Correct
feald	**field**	fery	**ferry****
fealing	**feeling**	fesable	**feasible**
feasco	**fiasco**	fesster	**fester**
Febuary	**February**	festavil	**festival**
fech	**fetch****	feter	**fetter**
fedd	**Fed, the**	fether	**feather**
fedderals	**Federales**	fetle	**fettle**
feddora	**fedora**	fettish	**fetish****
fedeback	**feedback**	feu	**few**
fedral	**federal**	feuneril	**funeral****
feeansay	**fiancé****	feurius	**furious**
feeasco	**fiasco**	feva	**fever**
feeblely	**feebly**	fiatrap	**firetrap**
feeline	**feline**	fibbrilation	**fibrillation**
feemale	**female**	fiberoid	**fibroid**
feend	**fiend****	fichnet	**fishnet**
feesability	**feasibility**	ficks	**fix**
feest	**feast****	ficktion	**fiction**
feesta	**fiesta**	fidle	**fiddle**
feeture	**feature**	fiebrus	**fibrous**
feetus	**fetus**	fieder	**feeder**
feild	**field**	fierbug	**firebug**
feirce	**fierce**	fierfiter	**firefighter**
fella	**fellow**	fiesty	**feisty**
fellony	**felony**	figahead	**figurehead**
fellt	**felt**	figet	**fidget**
femenine	**feminine**	figger	**figure**
femer	**femur**	figyative	**figurative**
femminism	**feminism**	fikil	**fickle**
feness	**finesse****	fiksation	**fixation**
fennder	**fender**	fikticious	**fictitious**
fenobarbital		filagree	**filigree**
	phenobarbital	filanderer	**philanderer**
fenomenal	**phenomenal**	filanthropy	**philanthropy**
fenomenon	**phenomenon**	filately	**philately**
fense	**fence**	filay	**filet**
fere	**fear**	fileal	**filial**
ferett	**ferret**	filharmonic	**philharmonic**
ferget	**forget**	fillay	**filet**
fergive	**forgive**	fille	**faille**
fernish	**furnish**	fillibuster	**filibuster**
fersake	**forsake**	fillter	**filter**
ferst-rate	**first-rate**	fillthee	**filthy**
ferthermore	**furthermore**	fillum	**film**
fertil	**fertile**	filmsy	**flimsy**
ferver	**fervor**	filosophy	**philosophy**

Incorrect	Correct	Incorrect	Correct
finanse	**finance****	flayk	**flake**
finanshil	**financial**	flaykee	**flaky**
finatic	**fanatic**	flebitis	**phlebitis**
finese	**finesse****	flech	**flesh****
fingatip	**fingertip**	flecksible	**flexible**
fingger	**finger**	fleckstime	**flextime**
finil	**final**	fleebag	**fleabag**
finilize	**finalize**	fleese	**fleece**
finly	**finely****	flegeling	**fledgling**
finngerprint	**fingerprint**	flem	**phlegm**
fireing	**firing**	flert	**flirt**
firey	**fiery**	flete	**fleet**
firlo	**furlough**	flie	**fly**
firment	**ferment****	flikker	**flicker**
firoshus	**ferocious**	flipint	**flippant**
firther	**further****	flipp	**flip**
firtilise	**fertilize**	flirtacious	**flirtatious**
fishion	**fission**	flite	**flight**
fisically	**physically**	flix	**flicks**
fisiology	**physiology**	flochart	**flowchart**
fisscle	**fiscal****	flok	**flock****
fite	**fight**	flone	**flown**
fith	**fifth**	flook	**fluke**
fiting	**fitting**	floot	**flute**
fium	**fume**	flopy	**floppy**
flabagasted	**flabbergasted**	flor	**flaw****
flabergas	**flabbergast**	flore	**floor****
flachulent	**flatulent**	floresent	**fluorescent**
fladjelation	**flagellation**	floride	**fluoride****
flagg ship	**flagship**	floris	**florist**
flaging	**flagging**	floriscope	**fluoroscope**
flaim	**flame**	florish	**flourish**
flale	**flail**	Florrida	**Florida**
flambay	**flambé**	flote	**float**
flamible	**flammable**	flownder	**flounder**
flammboyant	**flamboyant**	flownse	**flounce**
flammenco	**flamenco**	flubb	**flub**
flaper	**flapper**	flucks	**flux**
flapp	**flap**	flucktuation	**fluctuation**
flasid	**flaccid**	flud	**flood**
flatary	**flattery**	fludder	**flutter**
flaten	**flatten**	flued	**fluid**
flater	**flatter**	fluint	**fluent**
flattfoot	**flatfoot**	flukshuate	**fluctuate**
flaver	**flavor**	flurine	**fluorine**
flaygrent	**flagrant****	flury	**flurry**

Incorrect	Correct	Incorrect	Correct
flys	**flies**	formadable	**formidable**
fobb	**fob**	formaly	**formally****
fobia	**phobia**	forman	**foreman**
focit	**faucet****	formelism	**formalism**
focks	**fox**	forment	**foment****
focksy	**foxy**	formil	**formal**
foe pas	**faux pas**	formost	**foremost**
foke	**folk**	forperson	**foreperson**
fokil	**focal**	forrensic	**forensic**
fokis	**focus**	forrest	**forest**
foks	**folks**	forrgon	**foregone**
foksel	**forecastle**	fornication	
foled	**fold**		**fornication****
foleo	**folio**	forrum	**forum****
folicle	**follicle**	forsee	**foresee**
folige	**foliage**	forsful	**forceful**
foller	**follow**	forsight	**foresight**
foly	**folly**	forskin	**foreskin**
fom	**farm**	forstall	**forestall**
fome	**foam**	fortatude	**fortitude**
fomula	**formula**	forteen	**fourteen**
fondal	**fondle**	fosfate	**phosphate**
fonetic	**phonetic**	fosforescence	
fonics	**phonics**		**phosphorescence**
fonograph	**phonograph**	fosforus	**phosphorus**
fonte	**font****	fosil	**fossil**
fony	**phony**	fotagenic	**photogenic**
foolback	**fullback**	foto	**photo**
forcast	**forecast**	fotography	**photography**
forceable	**forcible**	fotosinthesis	
forchoon	**fortune**		**photosynthesis**
forck	**fork**	fountin	**fountain**
forclose	**foreclose**	fourthrite	**forthright**
forclozure	**foreclosure**	fourties	**forties**
forebid	**forbid**	fourtunately	**fortunately**
fored	**forehead**	fourtutuous	**fortuitous**
fore ever	**forever**	fourty	**forty**
forefit	**forfeit**	fow	**foe**
foremaldahide		foward	**forward****
	formaldehyde	fownd	**found****
foremer	**former**	fowndation	**foundation**
forfit	**forfeit**	foyble	**foible**
forgry	**forgery**	fraggment	**fragment**
forhead	**forehead**	fraim	**frame**
forin	**foreign**	fraim-up	**frame-up**
forje	**forge**	frajile	**fragile**

Incorrect	Correct	Incorrect	Correct
frakas	**fracas**	frought	**fraught**
frakcher	**fracture**	froun	**frown**
frale	**frail**	Froyd	**Freud**
frankfutter	**frankfurter**	froydian	**Freudian**
frannchize	**franchise**	frugl	**frugal**
frase	**phrase****	fruntend	**front-end**
frate	**freight**	fruntil	**frontal**
frawd	**fraud**	frusstate	**frustrate**
fraygrince	**fragrance**	frutful	**fruitful**
fraymwork	**framework**	Fryday	**Friday**
freaby	**freebie**	fue	**few**
freadom	**freedom**	fued	**feud**
freagint	**free agent**	fuedal	**feudal**
frealode	**freeload**	fugative	**fugitive**
freddy mack		fuge	**fugue**
	Freddie Mac	fuje	**fudge**
freek	**freak****	fulashus	**fallacious**
freese-dry	**freeze-dry**	fullfil	**fulfill**
frekel	**freckle**	fullfilment	**fulfillment**
frelance	**freelance**	fultime	**full-time**
frend	**friend****	fumbil	**fumble**
frendship	**friendship**	funcshin	**function**
frendsy	**frenzy**	fundew	**fondue**
frennetic	**frenetic**	fundimental	**fundamental**
frenonogy	**phrenology**	funel	**funnel**
frenship	**friendship**	funeril	**funeral****
frensic	**forensic**	fungis	**fungus**
frequincy	**frequency**	funkshunal	**functional**
freshin	**freshen**	funndementalist	
freway	**freeway**		**fundamentalist**
fricasee	**fricassee**	funy	**funny**
fricshin	**friction**	furee	**furry****
frier	**friar****	furlow	**furlough**
fril	**frill**	furm	**firm**
frinje	**fringe**	furnature	**furniture**
frite	**fright**	furst aide	**first aid**
friter	**fritter**	fusalege	**fuselage**
friternel	**fraternal**	fust	**first**
frivlous	**frivolous**	futball	**football**
frojalent	**fraudulent**	futil	**futile**
frok	**frock**	futlose	**footloose**
frollic	**frolic**	fuz	**fuzz****
fronteersman		fyancy	**fiancé****
	frontiersman	fyberglass	**fiberglass**
frontspiece	**frontispiece**	fyber optic	**fiber-optic**
frosen	**frozen**	fyfo	**FIFO**

Incorrect	Correct	Incorrect	Correct
fynite	**finite**	fyuror	**furor**
fyoog	**fugue**	fyushea	**fuchsia**
fyord	**fjord**	fyuture	**future**

G

Incorrect	Correct	Incorrect	Correct
gaberdeen	**gabardine**	garrish	**garish**
gaf	**gaffe****	gasalene	**gasoline**
gafilter fish	**gefilte fish**	gasha	**geisha**
gaget	**gadget**	gaskit	**gasket**
gail	**gale**	gasseous	**gaseous**
gaim	**game**	gasstritis	**gastritis**
gaitkeeper	**gatekeeper**	gastly	**ghastly**
galacksy	**galaxy**	gatfly	**gadfly**
galary	**gallery**	gauk	**gawk**
galeic	**Gaelic**	gavvel	**gavel**
galent	**gallant**	gawdy	**gaudy**
galick	**Gaelic**	gawge	**gorge**
galin	**gallon**	gawl	**gall**
galip	**gallop**	gawlbladder	**gallbladder**
gallaxy	**galaxy**	gawr	**gore**
gallvanize	**galvanize**	gawse	**gauze****
gally	**galley**	gaymee	**gamy**
galows	**gallows**	gaz	**gas**
galstone	**gallstone****	gazel	**gazelle**
gama globlin		gazet	**gazette**
	gamma globulin	gealogy	**geology**
gambul	**gamble****	geazer	**geezer**
gammer	**gamma**	geedesic	**geodesic**
gammit	**gamut****	geego	**GIGO**
ganda	**gander**	geehad	**jihad**
gangreen	**gangrene**	geeolegy	**geology**
ganishee	**garnishee**	geep	**jeep**
garantee	**guarantee****	geer	**gear**
gararge	**garage**	geestring	**G-string**
garbige	**garbage**	geetar	**guitar**
gard	**guard**	gelies	**jellies**
garder	**garter**	gellding	**gelding**
gardian	**guardian**	gemm	**gem**
gardin	**garden**	genacide	**genocide**
gardner	**gardener**	genarator	**generator**
garilus	**garrulous**	geneology	**genealogy**
garit	**garret**	genisis	**genesis**
garlick	**garlic**	gennerate	**generate**

Incorrect	Correct	Incorrect	Correct
genneric	**generic**	giography	**geography**
genrally	**generally**	giometry	**geometry**
genrus	**generous**	girdal	**girdle**
gentalia	**genitalia**	gise	**guise**
gentelman	**gentleman**	git	**get****
gentlely	**gently**	gittar	**guitar**
genuwine	**genuine**	givaway	**giveaway**
genyufleck	**genuflect**	givback	**giveback**
genyus	**genius****	gizzmo	**gizmo**
gerd	**gird**	glair	**glare**
geremiad	**jeremiad**	glajer	**glazier****
gergul	**gurgle**	glamerus	**glamorous**
gerl	**girl**	glammer	**glamour**
gerlfrend	**girlfriend**	glanse	**glance**
germain	**germane****	glase	**glaze**
Germin	**German****	glashul	**glacial**
gerrintology	**gerontology**	glass sealing	**glass ceiling**
gerrund	**gerund**	glawsy	**glossy**
gescher	**gesture****	gleem	**gleam**
geshtalt	**gestalt**	glew	**glue**
gess	**guess**	glich	**glitch****
gest	**guest****	glidder	**glider**
geswit	**Jesuit**	glimer	**glimmer**
gettaway	**getaway**	glimse	**glimpse**
getto	**ghetto**	gliserin	**glycerin**
gettset	**jet set**	gliter	**glitter**
gezundhite	**gesundheit**	glitratty	**glitterati****
giantism	**gigantism**	glits	**glitz****
gidance	**guidance**	globle	**global**
gide	**guide**	gloome	**gloom****
gidy	**giddy**	glorafy	**glorify**
gient	**giant**	glosary	**glossary**
gigal	**giggle**	glosies	**glossies**
gigg	**gig**	glotis	**glottis**
giggabit	**gigabit**	glowkoma	**glaucoma**
giggolo	**gigolo**	gluecose	**glucose**
gighurts	**gigahertz**	glutin	**glutton****
gilless	**guileless**	gnawshus	**nauseous**
gillotine	**guillotine**	goalden parashoot	
gilty	**guilty**		**golden parachute**
gimick	**gimmick**	goble	**gobble****
giminasium	**gymnasium**	goblit	**goblet**
gimnast	**gymnast**	goddless	**godless**
ginacology	**gynecology**	gode	**goad**
ginee	**guinea**	godess	**goddess**
gingam	**gingham**	goegoe	**go-go**

Incorrect	Correct	Incorrect	Correct
goenad	**gonad**	gramy	**Grammy**
goffer	**gopher****	granaid	**grenade**
gogles	**goggles**	grandaughter	
gokart	**gocart**		**granddaughter**
gole	**goal****	grandur	**grandeur**
golebrick	**goldbrick**	grane	**grain**
gon	**gone**	granfather	**grandfather**
gondala	**gondola**	granmal	**grand mal**
gonnarea	**gonorrhea**	grannmother	
goofee	**goofy**		**grandmother**
goolag	**gulag**	gransmanship	
goolash	**goulash**		**grantsmanship**
gooroo	**guru**	grany	**granny**
gootenburg	**Gutenberg**	granyule	**granule**
gord	**gourd**	grashus	**gracious**
gorgous	**gorgeous**	grassp	**grasp**
gormet	**gourmet**	gratooty	**gratuity**
gosamer	**gossamer**	grattis	**gratis**
goshe	**gauche****	gravaty	**gravity**
gosip	**gossip**	gravle	**gravel**
gosspel	**gospel**	grayhound	**greyhound**
gost	**ghost**	graysful	**graceful**
gote	**goat**	greanhouse	**greenhouse**
gotea	**goatee**	greatful	**grateful**
goten	**gotten**	greating	**greeting**
goun	**gown**	gredy	**greedy**
gowge	**gouge**	greengoe	**gringo**
gowss	**gauss**	greevence	**grievance**
goyter	**goiter**	greevus	**grievous**
grabb	**grab**	greif	**grief**
graber	**grabber**	greive	**grieve**
gradduate	**graduate**	greivence	**grievance**
graditude	**gratitude**	gremmlin	**gremlin**
gradjewal	**gradual**	grene	**green**
graf	**graph**	grenemail	**greenmail**
graffic	**graphic**	grete	**greet**
grafics	**graphics**	grewsome	**gruesome**
grafitti	**graffiti**	greze	**grease****
grafology	**graphology**	griddlock	**gridlock**
gragarious	**gregarious**	gridiern	**gridiron**
graid	**grade**	grill	**grille****
graipfruit	**grapefruit**	grimas	**grimace**
graive	**grave**	grinn	**grin**
grajuation	**graduation**	grissed	**grist**
gramer	**grammar**	gritt	**grit**
gramm	**gram**	gritz	**grits**

Incorrect	Correct	Incorrect	Correct
groanup	**grown-up**	gudlookin	**goodlooking**
groap	**grope**	gud will	**goodwill**
grone	**groan****	gufe	**goof**
groop	**group**	guidence	**guidance**
groopy	**groupie**	gullable	**gullible**
grose	**gross**	guner	**gunner**
grosry	**grocery**	gurder	**girder**
grotesk	**grotesque**	gurlee	**girlie**
grothe	**growth**	guse	**goose**
grovey	**groovy**	gussto	**gusto**
growch	**grouch**	guter	**gutter**
grownd	**ground**	guterul	**guttural**
grownwork	**groundwork**	gutts	**guts**
groyn	**groin**	guvernment	**government**
gruje	**grudge**	guvnor	**governor**
grume	**groom**	guynofobia	**gynophobia**
grummpy	**grumpy**	guyser	**geyser**
grunje	**grunge**	gwackamola	**guacamole**
grutootous	**gratuitous**	gwash	**gouache****
gruve	**groove****	gygerbite	**gigabyte**
gruvil	**grovel**	gyger counter	
gryme	**grime**		**Geiger counter**
grynd	**grind**	gyle	**guile**
guage	**gauge****	gypsim	**gypsum**

		H		

Incorrect	Correct	Incorrect	Correct
habbit	**habit**	halaluyah	**hallelujah**
habichawate	**habituate**	halatosis	**halitosis**
habillitate	**habilitate**	Halaween	**Halloween**
habitchual	**habitual**	halcean	**halcyon**
hach	**hatch**	hale mary	**Hail Mary**
hackneed	**hackneyed**	halfs	**halves**
hadick	**haddock**	halmark	**hallmark**
haf	**half**	haloosination	
haffway	**halfway**		**hallucination**
hagerd	**haggard**	halow	**hallow****
hagil	**haggle**	halsion	**halcyon**
hainus	**heinous****	halusinate	**hallucinate**
hairbrained	**harebrained**	halusinogen	**hallucinogen**
hairlip	**harelip**	hamberger	**hamburger**
hait	**hate**	hamer	**hammer**
hakk	**hack**	hamlit	**hamlet**
hakker	**hacker**	hammatoe	**hammer toe**

Incorrect	Correct	Incorrect	Correct
hammstring	**hamstring**	haterd	**hatred**
hanbag	**handbag**	havock	**havoc**
hanbook	**handbook**	Hawayi	**Hawaii**
hancraft	**handicraft**	hawse	**horse****
hancuffs	**handcuffs**	haybeas korpis	
handdriting	**handwriting**		**habeas corpus**
handel	**handle**	haylo	**halo****
handycap	**handicap**	hayness	**heinous****
handywork	**handiwork**	hayrdue	**hairdo**
hanful	**handful**	hayrim	**harem**
hangkerchif	**handkerchief**	haytee	**Haiti**
hanmedown		haytful	**hateful**
	hand-me-down	hayvin	**haven****
hanngover	**hangover**	hayzy	**hazy**
hanoocah	**Hanukah**	hazbin	**has-been**
hant	**haunt**	hazil	**hazel**
hapin	**happen**	hazzerd	**hazard**
happly	**happily**	headake	**headache**
haradin	**harridan**	headinist	**hedonist**
harange	**harangue**	headress	**headdress**
harber	**harbor**	hearafter	**hereafter**
harboild	**hardboiled**	heartally	**heartily****
hardisk	**hard disk**	hebroo	**Hebrew**
hardning	**hardening**	hecktic	**hectic**
harecut	**haircut****	heddy	**heady**
haredresser	**hairdresser**	hede	**heed****
haried	**harried**	hedhunter	**headhunter**
Harlacwin	**harlequin**	hedkwarters	**headquarters**
harmoenyus	**harmonious**	hedlight	**headlight**
harnis	**harness**	hedline	**headline**
harrass	**harass**	hed-on	**head-on**
harrdship	**hardship**	heeler	**healer**
harremless	**harmless**	heematoma	**hematoma**
harrvest	**harvest**	heep	**heap**
harrykrishna		heerby	**hereby**
	Hare Krishna	heero	**hero**
harth	**hearth**	heet	**heat**
hartware	**hardware**	heetstroke	**heatstroke**
harty	**hearty****	heffer	**heifer**
hary	**hairy**	heighth	**height**
hasard	**hazard**	heirarchy	**hierarchy**
hasen	**hasten**	heje	**hedge**
hasienda	**hacienda**	hejemonoy	**hegemony**
hasle	**hassle****	hekil	**heckle**
hassidim	**Hasidim**	heksigon	**hexagon**
hatchit	**hatchet****	hel	**hell****

Incorrect	Correct	Incorrect	Correct
helish	**hellish**	hevy	**heavy**
hellem	**helm**	hevywait	**heavyweight**
hellicopter	**helicopter**	hewmongis	**humongous**
hellmit	**helmet**	hiarkill file	
hellples	**helpless**		**hierarchical file**
hellyn	**hellion**	hi-ball	**highball**
helo	**hello**	hibonate	**hibernate**
helth	**health**	hibread	**hybrid**
hemaglobin	**hemoglobin**	hibrow	**highbrow**
hemeroids	**hemorrhoids**	hich	**hitch**
hemesphere	**hemisphere**	hickup	**hiccup or hiccough**
hemm	**hem**	hiden	**hidden**
hemmafilia	**hemophilia**	hidensity	**high density**
hemmorage	**hemorrhage**	hideus	**hideous**
h-em-oh	**HMO**	hidrafobia	**hydrophobia**
hena	**henna**	hidranja	**hydrangea**
hensfourth	**henceforth**	hidraulic	**hydraulic**
hepful	**helpful**	hidrint	**hydrant**
hepparin	**heparin**	hidrofoil	**hydrofoil**
heppetitis	**hepatitis**	hidrogen	**hydrogen**
herassment	**harassment**	hidrokloric acid	
heratige	**heritage**		**hydrochloric acid**
herbashus	**herbaceous**	hiejack	**hijack**
herdel	**hurdle****	hiemlick manoover	
hereoic	**heroic**		**Heimlich maneuver**
heresay	**hearsay**	hifen	**hyphen**
herild	**herald**	hi-fidelity	**high fidelity**
hering	**herring****	hi-frequensy	
herisy	**heresy**		**high frequency**
herl	**hurl**	higbernate	**hibernate**
hermafradite		highpothesis	**hypothesis**
	hermaphrodite	highskool	**high school**
hermatige	**hermitage**	highst	**heist**
heros	**heroes**	hight	**height**
herredity	**heredity**	hi-handed	**high-handed**
herron	**heron**	hikery	**hickory**
her's	**hers**	hi-level	**high-level**
herse	**hearse**	hillarius	**hilarious**
hert	**hurt**	himen	**hymen**
hertofore	**heretofore**	hinderance	**hindrance**
hesatate	**hesitate**	hindoo	**Hindu**
hetagenius	**heterogeneous**	hinesite	**hindsight**
hethin	**heathen**	hiness	**highness**
hetrosexual	**heterosexual**	hinj	**hinge**
heve	**heave**	hipadermic	**hypodermic**
heven	**heaven****		

Incorrect	Correct	Incorrect	Correct
hipathermia		hoamboy	homeboy
	hyperthermia	hoap	hope
hiper	hyper	hobbell	hobble
hiperaktive	hyperacative	hobsinz cherce	
hiperbolee	hyperbole		Hobson's choice
hipersensetive		hoby	hobby**
	hypersensitive	hocky	hockey**
hipertension	hypertension	hoddog	hotdog
hipertext	hypertext	hoemefobia	homophobia
hipnosis	hypnosis	hojpoj	hodgepodge
hipnotist	hypnotist	hokes	hoax
hipocricy	hypocrisy	holagram	hologram
hipocrite	hypocrite	holea	wholly**
hipocritic oath		holedings	holdings
	Hippocratic oath	holedout	holdout
hipoglycemia		holeharted	wholehearted
	hypoglycemia	holesale	wholesale
hipopotimis		holesome	wholesome
	hippopotamus	holeycause	holocaust
hipotnoose	hypotenuse	holindaze	hollandaise
hippee	hippy	hollicust	holocaust
hipphopp	hiphop	holliday	holiday**
hippokrit	hypocrite	hollistic	holistic
hirearky	hierarchy	holow	hollow**
hiredditery	hereditary	holyness	holiness
hireup	higher-up	homaker	homemaker
hirezolution		homaside	homicide
	high resolution	homegeneous	
hirise	high-rise		homogeneous**
hirling	hireling	homerfobia	homophobia
hiroglific	hieroglyphic	homless	homeless
hiroism	heroism	homly	homely
hirpeas	herpes	hommage	homage
hisself	himself	hommonim	homonym
hisstamine	histamine	homoesexual	homosexual
hissterical	hysterical	homsick	homesick
histeria	hysteria	homsted	homestead
histerictomoy		homwork	homework
	hysterectomy	honakah	Hanukah
histry	history	honerable	honorable
hite	height	honeydo	honeydew
hi-teck	high-tech	honist	honest
hivv	HIV	honner	honor
hiway	highway	honny	honey
hiyena	hyena	honrary	honorary
hizpanic	Hispanic	honshow	honcho

Incorrect	Correct	Incorrect	Correct
honymoon	**honeymoon**	howzes	**houses**
hoo	**who**	hoy polloy	**hoi polloi**
hoobress	**hubris**	hoyst	**hoist****
hoonta	**junta****	hoze	**hose****
hoor	**whore****	hoziery	**hosiery**
hoove	**hoof**	hubb	**hub**
hopefull	**hopeful**	hubbkap	**hubcap**
hopeing	**hoping**	hud	**hood**
hopless	**hopeless**	hudd	**HUD**
horafyd	**horrified**	hudel	**huddle**
horemone	**hormone**	huf	**hoof**
horenjus	**horrendous**	huk	**hook**
horey	**hoary****	hukelbery	**huckleberry**
horible	**horrible**	hukworm	**hookworm**
horizen	**horizon**	humain	**humane****
horney	**horny**	humbell	**humble****
hornit	**hornet**	humer	**humor**
horra	**horror**	humilliate	**humiliate**
horrizontal	**horizontal**	huming	**humming**
horrorscope	**horoscope**	hummanities	**humanities**
horsey	**horsy**	humpe	**hump**
horshoe	**horseshoe**	humrus	**humorous****
horspower	**horsepower**	hunderd	**hundred**
hortaculcher	**horticulture**	hungar	**hunger**
horty	**haughty**	hungery	**hungry****
hosh	**harsh**	hupbub	**hubbub**
hosheesh	**hashish**	huray	**hurray**
hosspice	**hospice**	huricane	**hurricane**
hosspital	**hospital****	hurnia	**hernia**
hosspitality	**hospitality**	hursoot	**hirsute**
hosstel	**hostel****	hury	**hurry**
hostige	**hostage**	husle	**hustle**
hostle	**hostile****	hussler	**hustler**
hothedded	**hotheaded**	hute	**hoot**
hothows	**hothouse**	hutzpah	**chutzpah**
hotileer	**hotelier**	huvel	**hovel**
hottbed	**hotbed**	huver	**hover**
hottel	**hotel**	huxter	**huckster**
houshold	**household**	huzbind	**husband**
houswife	**housewife**	huzy	**hussy**
houzbraker	**housebreaker**	hyatis	**hiatus**
houzing	**housing**	hygene	**hygiene**
howel	**howl**	hymnil	**hymnal**
howevver	**however**	hyoobriss	**hubris**
hownd	**hound**	hypacrite	**hypocrite**
howskeeper	**housekeeper**		

Incorrect	Correct	Incorrect	Correct
hypatheticle	**hypothetical**	hyumanity	**humanity**
hypocracy	**hypocrisy**	hyumid	**humid**
hystrung	**high-strung**	hyumidifer	**humidifier**
hyumanatarien		hyumility	**humility**
	humanitarian	hyuristics	**heuristics**

I

Incorrect	Correct	Incorrect	Correct
iadine	**iodine**	Ilinois	**Illinois**
ibaprofen	**ibuprofen**	iliterate	**illiterate**
icahn	**icon or ikon**	illagitimate	**illegitimate**
iceing	**icing**	illeetist	**elitist**
icey	**icy**	illiad	**Iliad**
ich	**itch**	illisit	**illicit****
idd	**id**	illude	**elude****
ideel	**ideal**	illyitis	**ileitis**
ideer	**idea**	ilness	**illness**
idendicle	**identical**	ilogigal	**illogical**
identafy	**identify**	iltempered	**illtempered**
ideosyncracy	**idiosyncrasy**	iluminate	**illuminate****
idget	**idiot**	ilusion	**illusion****
idiology	**ideology**	ilusstrious	**illustrious**
idium	**idiom**	ilustrate	**illustrate**
idollater	**idolater**	imaculate	**immaculate**
idylic	**idyllic**	imadgine	**imagine**
iern	**iron****	imagrint	**immigrant****
iffie	**iffy**	imatation	**imitation**
iggnite	**ignite**	imaterial	**immaterial**
ignamineus	**ignominious**	imature	**immature**
ignerant	**ignorant**	imbark	**embark**
ignor	**ignore**	imbezzler	**embezzler**
igominy	**ignominy**	imbicile	**imbecile**
igwana	**iguana**	imbiew	**imbue****
igzasprate	**exasperate**	imeasurable	
iknishun	**ignition**		**immeasurable**
ikon	**icon**	imediate	**immediate**
ikonaclass	**iconoclast**	imense	**immense**
ikthiology	**ichthyology**	imenslee	**immensely**
iland	**island**	imerging	**emerging**
ilastic	**elastic**	imerse	**immerse**
ile	**isle****	imidiately	**immediately**
ilectronic	**electronic**	imige	**image**
ilegal	**illegal**	imigry	**imagery**
ilegible	**illegible****	iminint	**imminent****

Incorrect	Correct	Incorrect	Correct
immagination	imagination	imployee	employee
immegration	immigration	importence	importance
immemrable	immemorable	imposibility	impossibility
immesh	enmesh	impower	empower
immodest	immodest	imprasario	impresario
immpact	impact	impres	impress
immperative	imperative	impreshin	impression
immplore	implore	improovment	improvement
import	import	impuin	impugn
immpregnate	impregnate	impurfect	imperfect
immpropriety	impropriety	imput	input**
immpulse	impulse	impyaty	impiety
immpuritiy	impurity	imune	immune
imobil	immobile	inable	enable**
imoleate	immolate	inacceptable	unacceptable
imoral	immoral**	inaddmissible	inadmissible
imortil	immortal	inadekwit	inadequate
impare	impair	inadsesible	inaccessible
imparshal	impartial	inain	inane**
impashent	impatient	inamel	enamel
impashoned	impassioned	inamored	enamored
impasition	imposition	inamy	enemy**
impass	impasse	inate	innate
impaterbable	imperturbable	inaugarate	inaugurate
impatus	impetus	inavertent	inadvertent
impecible	impeccable	inavoidable	unavoidable
impeech	impeach	inawdible	inaudible
impeed	impede	inbalance	imbalance
impeerial	imperial	inbieb	imbibe
impell	impel	inbrolio	imbroglio
impenitrible	impenetrable	incalcable	incalculable
impervize	improvise	incarnit	incarnate
impetense	impotence	incert	insert**
impetent	impotent	incesint	incessant
impicunius	impecunious	incet	inset**
impinje	impinge	inchant	enchant
impirtenant	impertinent	inchoir	enquire
impius	impious	incidently	incidentally
implament	implement	incidious	insidious
implaquable	implacable	incinsere	insincere
implie	imply	incipid	insipid
implisit	implicit	incircle	encircle
		inclanation	inclination
		inclemit	inclement

Incorrect	Correct	Incorrect	Correct
inclood	**include**	inditement	**indictment**
inclosher	**enclosure**	individuly	**individually**
inclyne	**incline**	indocternate	**indoctrinate**
incogneto	**incognito**	indomnitable	**indomitable**
incombent	**incumbent**	indores	**indoors**
incondecent	**incandescent**	indowment	**endowment**
incorijible	**incorrigible**	induce	**induce**
incourage	**encourage**	inducment	**inducement**
incrament	**increment**	induktive	**inductive**
incredable	**incredible**	indurance	**endurance**
increse	**increase**	industral	**industrial**
incroch	**encroach**	Indyan	**Indian**
incryption	**encryption**	inefable	**ineffable**
incum	**income**	inekscusible	**inexcusable**
incumpatable		iner	**inner**
	incompatible	inersha	**inertia**
incured	**incurred**	inervate	**innervate****
incuring	**incurring**	inevatable	**inevitable**
incyclopedia	**encyclopedia**	inexrable	**inexorable**
incyurible	**incurable**	infadel	**infidel**
indagent	**indigent**	infadelaty	**infidelity**
indagestion	**indigestion**	infalible	**infallible**
indago	**indigo**	infamashun	**information**
indalent	**indolent**	infanitly	**infinitely**
indascreet	**indiscreet****	infecshun	**infection**
indaspensible		infent	**infant**
	indispensable	inferaction	**infraction**
indastry	**industry**	infered	**infrared**
indavisible	**indivisible****	inferier	**inferior**
inddent	**indent**	inferm	**infirm**
indeesent	**indecent**	infermary	**infirmary****
indefensable	**indefensible**	infermation	**information**
indeks	**index**	inferstructure	
indelable	**indelible**		**infrastructure**
independant	**independent**	infimous	**infamous**
indesent	**indecent**	infinative	**infinitive**
indesirable	**undesirable**	infincy	**infancy**
indesposed	**indisposed**	infintile	**infantile**
indetted	**indebted**	infintry	**infantry**
indiferent	**indifferent**	infireority	**inferiority**
indiggnent	**indignant**	inflamable	**inflammable**
indight	**indite****	inflashin	**inflation**
indijinus	**indigenous****	infleckshun	**inflection**
indiketive	**indicative**	inflewenza	**influenza**
indiscrible	**indescribable**	inflooence	**influence**
indisisive	**indecisive**	influcks	**influx**

Incorrect	Correct	Incorrect	Correct
influinse	**influence**	inklined	**inclined**
influmatin	**inflammation**	inkognito	**incognito**
inforce	**enforce**	inkoherent	**incoherent**
inforemal	**informal**	inkompitent	**incompetent**
infrence	**inference**	inkomunicado	
infur	**infer**		**incommunicado**
infurtility	**infertility**	inkoncievable	
infuze	**infuse**		**inconceivable**
infyuriate	**infuriate**	inkongrous	**incongruous**
ingagement	**engagement**	inkonspicuous	
ingconclusive			**inconspicuous**
	inconclusive	inkontanent	**incontinent**
ingection	**injection**	inkorpperate	**incorporate**
ingine	**engine**	inkredulous	**incredulous**
Inglish	**English**	inkriminate	**incriminate**
ingrachiate	**ingratiate**	inkubater	**incubator**
ingrave	**engrave**	inkwest	**inquest**
ingreat	**ingrate**	inkwiry	**inquiry**
ingreedient	**ingredient**	inkwisitive	**inquisitive**
ingunction	**injunction**	inkyubater	**incubator**
inhabatint	**inhabitant**	inlighten	**enlighten**
inhabition	**inhibition**	innabsencha	**in absentia**
inhail	**inhale**	innacurate	**inaccurate**
inhancement		innaproriate	
	enhancement		**inappropriate**
inhanse	**enhance**	innarticulate	**inarticulate**
inherrit	**inherit**	inn as much as	
inhyuman	**inhuman**		**inasmuch as**
inibility	**inability**	innaugurate	**inaugurate**
inifective	**ineffective**	innauspicious	
iniksplicible	**inexplicable**		**inauspicious**
iniquality	**inequality**	innclusive	**inclusive**
inishal	**initial**	inncomprable	
inishialise	**initialize**		**incomparable**
inixipirienced		inncomprehensible	
	inexperienced		**incomprehensible**
injary	**injury**	innconvenient	
injeanius	**ingenious****		**inconvenient**
injek	**inject**	inndemnity	**indemnity**
injery	**injury**	inndenture	**indenture**
injestion	**ingestion**	innduction	**induction**
injoyment	**enjoyment**	inndulge	**indulge**
inkapable	**incapable**	innebreate	**inebriate**
inkapacitate	**incapacitate**	innechative	**initiative**
inkarserate	**incarcerate**	innedible	**inedible**
inkeruptible	**incorruptible**	innefishent	**inefficient**

Incorrect	Correct	Incorrect	Correct
innept	**inept****	innventer	**inventor**
innfekshious	**infectious**	innvest	**invest****
innfermercial	**infomercial**	innvestigatin	
	or **informercial**		**investigation**
innfinitive	**infinitive**	innvolve	**involve**
innfinity	**infinity**	innvulnable	**invulnerable**
innflate	**inflate**	inocense	**innocence**
innflexible	**inflexible**	inocuous	**innocuous**
innfluenza	**influenza**	inordinant	**inordinate**
innformant	**informant**	inormous	**enormous**
innfringe	**infringe**	inovate	**innovate**
innfusion	**infusion**	inpail	**impale**
innhospitible	**inhospitable**	inpediment	**impediment**
innitiation	**initiation**	inpenitent	**impenitent**
innjustise	**injustice**	inpersonal	**impersonal**
innlaw	**in-law**	inpersonate	**impersonate**
innlay	**inlay**	inpitigo	**impetigo**
innoculate	**inoculate**	inplant	**implant**
innraktable	**intractable**	inplawsible	**implausible**
innrem	**in rem**	inpolite	**impolite**
innsekticide	**insecticide**	inpractical	**impractical**
innsert	**insert****	inprapritey	**impropriety**
innsignia	**insignia**	inpregnable	**impregnable**
innsist	**insist**	inprinting	**imprinting**
innsitutionalization		inprison	**imprison**
	institutionalization	inprobable	**improbable**
innsolvent	**insolvent**	inpromtu	**impromptu**
innsomia	**insomnia**	inproper	**improper**
innspection	**inspection**	inprovident	**improvident**
innstalation		inpulsive	**impulsive**
	installation**	inpunitiy	**impunity****
innstitution	**institution**	inquier	**inquire**
innstruction	**instruction**	inrich	**enrich**
innsult	**insult**	insalate	**insulate****
inntegrity	**integrity**	insalent	**insolent**
inntegument	**integument**	insanaty	**insanity**
inntermediary		inscrewtable	**inscrutable**
	intermediary	inseck	**insect**
inntestine	**intestine**	insekure	**insecure**
inntolerant	**intolerant**	insemble	**ensemble**
inntransagent		insendery	**incendiary**
	intransigent	insense	**incense**
inntrinsic	**intrinsic**	insentive	**incentive**
inntruder	**intruder**	inseprable	**inseparable**
innuit	**Inuit**	inserjint	**insurgent**
innveetro	**in vitro**	insest	**incest****

Incorrect	Correct	Incorrect	Correct
insibordinate		intavention	**intervention**
	insubordinate	intavil	**interval**
insident	**incident**	integeral	**integral**
insied	**inside**	intelectual	**intellectual**
insiggnificant		intelegance	**intelligence**
	insignificant	intemprate	**intemperate**
insiminate	**inseminate**	intensafy	**intensify**
insinerator	**incinerator**	intenshun	**intention**
insipient	**incipient****	interceed	**intercede**
insise	**incise**	intercep	**intercept**
insision	**incision**	intercorse	**intercourse**
insisive	**incisive**	interduce	**introduce**
insistant	**insistent**	interferance	**interference**
insite	**insight****	intergration	**integration**
inskription	**inscription**	interlewd	**interlude**
insolluble	**insoluble**	intermitent	**intermittent**
insparation	**inspiration**	intermural	**intramural**
instagate	**instigate**	internul	**internal**
instalment	**installment**	interpalate	**interpolate****
instatute	**institute**	interpet	**interpret**
insted	**instead**	interrest	**interest**
instense	**instance**	intersede	**intercede**
instibility	**instability**	intersession	
instink	**instinct**		**intercession****
instintaneus		interspection	
	instantaneous		**introspection**
instrament	**instrument**	interupt	**interrupt**
instruk	**instruct**	interusion	**intrusion**
insufrable	**insufferable**	interuterine	**intrauterine**
insurtion	**insertion**	intervenous	**intravenous**
insyulin	**insulin**	intervert	**introvert**
insyzer	**incisor**	intervue	**interview**
intacomm	**intercom**	inthrall	**enthrall**
intadick	**interdict**	inthusiasm	**enthusiasm**
intaface	**interface**	intifere	**interfere**
intagrate	**integrate**	intirior	**interior****
intajection	**interjection****	intooishun	**intuition**
intamarry	**intermarry**	intoragate	**interrogate**
intamate	**intimate****	intoxacate	**intoxicate**
intamediete	**intermediate**	intraactive	**interactive**
intanational	**international**	intracacy	**intricacy**
intanet	**Internet**	intradependent	
intangle	**entangle**		**interdependent**
intanjible	**intangible**	intradisciplinary	
intaseck	**intersect**		**interdisciplinary**
intavenous	**intravenous**	intraface	**interface**

Incorrect	Correct	Incorrect	Correct
intrafereon	**interferon**	iradiation	**irradiation**
intranet	**Internet**	irafutable	**irrefutable**
intrap	**entrap**	irational	**irrational**
intrapersonal		iredeemable	**irredeemable**
	interpersonal	iredendist	**irredentist**
intraracial	**interracial**	ireguler	**irregular**
intreeg	**intrigue**	irelevence	**irrelevance**
intresting	**interesting**	iresistable	**irresistible**
intrist	**interest**	iresponsible	**irresponsible**
introod	**intrude**	irevocable	**irrevocable**
inturvene	**intervene**	irigate	**irrigate**
inuendo	**innuendo**	iriny	**irony**
inuendos	**innuendoes**	iritable	**irritable**
inumberable	**innumerable**	irn	**urn****
inurt	**inert**	irrascible	**irascible**
invallid	**invalid**	irregardless	**regardless**
invalyable	**invaluable**	irrelentless	**relentless**
invatation	**invitation**	irrevelant	**irrelevant****
invazhun	**invasion**	irridesent	**iridescent**
invegel	**inveigle**	isalate	**isolate**
invektive	**invective**	isberg	**iceberg**
invelop	**envelop****	isertope	**isotope**
invenerate	**inveterate**	ishue	**issue**
inveriably	**invariably**	ishuence	**issuance**
invesment	**investment**	ismus	**isthmus**
investagate	**investigate**	isreal	**Israel**
invey	**inveigh**	issometric	**isometric**
invidyus	**invidious**	ither	**either****
invigerate	**invigorate**	itily	**Italy**
invintory	**inventory**	itim	**item**
invironment	**environment**	itomise	**itemize**
invizable	**invisible****	ivary	**ivory**
invoise	**invoice**	ivey	**ivy****
invollintery	**involuntary**	I witness	**eyewitness**
invurtabrate	**invertebrate**	iyatrogenic	**iatrogenic**
inwerd	**inward**	i-you-d	**IUD**
ipacak	**ipecac**	Izlam	**Islam**
iradesense	**iridescence**	Izrael	**Israel**

<hr>

J

jac	**jack**	jackuzi	**jacuzzi**
jackel	**jackal**	jaewak	**jaywalk**
jacknife	**jackknife**	jagantic	**gigantic**

Incorrect	Correct	Incorrect	Correct
jaged	**jagged**	jenny may	**Ginnie Mae**
jagg	**jag**	jenoside	**genocide**
jagwar	**jaguar**	jentile	**gentile****
jaid	**jade**	jenyus	**genius****
jakass	**jackass**	jepordy	**jeopardy**
jaket	**jacket**	jeramide	**jeremiad**
jakpot	**jackpot**	jere	**jeer**
jale	**jail**	jermicide	**germicide**
jallopy	**jalopy**	jerney	**journey****
jamaca	**Jamaica**	jerontology	**gerontology**
jamberee	**jamboree**	jerrimander	**gerrymander**
janator	**janitor**	jersy	**jersey**
janetic	**genetic**	jeryatricks	**geriatrics**
jangel	**jangle**	jestation	**gestation**
Januwery	**January**	jetison	**jettison**
Jappenese	**Japanese**	jetsome	**jetsam**
jargin	**jargon**	jett	**jet**
jarver	**java**	jettlagg	**jet lag**
jassy	**jazzy**	jety	**jetty**
javvlin	**javelin**	jeu jitsoo	**jujitsu**
jawndis	**jaundice**	jewdo	**judo**
jawz	**jaws**	jewdyism	**Judaism**
jaylbrake	**jailbreak**	jewellary	**jewelry**
jayride	**joyride**	jewls	**jewels**
jaysee	**Jaycee**	jewsy	**juicy**
jaz	**jazz**	Jezuit	**Jesuit**
jazmin	**jasmine**	jieb	**jibe****
jeanyal	**genial**	jiffiebag	**jiffybag**
jear	**jeer**	jify	**jiffy**
jeehad	**jihad**	jigabute	**gigabyte**
Jefersonien	**Jeffersonian**	jigel	**jiggle**
jejewne	**jejune****	jiger	**jigger**
jekill and hide		jigg	**jig**
	Jekyll and Hyde	jiggsaw	**jigsaw**
jelatin	**gelatine**	jimnastics	**gymnastics**
jellus	**jealous****	jimy	**jimmy**
jely	**jelly**	jingel	**jingle**
jembellia	**jambalaya**	jingivitis	**gingivitis**
jenatype	**genotype**	jingoe	**jingo**
jender	**gender**	jinjer	**ginger**
jenecide	**genocide**	jinjiva	**gingiva**
jeneration	**generation**	jinnie mays	**Ginny Maes**
jeneric	**generic**	jip	**gyp**
jenes	**jeans****	jipsee	**gypsy**
jenesis	**genesis**	jiraf	**giraffe**
jenetalia	**genitalia**	jirascope	**gyroscope**

Incorrect	Correct	Incorrect	Correct
jiters	**jitters**	joyne	**join**
jittney	**jitney**	joynt	**joint**
joak	**joke**	joyst	**joist**
jobb	**job****	joyus	**joyous**
jober	**jobber**	jubalee	**jubilee**
jogg	**jog****	judgement	**judgment**
joiful	**joyful**	judishary	**judiciary**
jokend	**jocund**	judism	**Judaism**
jokey	**jockey**	juganaut	**juggernaut**
jokker	**joker**	juge	**judge**
jokstrap	**jockstrap**	juggalar	**jugular****
jokular	**jocular**	jugler	**juggler****
jolet	**jolt**	jukstapose	**juxtapose**
joly	**jolly**	jumaika	**Jamaica**
jondarm	**gendarme**	jumbel	**jumble**
jonre	**genre**	jummp	**jump**
joobilunt	**jubilant**	jungel	**jungle**
joodaika	**Judaica**	jungshin	**junction**
joodas	**Judas**	junkee	**junkie** or **junky**
joodishal	**judicial**	junkit	**junket**
joodoe	**judo**	junkture	**juncture**
jooish	**Jewish**	junnkbond	**junk bond**
joojoo	**juju**	junnter	**junta****
jook box	**jukebox**	junque	**junk**
joolie	**July**	jurey	**jury****
joolip	**julep**	jurk	**jerk**
jools	**jewels**	jurnal	**journal**
joon	**June**	jurnlist	**journalist**
joonyer	**junior**	jurrooslim	**Jerusalem**
joorisdicshun	**jurisdiction**	jushe	**Jewish**
joorist	**jurist**	juss	**juice****
joose	**juice****	justefy	**justify**
joot	**jute****	justise	**justice**
josle	**jostle**	juvinile	**juvenile**
joting	**jotting**	jwa de veever	**joi de vivre**
jouns	**jounce**	jymnast	**gymnast**
joveal	**jovial**	jyrate	**gyrate**
joynder	**joinder**	jyve	**jive**

K

Incorrect	Correct	Incorrect	Correct
kache	**cache****	kafee klotch	
kadet	**cadet**		**kaffeeklatsch**
kadish	**Kaddish****	kaff	**calf**

Incorrect	Correct	Incorrect	Correct
kahki	**khaki**	kenard	**canard**
kameleon	**chameleon**	Kenedy	**Kennedy**
kameo	**cameo**	kenel	**kennel**
kangeroo	**kangaroo**	keosk	**kiosk**
kanish	**knish**	keoty	**coyote**
kanoo	**canoe**	kep	**kept**
kao	**kayo or K.O.**	kepe	**keep**
kaos	**chaos**	kerasene	**kerosene**
kapput	**kaput**	kerser	**cursor**
kaptive	**captive**	kersh	**kirsch**
karacter	**character**	kerst	**cursed**
karateen	**carotene**	kertin	**curtain**
karisma	**charisma**	kerupt	**corrupt**
karmer	**karma**	kerve	**curve**
karof	**carafe**	ketch	**catch**
	Kaposi's sarcoma	ketel	**kettle**
karposee sarcoma		kettosis	**ketosis**
karsinoma	**carcinoma**	keyo plan	**Keogh plan**
kasm	**chasm**	kiak	**kayak**
katar	**catarrh**	kibbitzer	**kibitzer**
kaveat empter		kible	**kibble**
	caveat emptor	kichin	**kitchen**
kavel	**cavil**	kiddnap	**kidnap**
kayle	**kale**	kidnee	**kidney**
kaynine	**canine**	kiebosh	**kibosh**
kaypok	**kapok**	kik-off	**kickoff**
k'bob	**kebob**	kilacicle	**kilocycle**
keal	**keel**	kilagram	**kilogram**
kean	**keen**	kilbassa	**kielbasa**
keaper	**keeper**	kiler	**killer**
keapunch	**keypunch**	kiljoy	**killjoy**
keatone	**ketone**	killabite	**kilobyte**
kechup	**ketchup**	killen	**kiln****
kee	**key****	killerbawd	**kilobaud**
keebored	**keyboard**	killerhertz	**kilohertz**
keekback	**kickback**	killometre	**kilometer**
keelo	**kilo**	killowatt	**kilowatt**
keenote	**keynote**	kimona	**kimono**
keepunch	**keypunch**	kindel	**kindle**
keesh	**quiche**	kindergarden	
keestone	**keystone**		**kindergarten**
keewee	**kiwi**	kindrid	**kindred**
kegg	**keg**	kinely	**kindly**
kellp	**kelp**	kiness	**kindness**
Keltic	**Celtic**	kingdum	**kingdom**
ken	**can**		

Incorrect	Correct	Incorrect	Correct
kiniscope	**kinescope**	kolyumnist	**columnist**
kinnetic	**kinetic**	komfortable	**comfortable**
kinpin	**kingpin**	koming	**coming**
kiper	**kipper**	kommunist	**communist**
kiropedy	**chiropody**	konclusion	**conclusion**
kist	**kissed**	konosewer	**connoisseur**
kitastrofy	**catastrophe**	kool	**cool**
kitin	**kitten**	koris	**chorus**
kiyoty	**coyote**	korz	**corps****
klak	**claque**	koytis	**coitus**
klandestin	**clandestine**	kraft	**craft**
klassified	**classified**	kriptic	**cryptic**
kleek	**clique****	kriptology	**cryptology**
klenser	**cleanser**	kronic	**chronic**
kloan	**clone****	kubism	**cubism**
klorine	**chlorine**	kudgel	**cudgel**
kloy	**cloy**	kul-de-sac	**cul-de-sac**
kneonatal	**neonatal**	kulture	**culture**
knewral	**neural**	kumpendium	
knewrosis			**compendium**
knewspeak	**newspeak**	kurnel	**colonel****
knewt	**newt**	kurvashus	**curvaceous**
knewter	**neuter**	kusp	**cusp**
knifes	**knives**	kuspea	**cuspy**
knotation	**notation**	kwertee	**QUERTY**
knoted	**knotted**	kwier	**quire****
knowed	**knew****	kwik	**quick**
know-fault	**no-fault**	kwiksotic	**quixotic**
knowlege	**knowledge**	kwinella	**quinella**
knowmad	**nomad**	kwire	**choir****
kochere	**kosher**	kworem	**quorum**
kolic	**colic**	kwotidian	**quotidian**

L

Incorrect	Correct	Incorrect	Correct
labb	**lab**	lachkee kid	**latchkey kid**
labedo	**libido****	laciny	**larceny**
laber	**labor**	lacker	**lacquer**
labidinus	**libidinous**	lacksitive	**laxative**
labirinth	**labyrinth**	lacktose	**lactose**
lable	**label**	ladel	**ladle**
labotomy	**lobotomy**	lader	**ladder**
labratory	**laboratory**	ladys	**ladies**
lach	**latch**	laffable	**laughable**

Incorrect	Correct	Incorrect	Correct
laffter	**laughter**	larseny	**larceny**
lagard	**laggard**	lasatude	**lassitude**
lage	**large**	lase	**lace**
lagg	**lag**	laserate	**lacerate**
laging	**lagging**	lasivious	**lascivious**
lagune	**lagoon**	laso	**lasso**
lahiyime	**l'chaim**	lasseration	**laceration**
laim	**lame****	latatude	**latitude**
laim duck	**lame duck**	latenna	**Latina****
laison	**liaison**	laticework	**latticework**
lait	**late**	latly	**lately**
lakey	**lackey**	latril	**laetrile**
lakrimos	**lachrymose**	lattent	**latent**
laks	**lax**	latteral	**lateral**
laksadaysakle		lattin	**Latin**
	lackadaisical	lattino	**Latino****
laktation	**lactation**	laveleer	**lavaliere**
lakuna	**lacuna**	lavinder	**lavender**
lakwashus	**loquacious**	lavitory	**lavatory**
lamanate	**laminate**	lavva	**lava****
lambast	**lambaste**	lavvish	**lavish**
lamentible	**lamentable**	lawd	**lord****
lammentation		lawdanum	**laudanum**
	lamentation	lawdible	**laudable**
lamskin	**lambskin**	lawft	**loft**
lanalin	**lanolin**	lawnder	**launder**
langer	**languor**	lawndry	**laundry**
langwidge	**language****	lawnhand	**longhand**
langwish	**languish****	lawsoot	**lawsuit**
lanlady	**landlady**	layed	**laid**
lanlord	**landlord**	laytest	**latest**
lanmark	**landmark**	laytex	**latex**
lann	**LAN**	laywer	**lawyer**
lannedlocked	**landlocked**	lazyness	**laziness**
lanscape	**landscape**	leafs	**leaves**
lanse	**lance**	leakige	**leakage**
lantin	**lantern**	leanyent	**lenient**
lanyap	**lagniappe**	leasor	**lessor****
lanzheree	**lingerie**	leasure	**leisure**
lapce	**lapse**	leathil	**lethal**
lapell	**lapel**	leazon	**liaison**
laprascope	**laparoscope**	lecksacon	**lexicon**
laringitis	**laryngitis**	leconic	**laconic**
larinx	**larynx**	ledgislature	**legislature**
larrgess	**largesse**	leeder	**leader**
larrva	**larva****	leeg	**league**

Incorrect	Correct	Incorrect	Correct
leegenares disease		lettup	letup
	legionnaires' disease	levatation	levitation
leejon	legion	leve	leave**
lees	least**	leven	eleven
leese	lease	levey	levee**
leezon	lesion	levle	level
leff	left	levler	leveler
leffhanded	left-handed	levrage	leverage
leffovers	leftovers	levven	leaven
legallize	legalize	levver	lever
leger	ledger	lew	lieu
legil	legal	lewow	luau
legissy	legacy	leyoff	layoff
legitamate	legitimate	leyway	layaway
leif	leaf**	lez majesty	lese majesty
leige	liege	lezbian	lesbian
leisurly	leisurely	libaterian	libertarian
lejable	legible	libbity	liberty
lejend	legend	liber	LIBOR
lejerdeman	legerdemain	liberalizm	liberalism
lejjer	ledger	liberry	library
lejon	legion	libility	liability
lekcher	lecture	lible	libel**
lemenade	lemonade	libral	liberal
lemmen	lemon	libreto	libretto
lended	lent	lickrish	licorice
lenth	length	lickwidate	liquidate
lenz	lens	lieing	lying
leperd	leopard	lier	liar**
lepersy	leprosy	lifboat	lifeboat
leprakon	leprechaun	lifes	lives
lept	leaped	liffoff	liftoff
lerch	lurch	lifgard	lifeguard
lern	learn	liftime	lifetime
lesen	lessen**	ligiment	ligament
lessay fare	laissez-faire	ligiture	ligature
lesse majesty	lese majesty	likker	liquor**
lessithin	lecithin	likly	likely
letahead	letterhead	likness	likeness
letchery	lechery	lillac	lilac
leter	letter**	lilly	lily
lether	leather	lim	limb**
lethergy	lethargy	limazine	limousine
letice	lettuce	limba	limber
lets	let's	limbow	limbo
letterd	lettered	lime disease	Lyme disease

Incorrect	Correct	Incorrect	Correct
limf	**lymph**	littligious	**litigious**
limfoma	**lymphoma**	littmus	**litmus**
limlite	**limelight**	livegard	**lifeguard**
limmbic	**limbic**	liven	**enliven**
limmit	**limit**	livlihood	**livelihood**
lims	**limps**	livly	**lively**
linament	**liniment****	livry	**livery**
Lincon	**Lincoln**	livstock	**livestock**
lingweeny	**linguine**	livvid	**livid****
lingwist	**linguist**	lizzard	**lizard**
linier	**linear****	loab	**lobe**
linkd	**linked**	loball	**lowball**
linkige	**linkage**	lobbie	**lobby**
linnen	**linen**	lobbster	**lobster**
linnger	**linger**	lobbster shift	**lobster shift**
linnoleum	**linoleum**	lobey	**lobby**
linnt	**lint**	lobrow	**lowbrow**
linx	**lynx****	locallize	**localize**
lionman	**lineman**	locamotive	**locomotive**
lippstick	**lipstick**	loccation	**location**
lipsink	**lip-sync**	lockket	**locket**
liqued	**liquid**	loecal	**low-cal**
liquify	**liquefy**	lofer	**loafer**
liric	**lyric**	loffty	**lofty**
lirk	**lurk**	logerithm	**logarithm**
lisence	**license**	loggic	**logic**
lisenshus	**licentious**	log off	**log-off**
lisergic acid	**lysergic acid**	logon	**log-on**
lisome	**lissome**	loial	**loyal**
lissed	**list**	loiyer	**lawyer**
lissen	**listen**	loje	**lodge****
litabug	**litterbug**	lokate	**locate**
litchen	**lichen****	lokist	**locust****
lite	**light**	lokjaw	**lockjaw**
liteharted	**lighthearted**	lokkout	**lockout**
litemotif	**leitmotiv**	lokus	**locus****
lite pen	**light pen**	lolode	**loload**
litergical	**liturgical**	lon	**lawn**
litewait	**lightweight**	lonch	**launch**
litheum	**lithium**	loneshark	**loanshark**
litle	**little**	longgwinded	**long-winded**
litorary	**literary**	lonjeray	**lingerie**
litracy	**literacy**	lonjevaty	**longevity**
litrature	**literature**	lonjitude	**longitude**
littany	**litany**	lonliness	**loneliness**
litteral	**literal**		

Incorrect	Correct	Incorrect	Correct
lonly	**lonely**	lozer	**loser**
lonsome	**lonesome**	lubercate	**lubricate**
loocrative	**lucrative**	lucksury	**luxury**
lood	**lewd**	ludacrus	**ludicrous**
looftmensh	**luftmensch**	luet	**lute****
looje	**luge**	lufa	**loofah**
looloo	**lulu**	lugage	**luggage**
loonatic	**lunatic**	luke	**luck**
looner	**lunar**	lukeism	**lookism**
loopus	**lupus**	lukemia	**leukemia**
loor	**lure**	lukout	**lookout**
loosid	**lucid**	lukra	**lucre**
lootenant	**lieutenant**	lukshurient	**luxuriant****
loover	**louver**	lukwarm	**lukewarm**
Loovre	**Louvre**	lulaby	**lullaby**
looze	**lose****	luminecent	**luminescent**
lor	**lore****	lummpectomy	
lorel	**laurel**		**lumpectomy**
loresoot	**lawsuit**	lunasy	**lunacy**
lornyet	**lorgnette**	lunchin	**luncheon**
lorre	**law****	lunchinet	**luncheonette**
los	**loss****	lunng	**lung**
losenge	**lozenge**	luny	**loony**
loshun	**lotion**	lupehole	**loophole**
lothe	**loathe****	lushous	**luscious**
lothsum	**loathsome**	lusster	**luster**
loto	**lotto**	lusterous	**lustrous**
loveable	**lovable**	luv	**love**
loveing	**loving**	luxry	**luxury**
lovly	**lovely**	luzer	**loser**
lowd	**loud**	lydacaine	**lydocaine**
lowdspeaker	**loudspeaker**	lyeing	**lying**
lowgoe	**logo**	lykwise	**likewise**
lownje	**lounge**	lyme	**lime****
lowt	**lout**	lynchpin	**linchpin**
loyter	**loiter**	lynup	**lineup**
		lyon	**lion**

M

Incorrect	Correct	Incorrect	Correct
macanic	**mechanic**	maccaroni	**macaroni**
macarune	**macaroon**	machurashun	**maturation**
maccab	**macabre**	machure	**mature**
maccadim	**macadam**	macintosh	**mackintosh**

Incorrect	Correct	Incorrect	Correct
mackismo	**machismo**	malaze	**malaise**
mackrel	**mackerel**	malebox	**mailbox**
mackro	**macro**	maleman	**mailman**
madalion	**medallion**	malestorm	**maelstrom**
madd	**mad**	malfezence	**malfeasance**
maddame	**madame**	maliable	**malleable**
maddros	**madras**	maline	**malign**
madmwazel	**mademoiselle**	malingger	**malinger**
madona	**Madonna**	malishus	**malicious**
mafea	**Mafia**	mallady	**malady**
magesty	**majesty**	mallagusted	**maladjusted**
maggiler	**megillah**	mallaria	**malaria**
maggnanimous		mallformation	
	magnanimous		**malformation**
maggnesium	**magnesium**	mallignant	**malignant**
magizine	**magazine**	mallis	**malice**
magnatude	**magnitude**	mallnutrition	
magnifasense			**malnutrition**
	magnificence	mallpractice	**malpractice**
magnit	**magnet****	malpropism	**malapropism**
magot	**maggot**	mamagram	**mammogram**
mahchow	**macho**	mamal	**mammal**
mahiraja	**maharajah**	mamalade	**marmalade**
mahvlus	**marvelous**	mame	**maim**
maibe	**maybe****	mamell	**mammal**
maice	**mace**	mammery	**mammary**
maidnly	**maidenly**	mamosa	**mimosa**
mainger	**manger**	mamuth	**mammoth**
mainia	**mania**	manacure	**manicure**
maintainance		manafacture	**manufacture**
	maintenance	manafesto	**manifesto**
maionaize	**mayonnaise**	manafold	**manifold**
maitriarc	**matriarch**	managable	**manageable**
majer	**major**	managut	**manicotti**
majik	**magic**	manajer	**manager**
majistrat	**magistrate**	manakin	**mannequin**
majoraty	**majority**	mand	**manned**
Makavelian		mandable	**mandible**
	Machiavellian	manditory	**mandatory**
makeing	**making**	maneac	**maniac**
makismo	**machismo**	maneframe	**mainframe**
makrobiotic	**macrobiotic**	maneland	**mainland**
maksi	**maxi**	maner	**manner****
makup	**makeup**	manestream	**mainstream**
maladikshun	**malediction**	mangel	**mangle**
malaklusion	**malocclusion**	manginese	**manganese**

Incorrect	Correct	Incorrect	Correct
manicle	**manacle**	marvilus	**marvelous**
manje	**mange**	masaje	**massage**
manjer	**manger**	masaker	**massacre**
mannic depressive		masakist	**masochist**
	manic depressive	mascuelin	**masculine**
mannipulative		mashety	**machete**
	manipulative	mashinery	**machinery**
mannkind	**mankind**	Masichusetts	
manogamist	**monogamist**		**Massachusetts**
manoor	**manure**	masinry	**masonry**
manotinus	**monotonous**	masive	**massive**
manshun	**mansion**	maskerade	**masquerade**
mantlpeace	**mantelpiece**	maskuline	**masculine**
manule	**manual**	masooze	**masseuse**
manuscrip	**manuscript**	massala	**marsala**
manuver	**maneuver**	masscara	**mascara**
manyana	**mañana**	massokism	**masochism**
mapul	**maple**	masstektimy	**mastectomy**
maraskino	**maraschino**	masstermind	**mastermind**
marass	**morass**	masta	**master**
maratell	**marital****	mastacate	**masticate**
maratime	**maritime**	mastarpiece	**masterpiece**
marawana	**marijuana**	masterbait	**masturbate**
marawder	**marauder**	mastoyd	**mastoid**
marbel	**marble**	masur	**masseur**
marc	**mark****	matar	**matter**
marcdown	**markdown**	mater de	**maître d'**
mareen	**marine**	maternaty	**maternity**
marey	**marry****	mathamatics	
marige	**marriage****		**mathematics**
marjerin	**margarine**	matinay	**matinée**
marjin	**margin**	matramony	**matrimony**
markee	**marquis**	matrinly	**matronly**
markez	**marquise**	matris	**mattress**
markit	**market**	matterial	**material**
marksism	**Marxism**	mattriculate	**matriculate**
marow	**marrow**	maturnal	**maternal**
marragable	**marriageable**	mavrick	**maverick**
marrathon	**marathon**	mawdlin	**maudlin**
marrawder	**marauder**	maxamum	**maximum**
marrkup	**markup**	mayer	**mayor**
marryed	**married**	maylanje	**mélange**
marteeni	**martini**	maylay	**melée****
marter	**martyr**	maynage ataw	
martygra	**Mardi Gras**		**ménage à trois**
marune	**maroon**	mayntane	**maintain**

Incorrect	Correct	Incorrect	Correct
maysa	**mesa**	melow	**mellow**
mayteeay	**métier****	memberane	**membrane**
maytreeark	**matriarch**	mementum	**momentum**
maytricks	**matrix**	memmber	**member**
maytrix	**matrix**	memmento	**memento**
mayvin	**maven**	memmorial	**memorial**
mazoleum	**mausoleum**	memrable	**memorable**
meaness	**meanness**	memrandum	
meanyal	**menial**		**memorandum**
meca	**mecca** or **Mecca**	memry	**memory**
mecanic	**mechanic**	memwar	**memoir**
mecksikin	**Mexican**	menajery	**menagerie**
Medacare	**Medicare**	menapause	**menopause**
medamorfisis		menise	**menace**
	metamorphosis	menningitis	**meningitis**
medecine	**medicine**	mennora	**menorah**
medekade	**Medicaid**	mennstration	
medel	**medal****		**menstruation**
medeocker	**mediocre**	menshun	**mention**
medetate	**meditate**	menstrate	**menstruate**
Mediteranean		ment	**meant**
	Mediterranean	mentch	**mensch**
medle	**meddle****	mentle	**mental**
medly	**medley**	meny	**many**
medow	**meadow**	menyu	**menu**
medyation	**mediation**	merandise	**Mirandize**
meedea	**media**	merang	**meringue**
meediate	**mediate**	meratocricy	**meritocracy**
meedjum	**medium**	merchindize	**merchandise**
meeger	**meager**	mercinery	**mercenary**
meeteor	**meteor****	merder	**murder**
meet market	**meat market**	merderer	**murderer**
meggerbite	**megabyte**	merdger	**merger**
meglomania		meret	**merit**
	megalomania	merje	**merge**
mein	**mien****	merly	**merely**
mekanize	**mechanize**	mermer	**murmur**
meklizine	**meclizine**	merryland	**Maryland**
meksako	**Mexico**	merryly	**merrily**
meldown	**meltdown**	mersy	**mercy**
melincoly	**melancholy**	merth	**mirth**
mellanoma	**melanoma**	mesenger	**messenger**
mellenen	**melanin**	mesing	**messing**
mellodious	**melodious**	messcline	**mescaline**
mellodrama	**melodrama**	mesure	**measure**
mellon	**melon**	mesy	**messy**

Incorrect	Correct	Incorrect	Correct
mesyur	**monsieur**	miligram	**milligram****
metafor	**metaphor**	milinary	**millinery****
metamfetimine		milionaire	**millionaire**
	methamphetamine	millicha	**militia**
metefisics	**metaphysics**	millyou	**milieu**
meteocrity	**mediocrity**	milogram	**myelogram****
meterial	**material**	miloma	**myeloma**
Methadist	**Methodist**	minamize	**minimize**
methe	**meth**	minamum	**minimum**
methed	**method**	Minasota	**Minnesota**
methedone	**methadone**	minature	**miniature**
metripolitan	**metropolitan**	mingel	**mingle**
metroe	**metro**	miniral	**mineral**
mettabolism	**metabolism**	minis	**minus**
mettalic	**metallic**	miniscule	**minuscule**
mettastasis	**metastasis**	minit	**minute**
metticulous	**meticulous**	minnimum	**minimum**
mettre de	**maitre d'**	minnister	**minister**
mettric	**metric**	minnyseries	**miniseries**
meucus	**mucous**	minoksidil	**minoxidil**
mezaneen	**mezzanine**	minoraty	**minority**
mezels	**measles**	minse	**mince****
mezmerize	**mesmerize**	minusha	**minutiae**
miakulper	**mea culpa**	miny	**mini**
micerorganism		minycomputer	
	microorganism		**minicomputer**
micersurgery		miopia	**myopia**
	microsurgery	miopic	**myopic**
micrascope	**microscope**	miricle	**miracle**
miday	**midday**	mirky	**murky**
middel	**middle**	miror	**mirror**
middwife	**midwife**	mirraje	**mirage****
midevil	**medieval**	mirtle	**myrtle**
midnite	**midnight**	mischevous	**mischievous**
mikerchip	**microchip**	mischif	**mischief**
mikerfilm	**microfilm**	miselaneous	
mikrafone	**microphone**		**miscellaneous**
mikro	**micro**	mishigan	**Michigan**
mikrobiology		mishin	**mission**
	microbiology	mishnary	**missionary**
mikrowave	**microwave**	Mississippi	**Mississippi**
mikture	**mixture**	miskast	**miscast**
milage	**mileage**	mislayed	**mislaid**
milameter	**millimeter**	mispell	**misspell**
milatery	**military**	mispropriate	
milenium	**millennium**		**misappropriate**

Incorrect	Correct	Incorrect	Correct
misquito	**mosquito**	mobd	**mobbed**
misrable	**miserable**	mobill	**mobile**
misry	**misery**	mobillize	**mobilize**
misscarage	**miscarriage**	mocassin	**moccasin**
missconception		moch	**mosh**
	misconception	moddality	**modality**
missconduct	**misconduct**	modderate	**moderate**
missdemeaner		modifyer	**modifier**
	misdemeanor	modil	**model****
missel	**missile****	modis operande	
misselaneous			**modus operandi**
	miscellaneous	modist	**modest**
missfit	**misfit**	modren	**modern**
missfortune	**misfortune**	modrenism	**modernism**
missgiving	**misgiving**	moedem	**modem**
misshap	**mishap**	moffia	**Mafia**
missin	**missing**	mogill	**mogul**
missojiny	**misogyny**	Mohamedin	
misstake	**mistake**		**Muhammadan**
misster	**mister**	mohoginy	**mahogany**
misstrial	**mistrial**	mojulate	**modulate**
missunderstand		moka	**mocha**
	misunderstand	mokery	**mockery**
mistacizm	**mysticism**	moksy	**moxie**
mistate	**misstate**	molatto	**mulatto**
mistep	**misstep**	moler	**molar**
misterious	**mysterious**	molify	**mollify**
mistery	**mystery**	mollases	**molasses**
misthenia graves		mollecule	**molecule**
	myasthenia gravis	mollestation	**molestation**
mistic	**mystic**	mombo	**mambo**
mistify	**mystify**	mommentus	**momentous**
mistris	**mistress**	monalith	**monolith**
mitabilism	**metabolism**	monalog	**monologue**
mitagate	**mitigate****	monarail	**monorail**
miterm	**midterm**	monark	**monarch**
mith	**myth**	monatery	**monetary**
mithical	**mythical**	mone	**moan**
mittin	**mitten**	moneter	**monitor**
mizanthrope	**misanthrope**	monistery	**monastery**
mizer	**miser**	monitone	**monotone**
mizerable	**miserable**	monnakrone	
mizuri	**Missouri**		**monochrome**
moal	**mole**	monniter	**monitor**
moap	**mope**	monnopolly	**monopoly**
mobb	**mob**	monnster	**monster**

Incorrect	Correct	Incorrect	Correct
monsterous	**monstrous**	mowse	**mouse****
mony	**money**	mowthpeace	**mouthpiece**
monyument	**monument**	moyschur	**moisture**
moomoo	**muumuu**	mozaic	**mosaic**
moovie	**movie**	muchroom	**mushroom**
morano	**Marrano**	mudy	**muddy**
morebid	**morbid**	mufin	**muffin**
morebund	**moribund**	muger	**mugger**
Moreman	**Mormon**	mugg	**mug**
moreon	**moron**	mukkup	**mockup**
moretality	**mortality**	mula	**mullah**
morfeen	**morphine**	mulagatanny	
morg	**morgue**		**mulligatawny**
morgage	**mortgage**	muleish	**mulish**
mornfull	**mournful**	mulltemillionaire	
moroco	**Morocco**		**multimillionaire**
morover	**moreover**	mulltinational	
morralty	**morality**		**multinational**
morrbidity	**morbidity**	mulltiple sklerosis	
morsal	**morsel**		**multiple sclerosis**
mortafy	**mortify**	mulltiplier	**multiplier**
mortaly	**mortally**	multaplex	**multiplex**
morter	**mortar**	multaply	**multiply**
mortuery	**mortuary**	multatude	**multitude**
mose	**most**	multykultural	
moseltough	**mazeltov**		**multicultural**
moshin	**motion**	multymedia	**multimedia**
moshroom	**mushroom**	multytasking	
mosk	**mosque**		**multitasking**
moskeeto	**mosquito**	mumbel	**mumble**
mosy	**mossy**	mummy trak	
motavate	**motivate**		**mommy track**
moteef	**motif****	mundain	**mundane**
moter	**motor**	munday	**Monday**
motled	**mottled**	munk	**monk**
motocycle	**motorcycle**	munkey	**monkey**
motse	**matza or matzoh**	munth	**month**
motserela	**mozzarella**	murcery	**mercury**
motta	**motto**	murchant	**merchant**
moufwash	**mouthwash**	murfy's lore	
mough	**muff**		**Murphy's Law**
mountage	**montage**	murge	**merge**
moustache	**mustache**	murmer	**murmur**
movment	**movement**	murrel	**mural**
mowdem	**modem**	musell	**muscle****
mowntain	**mountain**		

Incorrect	Correct	Incorrect	Correct
musilije	**mucilage**	myestrow	**maestro**
muskular distrophy		mygrane	**migraine**
	muscular dystrophy	mygrate	**migrate**
mussnt	**mustn't**	myke	**mike**
musster	**muster**	mynority	**minority**
mustid	**mustard****	myootation	**mutation**
mutha	**mother****	mytamicin C	
mutny	**mutiny**		**mitomycin C**
muzeem	**museum**	mytosis	**mitosis**
muzik	**music**	myuni	**muni**
muzlin	**muslin****	myunicipal	**municipal**
muzzel	**muzzle**	myutant	**mutant**
myazma	**miasma**	myute	**mute****
mycroprocesser		myutule	**mutual**
	microprocessor	mzuma	**mazuma**

N

Incorrect	Correct	Incorrect	Correct
nabb	**nab**	narrerband	**narrowband**
nabor	**neighbor**	narsisist	**narcissist**
nacent	**nascent**	narsistic	**narcissistic**
nachurally	**naturally**	nasent	**nascent**
nachuropathy		nash	**gnash**
	naturopathy	nashunel	**national**
nack	**knack**	nastershum	**nasturtium**
nacotics	**narcotics**	nastyness	**nastiness**
naddy	**natty**	nat	**gnat**
nafairius	**nefarious**	natchur	**nature**
naftha	**naphtha****	nattivity	**nativity**
naged	**nagged**	nausha	**nausea**
naiborhood	**neighborhood**	navagible	**navigable**
naivtay	**naïveté**	navey	**navy**
nale	**nail**	naw	**gnaw**
namless	**nameless**	nawm	**norm**
namonia	**pneumonia**	nawty	**naughty****
nany	**nanny**	naybor	**neighbor**
napsack	**knapsack**	naydir	**nadir**
naraminded		naytive	**native**
	narrow-minded	nazal	**nasal**
naration	**narration**	nazdack	**NASDAQ**
narative	**narrative**	neady	**needy**
narkalepsy	**narcolepsy**	nebulus	**nebulous**
narled	**gnarled**	neccesery	**necessary**
narow	**narrow**	necesity	**necessity**

Incorrect	Correct	Incorrect	Correct
neckromansy		newmeric	**numeric**
	necromancy	newral	**neural**
nectereen	**nectarine**	newrologist	**neurologist**
nee	**knee**	newrosis	**neurosis**
neecap	**kneecap**	newsance	**nuisance**
neece	**niece**	newtor	**neuter**
needel	**needle**	newtral	**neutral**
neegrow	**Negro**	newtron	**neutron**
neelsens	**Nielsen's**	newvo rich	**nouveau riche**
neeo	**neo**	newzspaper	**newspaper**
neepotism	**nepotism**	nex	**next**
neersited	**nearsighted**	Niagra	**Niagara**
neet	**neat**	nializm	**nihilism**
neether	**neither****	nianderthal	**Neanderthal**
nefew	**nephew**	nible	**nibble****
nefritis	**nephritis**	nicateen	**nicotine**
negitive	**negative**	nich	**niche****
neglajence	**negligence**	nickle	**nickel**
negleck	**neglect**	nicknack	**knickknack**
neglegay	**negligee**	nicly	**nicely**
negoshiate	**negotiate**	nietmare	**nightmare**
Negros	**Negroes**	nieve	**naïve**
neice	**niece**	nife	**knife**
nekkid	**naked**	nigate	**negate**
nekrology	**necrology**	night errend	
neks	**next**		**knight errant**
neksis	**nexus**	nikname	**nickname**
nelagism	**neologism**	nileism	**nihilism**
nell	**knell****	nill	**nil**
nemisis	**nemesis**	nimbel	**nimble**
nemonic	**mnemonic**	nimf	**nymph**
nenersecond	**nanosecond**	nimmbee	**NIMBY****
neppotizm	**nepotism**	ninedy	**ninety**
nerosis	**neurosis**	nineth	**ninth**
nerse	**nurse**	ninfamaniac	
nerture	**nurture**		**nymphomaniac**
nervanna	**nirvana**	ninteen	**nineteen**
nerviss	**nervous**	nionatal	**neonatal**
nesecery	**necessary**	nippal	**nipple**
nesessity	**necessity**	nirsery	**nursery**
nesle	**nestle**	nise	**NYSE**
nettwerk	**network**	nite	**night****
neumonia	**pneumonia**	niteclub	**nightclub**
newbile	**nubile**	nitragen	**nitrogen**
newdist	**nudist**	nitting	**knitting**
newmatic	**pneumatic**	nives	**knives**

Incorrect	Correct	Incorrect	Correct
noatbook	**notebook**	noovo reesh	
nobb	**knob****		**nouveau riche**
nobles oblege		normel	**normal**
	noblesse oblige	normming	**norming**
noch	**notch**	northernly	**northerly**
nock	**knock****	noshun	**notion**
nocknee	**knock-knee**	nosis	**gnosis**
nock-offs	**knockoffs**	nosstril	**nostril**
nockternil	**nocturnal**	notafy	**notify**
noed	**node****	notchy	**gnocci**
noefrills	**no-frills**	notery	**notary**
noehitter	**no-hitter**	noth	**north**
noel	**knoll**	notible	**notable**
noesbleed	**nosebleed**	noticable	**noticeable**
noeshow	**no-show**	notise	**notice**
noevember	**November**	nottorious	**notorious**
nokshus	**noxious**	notworthy	**noteworthy**
nole	**knoll**	novacane	**Novocaine**
nolode	**no-load**	noval	**novel**
nomanal	**nominal**	noviss	**novice**
nome	**gnome**	no where	**nowhere**
nomminate	**nominate**	nowlege	**knowledge**
noneexempt	**nonexempt**	nown	**noun**
nonefat	**nonfat**	noyz	**noise**
nonesuport	**nonsupport**	nozgay	**nosegay**
nonndeductible		nozy	**nosy**
	nondeductible	nuckle	**knuckle**
nonnentity	**nonentity**	nucleous	**nucleus**
nonnprofit	**nonprofit**	nudal	**noodle****
nonock	**no-knock**	nudaty	**nudity**
nonshalant	**nonchalant**	nuetral	**neutral**
nonvilence	**nonviolence**	nukular	**nuclear**
noo	**new****	nulification	**nullification**
noobile	**nubile**	num	**numb**
nooclear	**nuclear**	numatic	**pneumatic**
nooge	**nudge**	numba	**number**
nooke	**nuke****	numb de plume	
noomatic	**pneumatic**		**nom de plume**
noomeral	**numeral**	nummerical	**numerical**
nooratic	**neurotic**	nummskull	**numskull**
nooron	**neuron**	numrous	**numerous**
noosance	**nuisance**	nuncom	**noncom**
noot	**newt**	nunery	**nunnery**
nooter	**neuter**	nunpairell	**nonpareil**
nootral	**neutral**	nunplus	**nonplus**

Incorrect	Correct	Incorrect	Correct
nunsektarian		nurve	**nerve**
	nonsectarian	nusecaster	**newscaster**
nunsekwiter	**non sequitur**	nusence	**nuisance**
nunsense	**nonsense**	nuspeak	**newspeak**
nunsizist	**nonsizist**	nustaljic	**nostalgic**
nunyou	**non-U**	nuthing	**nothing**
nupshal	**nuptial**	nutralise	**neutralize**
nuralja	**neuralgia**	nutrishon	**nutrition**
nurd	**nerd**	nuty	**nutty**
nurish	**nourish**	nyeev	**naïve**
nuritis	**neuritis**	nyether	**neither****
nuroligist	**neurologist**	nyew	**new****
nursary	**nursery**	nytffall	**nightfall**
nursmaid	**nursemaid**	nytragen	**nitrogen**

		0	
oaysis	**oasis**	obliderate	**obliterate**
obay	**obey**	oblidge	**oblige**
obayisence	**obeisance**	obligatto	**obbligato**
obbjecshun	**objection**	oblikwey	**obloquy****
obbligatory	**obligatory**	obnocshus	**obnoxious**
obblivus	**oblivious****	obo	**oboe**
obblong	**oblong**	obsalecent	**obsolescent**
obbservatory	**observatory**	obsaleet	**obsolete**
obbstruction	**obstruction**	obsavation	**observation**
obbsurv	**observe**	obseekweus	**obsequious**
obcelete	**obsolete**	obseen	**obscene**
obderit	**obdurate**	obseshun	**obsession**
obedeance	**obedience**	obskure	**obscure**
obeecity	**obesity**	obstatrishun	**obstetrician**
obees	**obese**	obstickal	**obstacle**
obfaskate	**obfuscate**	obstonite	**obstinate**
obgective	**objective**	obstruk	**obstruct****
obhorent	**abhorrent**	obtane	**obtain**
obichuary	**obituary**	obtoos	**obtuse**
obitrator	**arbitrator**	obtusive	**obtrusive**
obitter diktum		obveate	**obviate**
	obiter dictum	obvius	**obvious****
objeck	**object****	obvurse	**obverse**
objecshunable		obzervance	**observance**
	objectionable	ocasion	**occasion**
oblagation	**obligation**	occassionel	**occasional**
obleek	**oblique****		

Incorrect	Correct	Incorrect	Correct
occuler	**ocular**	ohpare	**au pair**
occulist	**oculist**	oister	**oyster**
occurance	**occurrence**	oklock	**o'clock**
oced	**OECD**	oklusion	**occlusion**
ociloscope	**oscilloscope**	oksymoron	**oxymoron**
octajenerion		oktal	**octal**
	octogenarian	oktane	**octane**
octapus	**octopus**	oktave	**octave**
ocult	**occult**	Oktober	**October**
ocupancy	**occupancy**	okupent	**occupant**
ocupyed	**occupied**	okyupation	**occupation**
ocurr	**occur****	olagarky	**oligarchy**
ocurred	**occurred**	olay	**olé**
od	**odd**	ole	**old**
oddisy	**odyssey**	oleboy network	
oddometer	**odometer**		**old-boy network**
odeous	**odious**	oledline	**old-line**
oder	**odor**	olefashioned	
oderus	**odorous**		**old-fashioned**
odlot	**odd lot**	olegirl network	
odorcolon	**eau de cologne**		**old-girl network**
ofbeet	**offbeat**	olfaktry	**olfactory**
ofer	**offer**	Olimpic	**Olympic**
offen	**often**	ollive	**olive**
offence	**offense**	ollygopoly	**oligopoly**
offring	**offering**	oltimer	**old-timer**
offshaw	**offshore**	omage	**homage**
ofhand	**offhand**	OME	**OEM**
ofice	**office****	ome	**ohm**
oficer	**officer**	omibus	**omnibus**
oficial	**official**	omishin	**omission**
ofishus	**officious**	omlet	**omelet**
ofline	**off-line**	omm	**om**
ofprice	**off-price**	ommbudsman	
ofputing	**off-putting**		**ombudsman**
ofsett	**offset**	omminous	**ominous**
ofspring	**offspring**	ommitt	**omit**
ofthamology		ommnipotent	**omnipotent**
	ophthalmology	omnepresent	**omnipresent**
of the record		omnishent	**omniscient**
	off-the-record	omniverus	**omnivorous**
ofyear	**off year**	onamatopea	
oggel	**ogle**		**onomatopoeia**
ogger	**ogre**	onarus	**onerous**
oh de colon		oncore	**encore**
	eau de cologne	onely	**only**

Incorrect	Correct	Incorrect	Correct
oneself	**oneself**	opptic	**optic**
onest	**honest**	opption	**option**
onis	**onus**	opra	**opera****
onkogene	**oncogene**	oprant	**operant**
on mass	**en masse**	oprate	**operate**
onncology	**oncology**	opress	**oppress**
onngoing	**ongoing**	opresser	**oppressor**
onnline	**on-line**	opreta	**operetta**
onnlooka	**onlooker**	oproprium	**opprobrium**
onnslawt	**onslaught**	opscurantism	
onofile	**oenophile**		**obscurantism**
onor	**honor**	opsequees	**obsequies**
onorable	**honorable**	opshen	**option**
onorary	**honorary**	opshinul	**optional**
onroot	**en route**	opsite	**op. cit.****
onsided	**one-sided**	opsteperus	**obstreperous**
onsomble	**ensemble**	optain	**obtain**
onsure	**onshore**	optamum	**optimum**
ontoroge	**entourage**	optishin	**optician**
ontraprenor	**entrepreneur**	optomism	**optimism**
ontray	**entrée**	optommotrist	**optometrist**
onvelope	**envelope**	opyulent	**opulent**
onwee	**ennui**	oragin	**origin****
ooz	**ooze**	orbut	**orbit**
opaik	**opaque**	orcherd	**orchard**
oparative	**operative**	orchester	**orchestra**
opatunist	**opportunist**	ordally	**orderly**
opeate	**opiate**	ordanation	**ordination**
opeck	**OPEC**	ordane	**ordain**
openess	**openness**	ordinence	**ordinance****
opin ended	**open-ended**	ordinry	**ordinary**
opin mined	**open-minded**	oredeal	**ordeal**
opinyun	**opinion**	oreganic	**organic**
opis	**opus**	oreint	**orient**
opner	**opener**	orentation	**orientation**
opning	**opening**	orevoir	**au revoir**
oponent	**opponent**	orfan	**orphan**
oportune	**opportune**	orful	**awful**
oportunity	**opportunity**	organisation	**organization**
opose	**oppose**	orgazm	**orgasm****
oposition	**opposition****	orgin	**organ****
opp-ed	**op-ed**	oricul	**oracle****
opperator	**operator**	orignal	**original**
oppeum	**opium**	oringe	**orange**
opponant	**opponent**	orjy	**orgy**
oppt	**opt****	orkid	**orchid**

Incorrect	Correct	Incorrect	Correct
ornathologist		outadate	out-of-date
	ornithologist	outkast	outcast
orniment	ornament	outkum	outcome
ornry	ornery	outlore	outlaw
orr	oar**	outtage	outage
orrator	orator	outter	outer
orrder	order	outtgoing	outgoing
orrganize	organize	outting	outing
ornate	ornate	outtlay	outlay
orrthapedist	orthopedist	outtlet	outlet
ors d'oeurves		outtlook	outlook
	hors d'oeuvres	outtpatient	outpatient
orthadentist	orthodontist	outtput	output
orthentik	authentic	outwerd	outward
ortherdox	orthodox	ovabaring	overbearing
orthorety	authority	ovabite	overbite
orthorize	authorize	ovacum	overcome
oryental	oriental	ovahead	overhead
oscullatory	osculatory	ovakill	overkill
oshan	ocean	ovalation	ovulation
osheanography		ovar	over
	oceanography	ovarole	overall
osher	OSHA	ovatime	overtime
osify	ossify	ovature	overture
osillate	oscillate	ovaview	overview
osite	oocyte	ovazelus	overzealous
oskar	Oscar	ovel	oval
ossiloscope	oscilloscope	overate	overrate
osstensible	ostensible	overdoo	overdo**
ossteporosis	osteoporosis	overeach	overreach
osstrasize	ostracize	overeksposure	
ostintashus	ostentatious		overexposure
ostritch	ostrich	overide	override
ostypath	osteopath	overnite	overnight
otaman	ottoman	overought	overwrought
ote couture	haute couture	overrbord	overboard
ottee cee	OTC	overrthrow	overthrow
oth	oath**	overser	overseer
othawise	otherwise	overule	overrule
otour	auteur**	overun	overrun
oudo	outdo	overwelm	overwhelm
oudoor	outdoor	overy	ovary
our glass	hourglass	ovir the cownter	
ourhand	hour hand		over-the-counter
our's	ours	ovurt	overt**
ourselfs	ourselves		

Incorrect	Correct	Incorrect	Correct
ovvercompensate		owtline	**outline**
	overcompensate	owtporing	**outpouring**
ovverlok	**overlook**	owtragous	**outrageous**
ovylate	**ovulate**	owtreach	**outreach**
owdated	**outdated**	owtsider	**outsider**
ownce	**ounce****	owtspoken	**outspoken**
owst	**oust**	owtstanding	**outstanding**
owt	**out****	owtwit	**outwit**
owtbord	**outboard**	oxagen	**oxygen**
owtbrake	**outbreak**	oxes	**oxen**
owtclass	**outclass**	oximoron	**oxymoron**
owtcry	**outcry**	oyl	**oil**
owtfeeld	**outfield**	oyntment	**ointment**
owtfit	**outfit**	ozmosis	**osmosis**

P

Incorrect	Correct	Incorrect	Correct
pachezi	**parcheesi**	pallit	**palate****
pachwerk	**patchwork**	pallsey	**palsy**
packige	**package**	palpatate	**palpitate**
Packistan	**Pakistan**	palpible	**palpable**
paddlock	**padlock**	palyative	**palliative**
padestrian	**pedestrian**	pam	**palm**
padjama	**pajama**	pament	**payment**
padray	**padre**	pamistry	**palmistry**
paeback	**payback**	pamphalet	**pamphlet**
paeyof	**payoff**	panaply	**panoply**
pagent	**pageant**	panash	**panache**
pailode	**payload**	pandamoneum	
pairent	**parent**		**pandemonium**
pajinate	**paginate**	pandar	**panda****
pakage	**package**	pandcake	**pancake**
pakking	**parking**	panerama	**panorama**
pakt	**pact****	panestaking	**painstaking**
palamino	**palomino**	panicea	**panacea**
palastine	**Palestine**	panicy	**panicky**
pallace	**palace**	panitela	**panatella**
pallacial	**palatial**	panjondum	**panjandrum**
pallasade	**palisade**	pankreas	**pancreas**
pallatable	**palatable**	panndemic	**pandemic**
palleontology		pannel	**panel**
	paleontology	pannhandle	**panhandle**
paller	**pallor**	panntheism	**pantheism**
pallindrome	**palindrome**	pantacostal	**Pentecostal**

Incorrect	Correct	Incorrect	Correct
pantamine	**pantomime**	parrenthasis	**parenthesis**
pantsnay	**pince-nez**	parrible	**parable**
panzy	**pansy**	parridy	**parody****
paola	**payola**	parrikeet	**parakeet**
papaloma	**papilloma**	parrish	**parish****
paper-mashay		parrishute	**parachute**
	papier-mâché	parrity	**parity****
papisy	**papacy**	parrking meter	
papp	**pap**		**parking meter**
pappaverine	**papaverine**	parrkinsons	**Parkinson's**
papperback	**paperback**	parrocheal	**parochial**
pappriker	**paprika**	parrole	**parole****
paprazy	**paparazzi**	parrson	**parson**
parafrase	**paraphrase**	parrthenogenesis	
paralise	**paralyze**		**parthenogenesis**
paraty	**parity****	parrturition	**parturition**
parce	**parse**	parrty	**party**
parchurition	**parturition**	parrymecium	
parden	**pardon**		**paramecium**
pardner	**partner**	parry-mutual	**pari-mutuel**
parfay	**parfait**	parsel	**parcel**
paridice	**paradise**	parshel	**partial**
paridime	**paradigm**	partasiple	**participle**
parifernalia		partickle	**particle**
	paraphernalia	partickuler	**particular**
parisite	**parasite**	partishun	**partition****
parkay	**parquet**	partisipate	**participate**
parlement	**parliament**	partizan	**partisan**
parler	**parlor**	partys	**parties**
Parmizan	**Parmesan**	parynoia	**paranoia**
parodocks	**paradox**	parypass	**pari passu**
parot	**parrot**	parypledgic	**paraplegic**
parraboler	**parabola**	parytal	**parietal**
parrade	**parade**	pasay	**passé**
parrafin	**paraffin**	pasenger	**passenger**
parragraf	**paragraph**	pashent	**patient**
parralel	**parallel**	pashion	**passion**
parralisis	**paralysis**	pasible	**passable****
parrameter	**parameter**	pasidge	**passage**
parramount	**paramount**	Pasific	**Pacific**
parraproffessional		pasify	**pacify**
	paraprofessional	pasive	**passive**
parrasychology		paso	**peso**
	parapsychology	pasover	**Passover**
parrathyon	**parathion**	pasport	**passport**
parratrooper	**paratrooper**	passay	**passé**

Incorrect	Correct	Incorrect	Correct
passification	**pacification**	paynter	**painter**
passifist	**pacifist**	payshent	**patient**
passta	**pasta**	paysley	**paisley**
passtell	**pastel**	paysmaker	**pacemaker**
passtime	**pastime**	paythos	**pathos****
passtrami	**pastrami**	paytriark	**patriarch**
pastachio	**pistachio**	paytron	**patron**
pasteing	**pasting**	paytronage	**patronage**
paster	**pastor****	payyee	**payee**
pastil	**pastille**	payyout	**payout**
pastrey	**pastry**	pean	**paean****
pasturize	**pasteurize**	peaphole	**peephole**
pastword	**password**	pearless	**peerless**
pastyer	**pasture****	peavish	**peevish**
patatoe	**potato**	pecunerary	**pecuniary**
patay	**pâté****	pedafilia	**pedophilia**
patermony	**patrimony**	pedagree	**pedigree**
patern	**pattern**	pedderast	**pederast**
patheing	**pathing**	peddiculosis	**pediculosis**
pathollogy	**pathology**	peddigog	**pedagogue**
paticular	**particular**	peddy	**petty**
patition	**petition****	pedent	**pedant**
patren	**patron**	pedistal	**pedestal**
patritism	**patriotism**	peeanist	**pianist**
patriyot	**patriot**	peeaza	**piazza**
patroleum	**petroleum**	peecee	**PC**
pattedifoigra		peecework	**piecework**
	pâté de foie gras	peech	**peach**
pattela	**patella**	peedyatrics	**pediatrics**
pattent	**patent**	peekant	**piquant**
patternal	**paternal**	pee-m-ess	**PMS**
pattio	**patio**	peenil	**penal****
pattrol	**patrol**	peenis	**penis**
pattronise	**patronize**	peenut	**peanut**
patune	**platoon**	peepul	**people**
paveing	**paving**	peeza	**pizza**
pavilon	**pavilion**	pegd	**pegged**
pavment	**pavement**	pegoda	**pagoda**
pawlbarer	**pallbearer**	peice	**piece****
pawltry	**paltry****	peicemeal	**piecemeal**
pawrter	**porter**	peirce	**pierce**
pawsity	**paucity**	pekan	**pecan**
pawtico	**portico**	peks	**pecs****
pawtray	**portray**	pektoral	**pectoral**
payecheck	**paycheck**	pelagra	**pellagra**
payed	**paid**	pelet	**pellet****

Incorrect	Correct	Incorrect	Correct
pellvis	**pelvis**	perdominant	
pemanship	**penmanship**		**predominant**
penalogy	**penology**	perel	**peril**
penant	**pennant**	perfer	**prefer****
penatenshary		perferate	**perforate**
	penitentiary	perfered	**preferred**
penatint	**penitent**	perfessor	**professor**
penatrate	**penetrate**	perfict	**perfect****
penatration	**penetration**	perfyume	**perfume**
penelty	**penalty**	pergatory	**purgatory**
pengwin	**penguin**	perge	**purge**
penife	**penknife**	peridontal	**periodontal**
penndyalum	**pendulum**	perliminary	**preliminary**
pennicilan	**penicillin**	perloin	**purloin**
penninsuler	**peninsula**	permenant	**permanent**
penntameter	**pentameter**	permenstrual	
penntathalon	**pentathlon**		**premenstrual**
penntegon	**Pentagon**	permiate	**permeate**
penntetok	**Pentateuch**	permisable	**permissible**
penntobarbital		permitt	**permit**
	pentobarbital	perogative	**prerogative**
penntup	**pent-up**	perpatrate	**perpetrate**
penoir	**peignoir**	perpatrater	**perpetrator**
penshent	**penchant**	perpensity	**propensity**
penshun	**pension**	perpetual	**perpetual**
pensil	**pencil**	perpicious	**propitious**
Pensylvania	**Pennsylvania**	perpindicular	
Pentacostal	**Pentecostal**		**perpendicular**
pentegram	**pentagram**	perple	**purple**
penus	**penis**	perponderant	
penyless	**penniless**		**preponderant**
peper	**pepper**	perport	**purport**
pepptic	**peptic**	perposterous	
perameter	**parameter**		**preposterous**
peraps	**perhaps**	perprietary	**proprietary****
percalator	**percolator**	perpubesent	**prepubescent**
percarious	**precarious**	perranum	**per annum**
percaution	**precaution**	perrascope	**periscope**
percept	**precept**	perrenial	**perennial**
percieve	**perceive**	perrifery	**periphery**
percise	**precise****	perrimter	**perimeter**
perclude	**preclude**	period	**period**
perculiar	**peculiar**	perrish	**perish****
percushion	**percussion**	perroxide	**peroxide**
perdikament	**predicament**	perrspective	**perspective**
		persacute	**persecute****

Incorrect	Correct	Incorrect	Correct
persavere	**persevere**	phaze	**phase****
perscribe	**prescribe****	Pheenix	**Phoenix**
perscription		pheenobarbatal	
	prescription**		**phenobarbital**
perse	**purse**	Philipino	**Filipino**
persent	**percent**	phillately	**philately**
persepectus	**prospectus**	Phillipines	**Philippines**
perser	**purser**	phinomenon	**phenomenon**
perserve	**preserve****	phisics	**physics**
persikute	**persecute****	phisionomy	**physiognomy**
persin	**person**	phisique	**physique****
persinality	**personality**	phisyology	**physiology**
perspacacous		phisyotherapy	
	perspicacious		**physiotherapy**
persue	**pursue**	phonettic	**phonetic**
persuit	**pursuit**	phonnics	**phonics**
persumption	**presumption**	phont	**font****
perswade	**persuade**	phosferous	**phosphorus**
pertanint	**pertinent**	phosforresence	
pertend	**pretend****		**phosphorescence**
perticulars	**particulars**	photagraph	**photograph**
pertonitis	**peritonitis**	phreek	**phreak****
peruet	**pirouette**	phylanthropy	
pervention	**prevention**		**philanthropy**
pervide	**provide**	physiclly	**physically**
pervue	**purview**	piana	**piano**
pesery	**pessary**	piarea	**pyorrhea**
pesimist	**pessimist**	piaza	**piazza**
pestaside	**pesticide**	picadilo	**peccadillo**
petteet	**petite**	piccyune	**picayune**
pettle	**petal**	pich	**pitch**
pettrify	**petrify**	pickcher	**picture****
pettulant	**petulant**	pickel	**pickle**
pettycoat	**petticoat**	picknic	**picnic**
petty mal	**petit mal**	picksel	**pixel**
peverse	**perverse****	picollo	**piccolo**
pezint	**peasant**	pidgeon	**pigeon****
phalus	**phallus**	pietty	**piety**
phamaceutical		piggeebak	**piggyback**
	pharmaceutical	piggment	**pigment**
phanntom lim		pijjin	**pigeon****
	phantom limb	pika	**pica****
phantastic	**fantastic**	piket	**picket**
Pharow	**Pharaoh**	pikkup	**pickup**
pharrinx	**pharynx**	pikpocket	**pickpocket**
phasician	**physician**	pilage	**pillage**

Incorrect	Correct	Incorrect	Correct
pilbox	**pillbox**	plaiyoff	**playoff**
pileing	**piling**	plajiarism	**plagiarism**
pilet	**pilot****	planetif	**plaintiff****
pilitis	**pyelitis**	plannet	**planet****
piller	**pillar****	plannetarium	
pillery	**pillory**		**planetarium**
pillfer	**pilfer**	planntation	**plantation**
pillgrim	**pilgrim**	plasa	**plaza**
pimmento	**pimento**	plasebo	**placebo**
pimpel	**pimple**	plasenta	**placenta**
pinacle	**pinnacle****	plassid	**placid**
pinapple	**pineapple**	plasster	**plaster**
pinkey	**pink eye**	plasstic	**plastic**
pinnochle	**pinochle****	plasted	**plastered**
pinnpoint	**pinpoint**	platow	**plateau**
pinnstripe	**pinstripe**	plattform	**platform**
pinnup	**pinup**	plattinum	**platinum**
pinsers	**pincers**	plattitude	**platitude**
pinurious	**penurious**	plattonic	**Platonic**
pionner	**pioneer**	plattoon	**platoon**
pipeing	**piping**	plausable	**plausible**
pipline	**pipeline**	plawdit	**plaudit**
piramid	**pyramid**	playwrite	**playwright**
pire	**pyre**	plazma	**plasma**
pirl	**purl****	pleab	**plebe**
piromaniac	**pyromaniac**	plebbacite	**plebiscite**
pirotechnics	**pyrotechnics**	plee	**plea**
pirpituity	**perpetuity**	pleed	**plead**
pisstil	**pistol****	pleet	**pleat**
pistin	**piston**	pleeze	**please****
pitchur	**picture****	plege	**pledge**
pitence	**pittance**	plenery	**plenary**
pittfall	**pitfall**	plenny	**plenty**
pittuitary	**pituitary**	plentyful	**plentiful**
pitty	**pity**	plesant	**pleasant**
pityful	**pitiful**	plesure	**pleasure**
pivit	**pivot**	pletherra	**plethora**
plaback	**playback**	pliewood	**plywood**
plabean	**plebeian**	plite	**plight**
placcate	**placate**	ploding	**plodding**
plackard	**placard**	ploi	**ploy**
placment	**placement**	ploorilism	**pluralism**
plad	**plaid**	plopp	**plop**
pladder	**platter**	plott	**plot****
plage	**plague****	plouw	**plow**
plaitlet	**platelet**	pluerisy	**pleurisy**

Incorrect	Correct	Incorrect	Correct
plugg	**plug**	polltagist	**poltergeist**
plukk	**pluck**	pollyethelene	
plumer	**plumber**		**polyethylene**
plunnder	**plunder**	pollygon	**polygon**
plurel	**plural**	pollygraf	**polygraph**
pluss	**plus**	polly si	**poli-sci**
pluttonium	**plutonium**	poltice	**poultice**
plya	**playa****	polute	**pollute**
plyable	**pliable**	polution	**pollution**
plye	**ply**	pome	**poem**
plyers	**pliers**	pommade	**pomade**
pockabook	**pocketbook**	pommel	**pummel**
pockit	**pocket**	pompidor	**pompadour**
podytry	**podiatry**	pompus	**pompous**
poetent	**potent**	poneytale	**ponytail**
poinyant	**poignant**	ponsho	**poncho**
poisin	**poison**	pontif	**Pontiff**
poit	**poet**	poobsesent	**pubescent**
poize	**poise**	pooding	**pudding**
poka	**polka****	poorim	**Purim**
polen	**pollen**	pooshup	**push-up**
polerise	**polarize**	pootsh	**putsch**
poletry	**poultry****	poppular	**popular****
Polianne	**Pollyanna**	poppulist	**populist**
poliglot	**polyglot**	popuree	**potpourri**
polisentric	**polycentric**	popyulation	**population**
polisy	**policy**	porcelin	**porcelain**
politikly korrect		poretal	**portal**
	politically correct	poridge	**porridge**
poliunsaturated		pornagraphy	
	polyunsaturated		**pornography**
pollar	**polar**	porposal	**proposal**
Pollaris	**Polaris**	porrthole	**porthole**
Pollaroid	**Polaroid**	portfollio	**portfolio**
pollemic	**polemic**	portible	**portable****
pollice	**police**	porto ricco	**Puerto Rico**
polliester	**polyester**	portrit	**portrait**
polligamy	**polygamy****	posative	**positive**
pollimer	**polymer**	poscard	**postcard**
pollio	**polio**	posedoffice	**post office**
pollip	**polyp**	posemortem	**postmortem**
pollish	**polish**	posepaid	**postpaid**
pollite	**polite**	posess	**possess**
pollitics	**politics**	posession	**possession**
pollity	**polity**	posible	**possible**
		posman	**postman**

Incorrect	Correct	Incorrect	Correct
pospone	**postpone**	precink	**precinct**
possefoot	**pussyfoot**	precoshious	**precocious**
possition	**position**	precure	**procure**
possta	**pasta**	predacate	**predicate**
possterity	**posterity**	predddnisone	**prednisone**
posstmaster	**postmaster**	preddesessor	**predecessor**
possy	**posse**	predeter	**predator**
postel	**postal**	predick	**predict**
postige	**postage**	predjidiss	**prejudice**
postirier	**posterior**	preeamble	**preamble**
postumus	**posthumous**	preech	**preach**
postyure	**posture**	preecher	**preacher**
potenshal	**potential**	preedictible	**predictable**
potery	**pottery**	preefabrikate	
poteum	**podium**		**prefabricate**
potry	**poetry**	preefered	**preferred**
pottasium	**potassium**	preemartial	**premarital**
potwhole	**pothole**	preemtory	**peremptory**
pouder	**powder**	preepare	**prepare**
pounse	**pounce**	preepuce	**prepuce**
pourus	**porous**	preesentation	
povety	**poverty**		**presentation**
powch	**pouch**	preesis	**paresis**
pownd	**pound**	preffer	**prefer****
powt	**pout**	prefice	**preface**
powwer	**power**	prefidious	**perfidious**
poynsetta	**poinsettia**	prefrence	**preference**
poyntless	**pointless**	pregenitor	**progenitor**
poyzin pill	**poison pill**	pregnent	**pregnant**
pozitron	**positron**	preist	**priest**
practologist	**proctologist**	prelood	**prelude**
prafound	**profound**	prema dona	**prima donna**
praggmatic	**pragmatic**	premere	**premier****
praier	**prayer**	preminent	**preeminent**
prairy	**prairie**	premiscuous	**promiscuous**
praize	**praise**	premiss	**premise**
praktical	**practical**	premiture	**premature**
praktise	**practice****	premival	**primeval**
praldahyde	**paraldehyde**	premmonition	
praliferate	**proliferate**		**premonition**
prataganist	**protagonist**	premyum	**premium**
pravincial	**provincial**	preocupation	
pravision	**provision**		**preoccupation**
preceed	**precede****	preperation	**preparation**
preceive	**perceive**	preposal	**proposal**
preception	**perception**		

Incorrect	Correct	Incorrect	Correct
prepposition		priviledge	**privilege**
	preposition**	privisy	**privacy**
preprietor	**proprietor**	privitazation	
presadent	**president****		**privatization**
Presbaterian		privite	**private**
	Presbyterian	privvy	**privy**
presedent	**precedent****	prizm	**prism**
preseed	**precede****	prizon	**prison**
presept	**precept**	proab	**probe**
preshent	**prescient**	proaktiv	**proactive**
preshure	**pressure**	probbate	**probate**
preshus	**precious**	probbity	**probity**
presice	**precise****	probible	**probable**
presipatate	**precipitate**	problim	**problem**
prespiration	**perspiration**	proccreate	**procreate**
prespire	**perspire**	procede	**proceed****
pressage	**presage**	proceedure	**procedure**
pressipiss	**precipice**	procent	**percent**
presstige	**prestige**	prochoyce	**pro-choice**
pretsell	**pretzel**	proclame	**proclaim**
prety	**pretty**	procter	**proctor**
prevade	**pervade**	proddigious	**prodigious**
prevale	**prevail**	proddigy	**prodigy****
prevelant	**prevalent**	produck	**product**
preversion	**perversion**	produktivity	**productivity**
previso	**proviso**	produse	**produce**
previus	**previous**	proe	**pro**
prevue	**preview**	proebation	**probation**
preycis	**precis****	proebono	**pro bono**
prezent	**present**	proechoyce	**pro-choice**
prezide	**preside**	proejesterone	
prezident	**president****		**progesterone**
prezume	**presume**	proelife	**pro-life**
priamplifier	**preamplifier**	profalactic	
prickley	**prickly**		**prophylactic****
pricless	**priceless**	profecy	**prophecy****
priemate	**primate**	profer	**proffer****
primative	**primitive**	profeshun	**profession**
primerrily	**primarily**	proffesor	**professor**
primery	**primary**	proffess	**profess**
primie	**preemie**	profficient	**proficient**
prinsess	**princess**	profille	**profile**
priorty	**priority**	proffit	**profit****
pritify	**prettify**	proflagate	**profligate**
prity	**pretty**	profuce	**profuse**
privaricate	**prevaricate**	profunctory	**perfunctory**

Incorrect	Correct	Incorrect	Correct
progection	**projection**	prosess	**process**
progeramer	**programmer**	prossecute	**prosecute****
proggnosis	**prognosis**	prosseser	**processor**
proggres	**progress**	prossession	**procession**
programm	**program****	prosspect	**prospect**
prohibbit	**prohibit**	prosstate	**prostate****
projeck	**project**	prosstatute	**prostitute**
projeny	**progeny**	prosstheesis	**prosthesis**
prokane	**procaine**	protatype	**prototype**
	procrastinate	proteck	**protect**
prokrastinate		protecoll	**protocol**
proktascope	**proctoscope**	protene	**protein**
prolive	**pro-life**	protezhay	**protégé**
proll	**prole**	prottaganist	**protagonist**
prollific	**prolific**	prottaplasm	**protoplasm**
prologgue	**prologue**	prottest	**protest**
prominade	**promenade**	Prottestent	**Protestant**
promisary	**promissory**	prottocoll	**protocol**
promm	**prom**	protton	**proton**
prommice	**promise**	protude	**protrude**
promminent	**prominent**	provadents	**providence**
prommiscuous		provoak	**provoke**
	promiscuous	provoe	**provost**
prommote	**promote**	provurb	**proverb**
promt	**prompt**	provvince	**province**
pronosticate		prowd	**proud****
	prognosticate	proxximity	**proximity**
pronounciation		proxxy	**proxy**
	pronunciation	prozaic	**prosaic**
prood	**prude**	pruddence	**prudence**
proove	**prove**	prufound	**profound**
properganda	**propaganda**	prunounce	**pronounce****
proppagate	**propagate**	prunto	**pronto**
proppel	**propel**	pruse	**peruse**
propper	**proper**	pruspectus	**prospectus**
propperty	**property****	prye	**pry**
propponent	**proponent**	pryemt	**preempt**
propportion	**proportion**	prymafacy	**prima facie**
proppose	**propose**	prymal scream	
propposition			**primal scream**
	proposition**	pryme	**prime**
propprietor	**proprietor**	pryority	**priority**
proppultion	**propulsion**	prypism	**priapism**
proprity	**propriety****	pryvitise	**privatize**
prosedure	**procedure**	psam	**psalm**
proseed	**proceed****	psico	**psycho**

Incorrect	Correct	Incorrect	Correct
psycology	**psychology**	purfector	**perfecta**
psyconalasis		purient	**prurient**
	psychoanalysis	puriferal	**peripheral**
pubb	**pub**	purile	**puerile**
pubblisity	**publicity**	puritis	**pruritis**
pubity	**puberty**	purjery	**perjury**
publacation	**publication**	purks	**perks**
publick	**public****	purmutation	**permutation**
puding	**pudding**	purnicious	**pernicious**
pudjy	**pudgy**	purp	**perp**
pue	**pew**	purpice	**purpose****
puggnatious	**pugnacious**	purplex	**perplex**
pulit	**pullet**	purquisite	**perquisite**
pulkritude	**pulchritude**	pursavere	**persevere**
pullminary	**pulmonary**	pursistance	**persistence**
pullp	**pulp**	pursona nongratis	
pullpit	**pulpit**		**persona non grata**
pullse	**pulse**	pursonnal	**personal****
pullser	**pulsar**	purspicacious	
pullverise	**pulverize**		**perspicacious**
pulside	**poolside**	pursuade	**persuade**
puly	**pulley**	purt	**PERT**
pumkin	**pumpkin**	purtain	**pertain**
pumpanickle		purterb	**perturb**
	pumpernickel	Purto Rico	**Puerto Rico**
punative	**punitive**	purvert	**pervert**
punctull	**punctual**	pussilanamous	
pungk	**punk**		**pusillanimous**
pungture	**puncture**	puthetic	**pathetic**
punjint	**pungent**	putina	**patina**
punktilious	**punctilious**	putred	**putrid**
punktuate	**punctuate**	putrify	**putrefy**
punnish	**punish**	puzzel	**puzzle**
punx	**punks**	pweblo	**pueblo**
pupe	**poop**	pyaneer	**pioneer**
pupet	**puppet**	pyedatear	**pied-à-terre**
pupull	**pupil****	pyela	**paella**
purception	**perception**	Pyric victory	
purch	**perch**		**Pyrrhic victory**
purchise	**purchase**	pyubes	**pubes**
pur deem	**per diem**	pyus	**pious****
purduction	**production**	pyutitive	**putative**

Incorrect	Correct	Incorrect	Correct

Q

Incorrect	Correct	Incorrect	Correct
quadd	**quad**	quepidity	**cupidity**
quaddrant	**quadrant**	quere	**queer**
quaddratic	**quadratic**	querk	**quirk****
quadrain	**quatrain**	queschun	**question**
quadrapledgic		questionaire	
	quadriplegic		**questionnaire**
quadrefonic		quibel	**quibble**
	quadrophonic	quicksotic	**quixotic**
quadrune	**quadroon**	quicsand	**quicksand**
quaf	**quaff**	quiddproko	
quafeur	**coiffure**		**quid pro quo**
quaik	**quake**	quier	**choir****
quak	**quack****	quik	**quick**
quakker	**Quaker**	quinntet	**quintet**
qualefy	**qualify**	quinntoplet	**quintuplet**
quallity	**quality****	quivver	**quiver****
quam	**qualm**	quized	**quizzed**
quanity	**quantity****	quizes	**quizzes**
quanntum	**quantum**	quizical	**quizzical**
quarc	**quark****	quizine	**cuisine**
quarel	**quarrel**	quodrangle	**quadrangle**
quarelled	**quarreled**	quoir	**choir****
quarentine	**quarantine**	quoshent	**quotient**
quarrtally	**quarterly**	quot	**quote****
quarrtet	**quartet**	quotashun	**quotation**
quary	**quarry****	quoter	**quota****
quashiokor	**kwashiorkor**	quynine	**quinine**
quater	**quarter**	qwadrepartite	
quawtaback	**quarterback**		**quadripartite**
quazar	**quasar**	qwantity	**quantity****
quazy	**quasi****	qwartz	**quartz****
qudrupul	**quadruple****	qwench	**quench**
queary	**query****	qwid	**quid**
queesh	**quiche**	qwill	**quill**
queezy	**queasy****	qwizz	**quiz**
quene	**queen****	qwurum	**quorum**
quepea	**kewpie**	qyayzar	**quasar**

Incorrect	Correct	Incorrect	Correct

R

Incorrect	Correct	Incorrect	Correct
rabbid	**rabid****	rajed	**raged**
rabees	**rabies****	rajeem	**regime**
rabi	**rabbi**	rakateer	**racketeer**
rabit	**rabbit****	raket	**racket**
rable	**rabble**	rakkish	**rakish**
racey	**racy**	rakoko	**rococo**
rachit	**ratchet**	rakontour	**raconteur**
raciosination		rakoon	**raccoon**
	ratiocination	raleroad	**railroad**
racizm	**racism**	ralley	**rally**
raconture	**raconteur**	rambil	**ramble**
racoon	**raccoon**	rameedial	**remedial**
raddicle	**radical**	ramm	**RAM****
raddiologist	**radiologist**	rammadam	**Ramadan**
raddish	**radish**	rammafication	
raddy	**ratty**		**ramification**
radeactivity	**radioactivity**	rammpage	**rampage**
radeation	**radiation**	rampint	**rampant**
radeator	**radiator**	randim	**random**
radeo	**radio**	ranecote	**raincoat**
radicks	**radix**	ranemaker	**rainmaker**
radiel	**radial**	rangle	**wrangle**
radient	**radiant**	rangler	**wrangler**
radisotope	**radioisotope**	ranje	**range**
radyis	**radius**	rankel	**rankle**
rafel	**raffle**	rannking	**ranking**
raff	**raft**	rannsak	**ransack**
rafia	**raffia**	ransid	**rancid**
rafined	**refined**	ransum	**ransom**
raform	**reform**	rapayshus	**rapacious**
ragga	**raga****	rapcher	**rapture**
ragid	**ragged**	rapel	**repel**
raglin	**raglan**	rapel	**rappel**
ragoo	**ragout****	rapore	**rapport**
rahtha	**rather**	rapp	**rap****
raign	**reign****	rappist	**rapist**
railling	**railing**	raproachment	
raindeer	**reindeer**		**rapprochement**
rainny	**rainy**	rapsody	**rhapsody**
raion	**rayon**	rarety	**rarity**
rait	**rate**	rarify	**rarefy**
raitable	**ratable**	rarly	**rarely**
raivin	**raven**	rascist	**racist**

Incorrect	Correct	Incorrect	Correct
rashanal	**rationale****	reanite	**reunite**
rashio	**ratio**	reapose	**repose**
rashnalize	**rationalize**	reapper	**reaper**
rashul	**racial**	reaserch	**research**
rashun	**ration**	reasessive	**recessive**
rasism	**racism**	reath	**wreath**
rasy	**racy**	reatort	**retort**
ratafy	**ratify**	reavaluate	**reevaluate**
rateing	**rating**	reawder	**reorder**
ratel	**rattle**	reazon	**reason**
rath	**wrath**	rebell	**rebel**
ratrap	**rattrap**	rebelyon	**rebellion**
rattlsnake	**rattlesnake**	reberthing	**rebirthing**
raught	**wrought**	rebiuk	**rebuke**
ravashing	**ravishing**	rebutil	**rebuttal**
raveel	**reveal**	recalsatrate	**recalcitrate**
ravije	**ravage**	recapichulate	**recapitulate**
ravnous	**ravenous**	recclamation	**reclamation**
ravvil	**ravel**	reccomend	**recommend**
ravvish	**ravish**	recconoyter	**reconnoiter**
rawkus	**raucous**	reccord	**record**
rawnchy	**raunchy**	reccreation	**recreation**
rawr	**raw****	reccumpense	**recompense**
rawshack	**Rorschach**	reccurrance	**recurrence**
rayce	**race**	recection	**resection**
raydar	**radar**	receed	**recede****
raydium	**radium**	receit	**receipt**
raydon	**radon**	recepy	**recipe**
raype	**rape**	reces	**recess**
rayshio	**ratio**	receshun	**recession**
raystrack	**racetrack**	recicle	**recycle**
rayth	**wraith**	recievable	**receivable**
rayting	**rating**	recieve	**receive**
rayz	**raze****	reck	**wreck****
rayzin	**raisin**	reckwisit	**requisite**
razer	**razor**	reclect	**recollect**
razidjual	**residual**	recloose	**recluse****
razon d'etre	**raison d'être**	reconisonce	
razzberry	**raspberry**		**reconnaissance**
reabuff	**rebuff**	reconize	**recognize**
reakshun	**reaction**	recooperate	**recuperate**
reakter	**reactor**	recovry	**recovery**
realaty	**reality**	recquire	**require**
realese	**release**	recrimnatory	
realise	**realize****		**recriminatory**
realy	**really**	recrute	**recruit**

Incorrect	Correct	Incorrect	Correct
rectafy	**rectify**	reep	**reap**
rectul	**rectal**	reepent	**repent**
reddhanded	**red-handed**	reeplacement	**replacement**
reddhearing	**red herring**	reeply	**reply****
reddline	**redline**	reeport	**report**
redekerate	**redecorate**	reeposess	**repossess**
redemshun	**redemption**	reepugnant	**repugnant**
reden	**redden**	reepulsive	**repulsive**
rederect	**redirect**	reesponse	**response**
redhed	**redhead**	reestriction	**restriction**
rediculous	**ridiculous**	reestrictive	**restrictive**
redily	**readily**	reetard	**retard**
reduceable	**reducible**	reetention	**retention**
redundent	**redundant**	reetred	**retread**
reduse	**reduce**	reetule	**retool**
redy	**ready**	reevene	**revenge**
reeact	**react**	reevoke	**revoke**
reebound	**rebound****	reevolver	**revolver**
reecapture	**recapture**	reevulsion	**revulsion**
reecepter	**receptor**	reeward	**reward**
reeceptionist	**receptionist**	reewind	**rewind**
reech	**reach**	referbish	**refurbish**
reeconstruct	**reconstruct**	refferendum	**referendum**
reedeme	**redeem**	reffermation	**reformation**
reeder	**reader**	reffugee	**refugee**
reed-only	**read-only**	reffuse	**refuse**
reedress	**redress**	refinment	**refinement**
reefraction	**refraction**	refirm	**reaffirm**
reefresher	**refresher**	refleks	**reflex**
reefund	**refund**	reflekshun	**reflection**
reeksamine	**reexamine**	refrance	**reference**
reelaps	**relapse**	refrane	**refrain**
reelent	**relent**	refree	**referee****
reel estate	**real estate**	refridgerator	**refrigerator**
reelizm	**realism**	refule	**refuel**
reeltor	**Realtor**	refun	**refund**
reem	**ream**	refuzal	**refusal**
reemarkable	**remarkable**	refuge	**refuge**
reematch	**rematch**	refyute	**refute**
reemorse	**remorse**	regail	**regale****
reemote	**remote**	regarder	**regatta**
reenforcement		regay	**reggae****
	reinforcement	regestrer	**registrar**
reenkarnation		reggard	**regard**
	reincarnation	regilate	**regulate**
reenvent	**reinvent**	reglar	**regular**

Incorrect	Correct	Incorrect	Correct
regreshun	**regression**	relm	**realm**
regretible	**regrettable**	relucktinse	**reluctance**
regul	**regal****	relyd	**relied**
regurjatate	**regurgitate**	relyible	**reliable**
rehabbilitate	**rehabilitate**	remane	**remain**
rehersel	**rehearsal**	reme	**ream**
rehurse	**rehearse**	remidy	**remedy**
reignbow	**rainbow**	reminiss	**reminisce**
reishue	**reissue**	remishun	**remission**
rejament	**regiment**	remitence	**remittance**
rejensy	**regency**	remm	**REM**
rejestration	**registration**	remmark	**remark**
rejeuvanate	**rejuvenate**	remmember	**remember**
rejister	**register**	remmit	**remit**
rejon	**region**	remmonstate	**remonstrate**
rejoyse	**rejoice**	remnint	**remnant**
rekall	**recall**	remoat	**remote**
rekapture	**recapture**	remoonerate	**remunerate**
rekin	**reckon**	remorsful	**remorseful**
rekline	**recline**	removeable	**removable**
reklis	**reckless**	removil	**removal**
reknown	**renown**	renact	**reenact**
rekombinant DNA		renagaid	**renegade**
	recombinant DNA	renaysense	**renascence**
rekonsile	**reconcile**	rendayvous	**rendezvous**
rekoop	**recoup**	reneg	**renege**
rekord	**record**	renevate	**renovate**
rektangul	**rectangle**	renforce	**reenforce**
rektim	**rectum**	renjin	**Roentgen**
rekwest	**request**	rennasonse	**renaissance**
rekweum	**requiem**	renownce	**renounce**
rekwital	**requital**	rentel	**rental**
rekwizit	**requisite**	rentry	**reentry**
relaition	**relation**	renue	**renew**
relakate	**relocate**	reoose	**reuse**
relaks	**relax**	reorgenise	**reorganize**
relavent	**relevant**	reostat	**rheostat**
relection	**reelection**	repare	**repair**
releif	**relief**	repatishun	**repetition**
releive	**relieve**	repatory	**repertory**
relie	**rely**	repawter	**reporter**
relient	**reliant**	repaytriate	**repatriate**
relinkwish	**relinquish**	repear	**reappear**
relitive	**relative**	repeel	**repeal**
rellegate	**relegate**	repelant	**repellent**
rellish	**relish**	reperation	**reparation**

Incorrect	Correct	Incorrect	Correct
reperbate	**reprobate**	resipient	**recipient**
reperduce	**reproduce**	resipracal	**reciprocal**
reperductive	**reproductive**	resiprosity	**reciprocity**
reperhensable		resitashun	**recitation**
	reprehensible	resle	**wrestle**
repersent	**represent**	resorse	**resource**
repetative	**repetitive**	resparator	**respirator**
repete	**repeat**	respectible	**respectable**
repetwar	**repertoire**	respit	**respite**
replaka	**replica**	responsable	**responsible**
replaysment	**replacement**	ressipea	**recipe**
repleet	**replete**	ressle	**wrestle**
repozatory	**repository**	resstriction	**restriction**
reppakushin	**repercussion**	resstructure	**restructure**
reppatee	**repartee**	restablish	**reestablish**
reppetition	**repetition**	restatution	**restitution**
repplenish	**replenish**	resterant	**restaurant**
repplicate	**replicate**	resteration	**restoration**
repport	**report**	restrane	**restrain**
reppublican	**Republican**	restrik	**restrict**
repputible	**reputable**	resumtion	**resumption**
reprable	**reparable**	resure	**reassure**
repramand	**reprimand**	resurtify	**recertify**
repreive	**reprieve**	resusitate	**resuscitate**
represed	**repressed**	resytul	**recital**
repreze	**reprise**	retale	**retail**
reprizal	**reprisal**	retalliate	**retaliate**
reproche	**reproach**	retane	**retain**
reproove	**reprove**	retaut	**retort**
reptil	**reptile**	retern	**return**
repyudiate	**repudiate**	retier	**retire**
rerite	**rewrite**	retirment	**retirement**
resadense	**residence**	retisent	**reticent**
resaleable	**resalable**	retna	**retina**
resalution	**resolution**	retorick	**rhetoric**
reseever	**receiver**	retreet	**retreat**
reseption	**reception**	retreive	**retrieve**
reserch	**research**	retroefit	**retrofit**
resessive	**recessive**	retrosay	**retroussé**
resevation	**reservation**	rettape	**red tape**
resevwar	**reservoir**	retterovirus	**retrovirus**
reshur	**reissue**	rettraction	**retraction**
residivism	**recidivism**	rettribushun	**retribution**
resind	**rescind****	rettroactive	**retroactive**
resint	**recent****	rettroe	**retro**

Incorrect	Correct	Incorrect	Correct
rettrogreshun		ricorder	**recorder**
	retrogression	ridel	**riddle**
rettrospeck	**retrospect**	ridence	**riddance**
retuch	**retouch**	ridgid	**rigid**
reveer	**revere**	rie	**rye****
revelle	**reveille****	RIET	**REIT**
revelution	**revolution**	rieterate	**reiterate**
revijun	**revision**	rifel	**rifle****
revilation	**revelation**	rigermarole	**rigmarole**
revinew	**revenue**	rigerus	**rigorous**
revivle	**revival**	rigg	**rig**
revize	**revise**	right-in	**write-in**
revokashun	**revocation**	right-protect	
revrent	**reverent****		**write-protect**
revolt	**revolt**	rigle	**wriggle**
revursible	**reversible**	rigur	**rigor**
revurt	**revert**	riht	**right****
revvarie	**reverie****	rije	**ridge**
revvolve	**revolve**	rikity	**rickety**
revyoo	**revue****	rikoshay	**ricochet**
reynion	**reunion**	rikota	**ricotta**
rezanense	**resonance**	rikshaw	**rickshaw**
rezemblence	**resemblance**	rilation	**relation**
rezent	**resent****	rilegious	**religious**
rezerve	**reserve**	rince	**rinse**
rezerve	**reserve**	rinestone	**rhinestone**
rezidew	**residue**	ringger	**ringer**
rezign	**resign**	ringwurm	**ringworm**
rezilyens	**resilience**	rinitis	**rhinitis**
rezin	**resin**	rinkel	**wrinkle**
rezistable	**resistible**	rinocerus	**rhinoceros**
rezistance	**resistance**	rinseing	**rinsing**
reznable	**reasonable**	riple	**ripple**
rezolve	**resolve**	rippen	**ripen**
rezort	**resort**	rippof	**rip-off**
rezult	**result**	ripublic	**republic**
rezume	**resume**	riquire	**require**
rezurecshun	**resurrection**	riseing	**rising**
rhime	**rhyme****	riskay	**risqué**
riaktionary	**reactionary**	riskchip	**risc chip**
ribben	**ribbon**	rist	**wrist**
ribbuld	**ribald**	rit	**writ**
richous	**righteous**	ritch	**rich**
richual	**ritual**	riteful	**rightful**
rickashay	**ricochet**	riteoff	**write-off**

Incorrect	Correct	Incorrect	Correct
riter	**writer**	rooves	**roofs**
rithe	**writhe**	roring	**roaring**
rithem	**rhythm****	rosay	**rosé****
ritowork	**right-to-work**	rosery	**rosary**
ritten	**written**	Rosevelt	**Roosevelt**
riut	**riot**	rosey	**rosy**
rivaluation	**revaluation**	roshes	**rushes**
rivel	**rival**	rost	**roast**
rivishonism	**revisionism**	rotait	**rotate**
rivit	**rivet**	rotery	**rotary**
rize	**rise**	roth	**wroth**
rizome	**rhizome**	rotha	**rather**
roadio	**rodeo**	rotin	**rotten**
roarshock	**Rorschach**	roudy	**rowdy**
robbin	**robin**	roughian	**ruffian**
robery	**robbery**	roveing	**roving**
roche hashanah		royaly	**royally**
	Rosh Hashanah	roze	**rose****
Rockerfellow	**Rockefeller**	rozin	**rosin**
rodeblok	**roadblock**	rubar	**rubber**
rododendrum		rubarb	**rhubarb**
	rhododendron	rubiola	**rubeola**
roebot	**robot**	rubish	**rubbish**
roedent	**rodent**	ruf	**rough****
roeman	**Roman**	ruffneck	**roughneck**
roge	**rogue**	ruge	**rouge**
rogish	**roguish**	rumatism	**rheumatism**
roial	**royal****	rumba	**rhumba**
rokkit	**rocket**	rumbil	**rumble**
rokk n role	**rock and roll**	rumer	**rumor****
roleout	**rollout****	rumije	**rummage**
rollplay	**roleplay**	rumy	**rummy**
rolover	**rollover****	runer	**runner**
romanse	**romance**	runing	**running**
romb	**ROM****	runnaway	**runaway**
rome	**roam****	runne-down	**run down****
rong	**wrong**	runtyen	**Roentgen**
roo	**rue**	rupcher	**rupture**
rooay	**roué**	rurel	**rural**
roobarb	**rhubarb**	rusbelt	**rustbelt**
rood	**rude****	ruset	**russet**
rooler	**ruler**	Rusha	**Russia**
roolet	**roulette**	rusil	**rustle**
roomate	**roommate**	russty	**rusty**
roomatism	**rheumatism**	rustik	**rustic**
roon	**ruin****	rutine	**routine**

Incorrect	Correct	Incorrect	Correct
rutter	**rudder**	ryitus	**riotous**
ruwanda	**Rwanda**	rype	**ripe**
ryenoserus	**rhinocerus**	rythm	**rhythm****

S

Incorrect	Correct	Incorrect	Correct
Sabath	**Sabbath****	sangwin	**sanguine**
sabatical	**sabbatical**	sanktity	**sanctity**
sabature	**saboteur**	sanlot	**sandlot**
sabbotage	**sabotage**	sanstone	**sandstone**
sacarin	**saccharin**	sargent	**sergeant**
sacerment	**sacrament**	sarkastic	**sarcastic**
sacherated	**saturated**	sassage	**sausage**
sacreligous	**sacrilegious**	sassiety	**society**
saffarry	**safari**	sassparilla	**sarsaparilla**
safire	**sapphire**	sasy	**sassy**
safrun	**saffron**	Sataday	**Saturday**
safty	**safety**	satasfactory	**satisfactory**
saif	**safe**	satinism	**Satanism**
saige	**sage**	sattelite	**satellite**
sailsperson	**salesperson**	sattisfaction	**satisfaction**
sakred	**sacred**	saught	**sought**
sakrifice	**sacrifice**	sausidge	**sausage**
saksafone	**saxophone**	saveing	**saving**
salammi	**salami**	savey	**savvy**
salieva	**saliva**	savige	**savage**
sallary	**salary****	sawcy	**saucy**
sallmenela	**salmonella**	sawdfish	**swordfish**
sallvation	**salvation**	sawdof	**sawed-off**
salm	**psalm**	sawdy araby	
saloot	**salute****		**Saudi Arabia**
salser	**salsa**	sawftwear	**software**
salyatation	**salutation**	sayder	**Seder**
samareye	**samurai**	saydist	**sadist**
samitic	**Semitic**	sayed	**said**
sammon	**salmon**	saynt	**saint**
sampel	**sample**	scaresity	**scarcity**
sanatashun	**sanitation**	scarsely	**scarcely**
sanaty	**sanity**	scatebored	**skateboard**
sanbag	**sandbag**	scedule	**schedule**
sandwidge	**sandwich**	sceleton	**skeleton**
sangshun	**sanction**	scenry	**scenery**
sangtimonious		sceptical	**skeptical**
	sanctimonious	schock	**shock**

Incorrect	Correct	Incorrect	Correct
schotch	**scotch**	sekwence	**sequence**
scithe	**scythe**	seldem	**seldom**
scizzers	**scissors**	selebrait	**celebrate**
scolastic	**scholastic**	selerity	**celerity**
scool	**school**	selery	**celery****
scrable	**scrabble**	seleschul	**celestial**
scrach	**scratch**	selfs	**selves**
Scripchure	**Scripture**	self steam	**self-esteem**
scuzzy port	**SCSI port**	selibacy	**celibacy**
seady	**seedy**	seliva	**saliva**
seberb	**suburb****	sellar	**cellar****
seceed	**secede**	sellefane	**cellophane**
secendrate	**second-rate**	sellfdiscipline	
secertery	**secretary**		**self-discipline**
secksism	**sexism**	sellfish	**selfish**
secum	**succumb**	sellibate	**celibate****
seddentary	**sedentary**	sellular	**cellular**
seditive	**sedative**	sellulite	**cellulite**
seduse	**seduce**	selluloid	**celluloid**
see art tea	**CRT**	selser	**seltzer**
seecurities	**securities**	seme	**seem****
seedan	**sedan**	semenary	**seminary**
seedy rom	**CD-ROM**	sement	**cement**
seekretive	**secretive**	semetary	**cemetery****
seekwell	**sequel**	semmester	**semester**
seel	**seal**	semminar	**seminar**
seelect	**select**	semyautomatic	
seenario	**scenario**		**semiautomatic**
seeries	**series**	senceless	**senseless**
seeson	**season**	sene	**scene****
seetbelt	**seatbelt**	seneter	**senator**
seeve	**sieve**	senic	**scenic**
see-y-a	**CYA**	senntence	**sentence**
seeze	**seize****	senota	**sonata**
seffhelp	**self-help**	sensative	**sensitive**
segragate	**segregate**	senser	**sensor**
segwee	**segue**	sentaria	**santeria**
seige	**siege**	sentement	**sentiment**
seing	**seeing**	sentenial	**centennial**
seinse	**science**	sentimeter	**centimeter**
seive	**sieve**	sentury	**century**
sekend	**second**	senyer	**senior****
sekret	**secret**	seperate	**separate**
sekskapade	**sexcapade**	sepport	**support**
sekular	**secular**	sepress	**surpress**
sekurety	**security**	serch	**search**

Incorrect	Correct	Incorrect	Correct
sereal	**cereal****	shantoosee	**chanteuse**
serebrally	**cerebrally**	shaperone	**chaperon**
sereise	**series**	shapo	**chapeau**
serface	**surface**	sharade	**charade**
serfing	**surfing**	shardonay	**chardonnay**
sergery	**surgery**	sharewear	**shareware**
sergical	**surgical**	sharlatin	**charlatan**
serjon	**surgeon**	shartroose	**chartreuse**
sermen	**sermon**	shasee	**chassis**
sermize	**surmise**	shato	**château**
serplus	**surplus****	shawt	**short**
serprize	**surprise**	shecana	**Chicana**
serrendipity	**serendipity**	shef	**chef**
sertificate	**certificate**	sheild	**shield**
servalanse	**surveillance**	sheke	**chic****
servay	**survey**	shelfs	**shelves**
servicable	**serviceable**	shellter	**shelter**
servise	**service**	sheneel	**chenille**
servive	**survive**	shenyon	**chignon**
servix	**cervix**	sheperd	**shepherd**
seseed	**secede**	sherbert	**sherbet**
sesession	**secession**	sherif	**sheriff****
sessemee	**sesame**	sheth	**sheath**
sesspool	**cesspool**	shevron	**chevron**
Setember	**September**	shez	**chaise**
sety	**settee**	Shicago	**Chicago**
seudo	**pseudo**	shicanery	**chicanery**
seudonym	**pseudonym**	shicano	**Chicano**
seveer	**severe**	shiek	**sheik****
sevinth	**seventh**	shiffon	**chiffon**
sevral	**several**	shillaylee	**shillelagh**
sexsy	**sexy**	shineing	**shining**
sez	**says**	shipd	**shipped**
sfardim	**Sephardim**	shippment	**shipment**
sfere	**sphere**	shiskabob	**shish kebab**
sfinx	**sphinx**	shizm	**schism**
shagrin	**chagrin**	shlok	**schlock**
shairwear	**shareware**	shoffer	**chauffeur**
shakk	**shack**	sholders	**shoulders**
shaley	**chalet**	shommus	**shamus**
shameleon	**chameleon**	shoodn't	**shouldn't**
shamise	**chemise**	shoostring	**shoestring**
shampain	**champagne**	shoredhand	**shorthand**
shamy	**chamois**	shott	**shot**
shandaleir	**chandelier**	showvinizm	**chauvinism**
shanker	**chancre**	shreik	**shriek****

Incorrect	Correct	Incorrect	Correct
shrein	**shrine**	simantics	**semantics**
shrubry	**shrubbery**	simbal	**symbol****
shtroodle	**strudel**	simester	**semester**
shud	**should**	simetry	**symmetry****
shudown	**shutdown**	similer	**similar**
shugar	**sugar**	simpathy	**sympathy**
shunn	**shun**	simphony	**symphony**
shure	**sure**	simton	**symptom**
shurt	**shirt****	simyalate	**simulate**
shutel	**shuttle**	sinamin	**cinnamon**
shuttout	**shutout**	sinario	**scenario**
shuv	**shove**	sinch	**cinch**
sibbling	**sibling**	sinder	**cinder**
sibercrud	**cybercrud**	sinderella	**cinderella**
siberculchur	**cyberculture**	sindicate	**syndicate**
sickel	**sickle**	sinema	**cinema**
sicure	**secure**	sinergetics	**synergetics**
sidarm	**sidearm**	singel	**single**
sidds	**SIDS**	sinicure	**sinecure**
side bar	**sidebar**	sinigog	**synagogue**
siedline	**sideline**	sinis	**sinus**
sience	**science**	sinn	**sin**
sieze	**seize****	sinncerly	**sincerely**
si-fi	**sci-fi**	sinnic	**cynic**
sigar	**cigar**	sinonym	**synonym**
sigarette	**cigarette**	sinopsis	**synopsis**
siggnificant	**significant**	sinosure	**cynosure**
sightrack	**sidetrack**	sinse	**since**
signerture	**signature**	sinsere	**sincere**
sikedelic	**psychedelic**	sintacks	**syntax**
sikly	**sickly**	sinthetic	**synthetic**
siko	**psycho**	sintilate	**scintillate**
sikofant	**sycophant**	sipher	**cipher**
sikosomatic		siramics	**ceramics**
	psychosomatic	sircumcision	**circumcision**
silacious	**salacious**	sircumstance	
silacone	**silicone**		**circumstance**
silance	**silence**	sirfit	**surfeit**
silf	**sylph**	sirious	**serious**
silible	**syllable**	sirkit	**circuit**
sillabus	**syllabus**	sirrup	**syrup**
sillverwear	**silverware**	sirynge	**syringe**
sillycon	**silicon**	sisk chip	**cisc chip**
silouette	**silhouette**	sisors	**scissors**
silva	**silver**	siss	**sis**
sim	**SIMM**	sist	**cyst**

Incorrect	Correct	Incorrect	Correct
sistem	**system**	skue	**skew**
sistern	**cistern**	skum	**scum**
sitadel	**citadel**	skurlus	**scurrilous**
sitaplasm	**cytoplasm**	skuttel	**scuttle**
siticosis	**psittacosis**	skwad	**squad**
sitizen	**citizen**	skware	**square**
sittuation	**situation**	skwat	**squat**
sivick	**civic**	skweeze	**squeeze**
sivilisation	**civilization**	slakk	**slack**
sivil rites	**civil rights**	slane	**slain**
sixt	**sixth**	slavry	**slavery**
sizemic	**seismic**	slax	**slacks**
sizle	**sizzle**	slayed	**slain**
sizm	**schism**	slimm	**slim**
sizmograph	**seismograph**	slipry	**slippery**
skab	**scab**	slite	**slight****
skalable	**scalable**	sloap	**slope**
skandal	**scandal**	slodown	**slowdown**
skane	**skein**	slugish	**sluggish**
skanner	**scanner**	smeer	**shmear**
skapegote	**scapegoat**	smuck	**schmuck**
skar	**scar**	smugg	**smug**
skarce	**scarce**	smujj	**smudge**
skare	**scare**	smuther	**smother**
skarf	**scarf**	snaffoo	**snafu**
skavenger	**scavenger**	snakk	**snack**
skedule	**schedule**	snall	**snarl**
skeematic	**schematic**	snapp	**snap**
skeme	**scheme**	snappshot	**snapshot**
skif	**skiff**	snawkle	**snorkel**
skilfill	**skillful**	snawt	**snort**
skism	**schism**	snobird	**snowbird**
sklerosis	**sclerosis**	snomobile	**snowmobile**
skoap	**scope**	snops	**schnaps**
skoflaw	**scofflaw**	sodder	**solder****
skone	**scone**	sodeum	**sodium**
skool	**school**	sofen	**soften**
skoolmate	**schoolmate**	sofer	**sofa**
skooner	**schooner**	sofisticate	**sophisticate**
skout	**scout**	sofwear	**software**
skreme	**scream**	soladarity	**solidarity**
skrole	**scroll**	solem	**solemn**
skrub	**scrub**	soler	**solar**
skrue	**screw**	solinoid	**solenoid**
skruplous	**scrupulous**	solisit	**solicit**
skuba	**scuba**	sollid	**solid**

Incorrect	Correct	Incorrect	Correct
sollis	**solace**	spewmoney	**spumoni**
sollution	**solution**	spifee	**spiffy**
solsoe	**solo**	spinn	**spin**
somba	**samba**	spinnof	**spinoff**
sooper	**super**	spirichule	**spiritual**
sooter	**suitor**	spiril	**spiral**
sopes	**soaps**	spirrit	**spirit**
sophmore	**sophomore**	splach	**splash**
sorce	**source****	sponser	**sponsor**
sord	**sword**	sportkast	**sportscast**
sorisis	**psoriasis**	spotlite	**spotlight**
sorow	**sorrow**	spowsal	**spousal**
sory	**sorry**	spowse	**spouse**
soseology	**sociology**	sprea	**spree**
soshalist	**socialist**	sprily	**spryly**
soshill	**social**	spufe	**spoof**
soshiopath	**sociopath**	spuller	**spooler**
sosiety	**society**	spurm	**sperm**
sotay	**sauté**	spurr	**spur**
sothern	**southern**	spye	**spy**
sourkraut	**sauerkraut**	spyurious	**spurious**
sovrin	**sovereign**	sqallid	**squalid**
sovrinty	**sovereignty**	sqwash	**squash**
sownd	**sound**	sree lanker	**Sri Lanka**
spagetti	**spaghetti**	stabb	**stab**
Spannish	**Spanish**	stabbility	**stability**
sparow	**sparrow**	staflococcus	
spasstic	**spastic**		**staphylococcus**
spatt	**spat**	stail	**stale**
spawtsware	**sportswear**	stakout	**stakeout**
spazm	**spasm**	stammp	**stamp**
speach	**speech**	stampeed	**stampede**
spead	**speed**	stanby	**standby**
specktaculer	**spectacular**	standerd	**standard**
speekafone	**speakerphone**	stanser	**stanza**
speeker	**speaker**	starberd	**starboard**
speeshus	**specious**	stardup	**startup**
spektator	**spectator**	starrk	**stark**
spekticle	**spectacle**	starrship	**starship**
spektrum	**spectrum**	stateing	**stating**
spekulate	**speculate**	statment	**statement**
speler	**speller**	statis	**status**
speshialty	**specialty****	stattic	**static**
speshul	**special****	stattistic	**statistic**
spesify	**specify**	statts	**stats**
spesiman	**specimen**	stawk	**stalk****

Incorrect	Correct	Incorrect	Correct
staytis kwo	**status quo**	subbliminal	**subliminal**
stedy	**steady**	subbsistance	**subsistence**
stelth	**stealth**	subburban	**suburban**
stelthy	**stealthy**	suberb	**suburb****
stensh	**stench**	sublyme	**sublime**
sterotipe	**stereotype**	subordnate	**subordinate**
sterrilize	**sterilize**	subumate	**sublimate**
sterritype	**stereotype**	subvursive	**subversive**
stiggma	**stigma**	succede	**succeed**
stilis	**stylus**	sucsess	**success**
stilleto	**stiletto**	sucum	**succumb**
stimmulus	**stimulus**	sufferage	**suffrage**
stine	**stein**	suffishent	**sufficient**
stiph	**stiff**	sufix	**suffix**
stipyalate	**stipulate**	suggest	**suggest**
stirio	**stereo**	sujjestion	**suggestion**
stokbroker	**stockbroker**	sukceser	**successor**
stokk	**stock**	suksinct	**succinct**
stomick	**stomach**	sullfur	**sulfur** or **sulphur****
stooper	**stupor**	sumaratan	**Samaritan**
stoped	**stopped**	sumary	**summary**
storege	**storage**	sumbody	**somebody**
storee	**story**	sumins	**summons**
stox	**stocks**	sumit	**summit**
stradle	**straddle**	summarine	**submarine**
strate	**straight****	sumshus	**sumptuous**
strate-jacket	**strait-jacket**	sune	**soon**
strech	**stretch**	supacomputer	
streeker	**streaker**		**supercomputer**
strenth	**strength**	supastitious	**superstitious**
strenyous	**strenuous**	supena	**subpoena**
stricly	**strictly**	supercede	**supersede**
stripteez	**striptease**	supireor	**superior**
stroab	**strobe**	suply	**supply**
stroak	**stroke**	suport	**support**
strugle	**struggle**	supose	**suppose**
strutegic	**strategic**	supperfluous	**superfluous**
stryfe	**strife**	supperman	**superman**
strykbraker	**strikebreaker**	supplys	**supplies**
stuble	**stubble**	supprise	**surprise**
studdy	**study**	supranatural	
studeying	**studying**		**supernatural**
stuf	**stuff**	supravise	**supervise**
stuped	**stupid**	supress	**suppress**
stypend	**stipend**	suprintendent	
subbern	**suborn**		**superintendent**

Incorrect	Correct	Incorrect	Correct
supscribtion	**subscription**	syatica	**sciatica**
suregate	**surrogate**	syberculture	**cyberculture**
surkit	**circuit**	sybernetic	**cybernetic**
suround	**surround**	sybil	**sibil**
survise	**service**	syborg	**cyborg**
suspishon	**suspicion**	sybot	**cybot**
susspect	**suspect**	syche	**psyche**
susspend	**suspend**	sychiatrist	**psychiatrist**
suth	**soothe**	sychic	**psychic**
sutle	**subtle****	sychology	**psychology**
sutract	**subtract**	sychosis	**psychosis**
suvenir	**souvenir**	sycobabble	**psychobabble**
suvvival	**survival**	sycotherepy	
swade	**suede****		**psychotherapy**
swair	**swear**	sydebar	**sidebar**
sware	**swear**	sykopath	**psychopath**
swave	**suave**	symetrical	**symmetrical**
sweaps	**sweeps**	symtom	**symptom**
sweapstakes	**sweepstakes**	syndacation	**syndication**
sweathart	**sweetheart**	synic	**cynic**
swerl	**swirl**	syst	**cyst**
swetshirt	**sweatshirt**	systerhud	**sisterhood**
swetshop	**sweatshop**	sytrack	**sidetrack**

T

Incorrect	Correct	Incorrect	Correct
tabanacle	**tabernacle**	taktill	**tactile**
tabb	**tab**	tallent	**talent**
tabblet	**tablet**	tallmid	**Talmud**
tabbulate	**tabulate**	tamata	**tomato**
tabelspoon	**tablespoon**	tammper	**tamper**
tabloyd	**tabloid****	tammpon	**tampon**
tabu	**taboo**	tanduri	**tandoori**
tacks lean	**tax lien**	tangable	**tangible**
tafeta	**taffeta**	tanjent	**tangent**
tailer	**tailor**	tanntalize	**tantalize**
tailite	**taillight**	tanntrum	**tantrum**
taipworm	**tapeworm**	targit	**target**
takeing	**taking**	tarmigan	**ptarmigan**
takkle	**tackle**	tarrdy	**tardy**
takout	**take-out**	tarrif	**tariff**
takover	**takeover**	tarrnish	**tarnish**
takt	**tact****	tarrow	**tarot****
taktics	**tactics**	tarrter	**tartar****

Incorrect	Correct	Incorrect	Correct
taseless	**tasteless**	teltale	**telltale**
tassit	**tacit**	temmerity	**temerity**
tasteing	**tasting**	temmp	**temp****
tatered	**tattered**	temmplit	**template**
tatle	**tattle**	temperarily	**temporarily**
tatoo	**tattoo**	temperment	**temperament**
taudry	**tawdry**	tempral lobe	
tavren	**tavern**		**temporal lobe**
taxible	**taxable**	temprary	**temporary**
taxxpayer	**taxpayer**	temprature	**temperature**
taynt	**taint****	temprence	**temperance**
tean's	**teens**	temt	**tempt****
teapea	**tepee**	temtation	**temptation**
teara	**tiara**	tenament	**tenement**
teater	**teeter**	tenasity	**tenacity**
techst	**text**	tendafoot	**tenderfoot**
tecksture	**texture**	tendancy	**tendency**
tecnical	**technical**	tenden	**tendon**
tee bills	**T-bills**	tendonitis	**tendinitis**
tee cell	**t-cell**	tenent	**tenant****
teech	**teach**	tener	**tenor****
teemmate	**teammate**	tenible	**tenable**
teemster	**teamster**	tenit	**tenet****
teemwork	**teamwork**	tennacious	**tenacious**
teenadger	**teenager**	tenndenshous	**tendentious**
teer	**tier****	tennderharted	
teerful	**tearful**		**tenderhearted**
teese	**tease****	tennsion	**tension**
teespoon	**teaspoon**	tennuous	**tenuous**
tejious	**tedious**	tenticle	**tentacle**
tekela	**tequila**	tentitive	**tentative**
teknik	**technique**	teppee	**tepee**
teknology	**technology**	teppid	**tepid**
tekstile	**textile**	terakote	**terra cotta**
telacompute	**telecompute**	terane	**terrain**
telagram	**telegram**	teratory	**territory**
tellacast	**telecast**	terbojet	**turbojet**
tellecomunication		tererist	**terrorist**
	telecommunication	terestrial	**terrestrial**
tellephone	**telephone**	terf	**turf**
tellescope	**telescope**	terible	**terrible**
tellethon	**telethon**	terific	**terrific**
tellevision	**television**	terify	**terrify**
tellex	**telex**	teritorial	**territorial**
tellmarketing		terkey	**turkey**
	telemarketing	termoil	**turmoil**

Incorrect	Correct	Incorrect	Correct
terncoate	**turncoat**	theiter	**theater**
terndown	**turndown**	themselfs	**themselves**
terniket	**tourniquet**	therafter	**thereafter**
ternip	**turnip**	theriputic	**therapeutic**
ternover	**turnover**	thermanooklear	
ternpike	**turnpike**		**thermonuclear**
ternround	**turnaround**	thermistat	**thermostat**
terodactil	**pterodactyl**	therrby	**thereby**
terpentine	**turpentine**	thersday	**Thursday**
terpetude	**turpitude**	thersty	**thirsty**
terpitude	**turpitude**	therteen	**thirteen**
terrasore	**pterosaur**	thery	**theory**
terrer	**terror****	thesawris	**thesaurus**
terribally	**terribly**	thesus	**thesis**
terris	**terrace**	theze	**these**
terrorbite	**terabyte**	thiefs	**thieves**
terryackid	**teriyaki**	thikskinned	**thick-skinned**
tesstickle	**testicle**	thimbell	**thimble**
tesstis	**testis**	thimus	**thymus**
tesstosterone	**testosterone**	thingpad	**thinkpad**
testafy	**testify**	thinnsksind	**thin-skinned**
testamony	**testimony**	thiroid	**thyroid**
testiment	**testament**	thogh	**though**
testube	**test tube**	thoro	**thorough**
testube baby		thorrax	**thorax**
	test-tube baby	thousind	**thousand**
tetatet	**tête-à-tête**	thred	**thread**
tetsee	**tsetse**	threshhold	**threshold**
tettrasiklin	**tetracycline**	thret	**threat**
Teusday	**Tuesday**	thriftey	**thrifty**
texbook	**textbook**	thriling	**thrilling**
thallidomide	**thalidomide**	thriveing	**thriving**
thalmus	**thalamus**	thrommbosis	**thrombosis**
thangsgiving		throte	**throat**
	Thanksgiving	thru	**through****
thawt	**thought**	thugg	**thug**
thawtful	**thoughtful**	thum	**thumb**
theem	**theme**	thummtack	**thumbtack**
theeology	**theology**	thunnder	**thunder**
theeretical	**theoretical**	thunnderstorm	
theerum	**theorem**		**thunderstorm**
thef	**theft**	thurd person	**third person**
theif	**thief**	thurmometer	
theirfore	**therefor****		**thermometer**
their's	**theirs**	thurrowfare	**thoroughfare**
theirselves	**themselves**	thurty	**thirty**

Incorrect	Correct	Incorrect	Correct
thwort	**thwart**	togle kee	**toggle key**
Tibbet	**Tibet**	toilit	**toilet****
tibbia	**tibia**	tokin	**token**
tickel	**tickle**	toksic	**toxic**
tiecoon	**tycoon**	tole	**toll****
tieing	**tying**	tollerant	**tolerant**
tiepist	**typist**	tomagraphy	**tomography**
tietan	**titan**	tomaine	**ptomaine**
tietfisted	**tightfisted**	tomali	**tamale**
tif	**tiff**	tommboy	**tomboy**
tifoid	**typhoid**	tommorow	**tomorrow**
tifus	**typhus**	tonage	**tonnage**
til	**till**	tonnic	**tonic**
timerity	**temerity**	tonnsil	**tonsil**
timmerous	**timorous**	tonsalectomey	
timmid	**timid**		**tonsillectomy**
timtale	**timetable**	toobal	**tubal**
tiney	**tiny****	tooberkulosis	
tingel	**tingle**		**tuberculosis**
tinitis	**tinnitus**	toogether	**together**
tinkture	**tincture**	tooition	**tuition**
tinnsel	**tinsel**	toolip	**tulip**
tipe	**type**	toom	**tomb****
tipical	**typical**	toomer	**tumor**
tipist	**typist**	toomesence	**tumescence**
tipography	**typography****	toomstone	**tombstone**
tippoff	**tip-off**	toonight	**tonight**
tiranical	**tyrannical**	toopay	**toupee****
tirant	**tyrant**	toor	**tour****
tirany	**tyranny**	Toosday	**Tuesday**
tirms	**terms**	toosh	**tush**
tishew	**tissue**	tooshay	**touché**
tite	**tight**	toothe	**tooth**
titel	**title**	tootie frootie	**tutti frutti**
tittalate	**titillate**	tootoo	**tutu**
tittular	**titular**	tootpick	**toothpick**
tobbaco	**tobacco**	toppic	**topic**
tobogun	**toboggan**	tora	**Torah**
tocko	**taco**	torador	**toreador**
to-day	**today**	torchure	**torture**
todey	**toady**	torement	**torment**
todler	**toddler**	torenado	**tornado**
toekinism	**tokenism**	torepedo	**torpedo**
toetalatarian	**totalitarian**	torid	**torrid**
togga	**toga**	torint	**torrent**
toggether	**together**	tork	**torque**

Incorrect	Correct	Incorrect	Correct
torper	**torpor**	treeage	**triage**
torrso	**torso**	treety	**treaty**
totling	**totaling**	treezon	**treason**
tott	**tot****	trekie	**trekkie**
tottem	**totem**	tremmer	**tremor**
tousand	**thousand**	treo	**trio**
towhold	**toehold**	treshure	**treasure**
tractball	**trackball**	tresspas	**trespass**
tradegy	**tragedy**	tressury	**treasury**
tradin	**trade-in**	tresurer	**treasurer**
trafick	**traffic**	trewsew	**trousseau**
traidmark	**trademark**	tribyatery	**tributary**
trakea	**trachea**	triger	**trigger**
traktion	**traction**	trilligy	**trilogy**
tramatic	**traumatic**	trimendous	**tremendous**
tranceparent	**transparent**	trimm	**trim**
trane	**train**	tripplecate	**triplicate**
trankwilizer	**tranquilizer**	trist	**tryst**
trannslait	**translate**	trivvial	**trivial**
trannsmit	**transmit**	trole	**troll**
trannsport	**transport**	troppical	**tropical****
trannsposition	**transposition**	trowma	**trauma**
transend	**transcend**	trowsers	**trousers**
transexual	**transsexual**	truble	**trouble**
transfrence	**transference**	trudition	**tradition**
transhent	**transient**	truefully	**truthfully**
transkrip	**transcript**	truely	**truly**
transsfer	**transfer**	trujectory	**trajectory**
tranzaction	**transaction**	trummpet	**trumpet**
tranzcription	**transcription**	tryad	**triad**
tranzfusion	**transfusion**	tryangle	**triangle**
tranzister	**transistor**	trybe	**tribe**
tranzit	**transit**	trycicle	**tricycle**
tranzition	**transition**	tryed	**tried**
tranzlater	**translator**	trymester	**trimester**
tranzplant	**transplant**	tryseps	**triceps**
tranzvestite	**transvestite**	tryumph	**triumph**
traser	**tracer**	tuchdown	**touchdown**
travvesty	**travesty**	tuff	**tough**
traydname	**trade name**	tumer	**tumor**
trayter	**traitor**	tummul	**tumult**
trecherus	**treacherous**	tumy	**tummy**
trechery	**treachery**	tunell	**tunnel**
treck	**trek**	tung	**tongue****
		tunnage	**tonnage**

Incorrect	Correct	Incorrect	Correct
turist	**tourist**	tweaser	**tweezer**
turkoise	**turquoise**	tweek	**tweak**
turminate	**terminate**	twich	**twitch**
turminel	**terminal**	twilite	**twilight**
turmite	**termite**	tydings	**tidings**
turms	**terms**	tyin	**tie-in**
turniket	**tourniquet**	tyming	**timing**
turrntable	**turntable**	tympany	**timpani** or
turse	**terse**		**tympani**
tursely	**tersely**	typeriter	**typewriter**
turtiary	**tertiary**	tyrade	**tirade**
tuthepaste	**toothpaste**	tythe	**tithe**
twealth	**twelfth**	tytrope	**tightrope**

U

Incorrect	Correct	Incorrect	Correct
ubbiquitous	**ubiquitous**	unalatteral	**unilateral**
ubjective	**objective**	unalienable	**inalienable**
ucharist	**Eucharist**	unamed	**unnamed**
uforia	**euphoria**	unamurican	**un-American**
uge	**huge**	unanamus	**unanimous**
ugenics	**eugenics**	unapeeling	**unappealing**
ukalalee	**ukulele**	unason	**unison**
Ukreign	**Ukraine**	Unatarian	**Unitarian****
ulltimite	**ultimate****	unatural	**unnatural**
ulltirior	**ulterior**	unaverse	**universe**
ulogy	**eulogy**	unawganized	**unorganized**
ulser	**ulcer**	unbeelievable	
ultamatum	**ultimatum****		**unbelievable**
ultersound	**ultrasound**	unclowded	**unclouded**
ultervilet	**ultraviolet**	unconshus	**unconscious**
umanatarien		unconsolable	
	humanitarian		**inconsolable**
umane	**humane**	uncumftable	
umanity	**humanity**		**uncomfortable**
umberella	**umbrella**	undadog	**underdog**
umble	**humble****	undagrad	**undergrad**
umbridge	**umbrage**	undaprivilledged	
umid	**humid**		**underprivileged**
umidifer	**humidifier**	undataker	**undertaker**
umility	**humility**	unddress	**undress**
ummbillical	**umbilical**	undegraduate	
ummpire	**umpire****		**undergraduate**
umpopular	**unpopular**	undeground	**underground**

Incorrect	Correct	Incorrect	Correct
underiter	**underwriter**	unkle	**uncle**
underrline	**underline****	unkonditionel	
underware	**underwear**		**unconditional**
undigestible	**indigestible**	unkonscious	**unconscious**
undinyable	**undeniable**	unkonventional	
undisirable	**undesirable**		**unconventional**
undoo	**undue****	unkooth	**uncouth**
undoubtably	**undoubtedly**	unkshus	**unctuous**
unduely	**unduly**	unlode	**unload**
undyeing	**undying**	unlysensed	**unlicensed**
uneek	**unique****	unnacustomed	
uneiform	**uniform**		**unaccustomed**
unempeachible		unnattached	**unattached**
	unimpeachable	unncommon	**uncommon**
unering	**unerring**	unndergo	**undergo**
unerned	**unearned**	unnderhanded	
unerth	**unearth**		**underhanded**
unescapable	**inescapable**	unnderworld	**underworld**
unesessary	**unnecessary**	unneqil	**unequal****
uneversly	**universally**	unnering	**unerring**
unexpensive	**inexpensive**	unnerstand	**understand**
unezy	**uneasy**	unnfavrable	**unfavorable**
unfagetible	**unforgettable**	unnit	**unit**
unfare	**unfair**	Unnited Nashuns	
unferl	**unfurl**		**United Nations**
unfinnished	**unfinished**	unnlawful	**unlawful**
unfitt	**unfit**	unnocupied	**unoccupied**
unfotunate	**unfortunate**	unnowable	**unknowable**
unfrendly	**unfriendly**	unnpreguced	
unfrequent	**infrequent**		**unprejudiced**
unganely	**ungainly**	unnprincipaled	
ungarded	**unguarded**		**unprincipled**
ungoddly	**ungodly**	unown	**unknown**
ungreatful	**ungrateful**	unparralelled	
unhelthy	**unhealthy**		**unparalleled**
unholey	**unholy**	unperceptibel	
unick	**eunuch****		**imperceptible**
unidulterated		unplesent	**unpleasant**
	unadulterated	unpresidented	
unifey	**unify**		**unprecedented**
uniquivikal	**unequivocal**	unredeemable	
unitey	**unity**		**irredeemable**
Unittid Stats		unrooly	**unruly**
	United States	unsertin	**uncertain**
univercity	**university**	unskryupulous	
unkemp	**unkempt**		**unscrupulous**

Incorrect	Correct	Incorrect	Correct
untill	**until**	uristics	**heuristics**
unumployed	**unemployed**	urocentric	**Eurocentric**
ununhibited	**uninhibited**	urodollar	**Eurodollar**
unuptrusive	**unobtrusive**	uronalisis	**urinalysis**
unutached	**unattached**	Urope	**Europe**
unvale	**unveil**	urranium	**uranium**
unyun	**union****	urvra	**oeuvre**
upers	**uppers**	useable	**usable**
uphology	**ufology**	usefull	**useful**
uppgrade	**upgrade**	useing	**using**
upproar	**uproar**	use to	**used to**
uproute	**uproot**	usige	**usage**
uptical	**optical**	usualy	**usually**
uptite	**uptight**	uther	**other**
uptix	**upticks**	uthinasia	**euthanasia**
upwrite	**upright**	utterus	**uterus**
uranal	**urinal**	uttility	**utility**
Urasian	**Eurasian**	uzenet	**Usenet**
urb	**herb**	uzer frendly	
ureeka	**eureka**		**user-friendly**
uria	**urea**	uzury	**usury**

V

Incorrect	Correct	Incorrect	Correct
vaccilate	**vacillate**	vandel	**vandal**
vaccuous	**vacuous**	vaneer	**veneer**
vacincy	**vacancy**	vanesh	**vanish**
vacinnation	**vaccination**	vangard	**vanguard**
vacume	**vacuum**	vankwish	**vanquish**
vail	**veil**	vannila	**vanilla**
vajina	**vagina**	vanntage	**vantage****
vajinitis	**vaginitis**	vantrillokwist	
vakant	**vacant**		**ventriloquist**
vakation	**vacation****	vaped	**vapid**
valadate	**validate**	varacose	**varicose**
valadictory	**valedictory**	varrnish	**varnish**
valer	**valor****	varyence	**variance****
valintine	**valentine**	varyible	**variable**
vallid	**valid**	vasilate	**vacillate**
vallium	**Valium**	vassectomy	**vasectomy**
valuble	**valuable****	vassel	**vassal****
valv	**valve**	Vatecan	**Vatican**
vammpire	**vampire**	vayper	**vapor**
vanaty	**vanity**	vaze	**vase**

Incorrect	Correct	Incorrect	Correct
vazleen	**vaseline**	verible	**variable**
vear	**veer**	verilaty	**virility**
vecablerry	**vocabulary**	verious	**various**
vecks	**vex**	vermen	**vermin**
vecter	**vector****	vermooth	**vermouth**
vedgetarian	**vegetarian**	Vermount	**Vermont**
veedee	**VD**	versafy	**versify****
veedio	**video**	Versighs	**Versailles**
veel	**veal**	vertabra	**vertebra****
veenel	**venal****	vertabrate	**vertebrate****
veeva	**viva**	vertabril	**vertebral**
vegitable	**vegetable**	verticle	**vertical**
vehimint	**vehement**	vertue	**virtue****
veicle	**vehicle**	vertule realaty	**virtual reality**
vejee	**veggie** or **vegie**	verufyible	**verifiable**
vellcrow	**velcro**	vesinety	**vicinity**
vellem	**vellum**	vesle	**vessel****
vellvet	**velvet**	vesst	**vest**
velosity	**velocity**	vestabule	**vestibule**
velupchus	**voluptuous**	vestage	**vestige**
venchure	**venture**	vestid	**vested**
vender	**vendor**	vetaranery	**veterinary**
Veneetion	**Venetian**	Vet Nam	**Viet Nam**
venella	**vanilla**	vetos	**vetoes**
vengance	**vengeance**	vetrans	**veterans**
venim	**venom**	vew	**view**
venntrikle	**ventricle**	Veyenna	**Vienna**
venorashun	**veneration**	vi	**vie**
venorible	**venerable****	vibrent	**vibrant**
ventellate	**ventilate**	vicker	**vicar**
ventellation	**ventilation**	vicksin	**vixen**
venul	**venal****	victem	**victim**
venum	**venom**	victer	**victor****
venumus	**venomous**	victry	**victory**
venus	**venous**	vidiocasset	**videocassette**
venyue	**venue**	vieduck	**viaduct**
verafiable	**verifiable**	vieing	**vying**
verafucation	**verification**	vien	**vein****
verafy	**verify****	vienell	**vinyl**
verassity	**veracity****	vigel	**vigil**
veraty	**verity****	vigelence	**vigilance**
verbil	**verbal**	viger	**vigor**
verbily	**verbally**	vigerous	**vigorous**
verchill	**virtual****	vilage	**village**
vergin	**virgin**	vilense	**violence**
veriaty	**variety**		

Incorrect	Correct	Incorrect	Correct
vilet	**violet****	voegue	**vogue****
vilinist	**violinist**	voiagere	**voyageur**
villify	**vilify**	voiyer	**voyeur**
villin	**villain**	volentary	**voluntary**
vinager	**vinegar**	voletell	**volatile**
vindacate	**vindicate****	volyum	**volume**
vinear	**veneer**	vomet	**vomit**
vinella	**vanilla**	vosiferus	**vociferous**
vinntner	**vintner**	vowcher	**voucher**
vinyet	**vignette**	vowl	**vowel**
violon	**violin**	voyce	**voice**
vipar	**viper**	voyce male	**voice mail**
viris	**virus**	vudka	**vodka**
virrility	**virility**	vuedue	**voodoo**
virulance	**virulence**	vuepoint	**viewpoint**
virulant	**virulent**	vulchur	**vulture**
vishious	**vicious**	vulger	**vulgar**
visiate	**vitiate**	vuluptuos	**voluptuous**
visige	**visage**	vulver	**vulva**
visinnity	**vicinity**	vuntrilloquist	
viskis	**viscous**		**ventrilloquist**
vissera	**viscera**	vurb	**verb**
vissid	**viscid**	vurdict	**verdict**
vissta	**vista**	vurnaculer	**vernacular**
vitaman	**vitamin**	vurs	**verse**
vitel	**vital**	vursatil	**versatile**
vitely	**vitally**	vursion	**version**
vito	**veto**	vursus	**versus****
vittles	**victuals**	vurtigo	**vertigo**
vivod	**vivid**	vusinaty	**vicinity**
vizable	**visible**	vyabel	**viable**
vizhun	**vision**	vyalin	**violin**
vizhunary	**visionary**	vybrater	**vibrator****
vizual	**visual**	vycarious	**vicarious**
vodvil	**vaudeville**	vyoofinder	**viewfinder**

	W		
wafur	**wafer**	waler	**whaler**
waggon	**wagon**	walet	**wallet**
waine	**wane**	wallnut	**walnut**
waitism	**weightism**	walts	**waltz**
waje	**wage**	walup	**wallop**
wakon	**waken**	wantabee	**wannabee**

Incorrect	Correct	Incorrect	Correct
wantin	**wanton****	wership	**worship**
warbel	**warble**	werth	**worth**
wardon	**warden**	westurn	**western**
warent	**warrant**	weteware	**wetware**
warr	**war****	wether	**weather****
warrantee	**warranty**	weylay	**waylay**
warreor	**warrior**	wherehouse	**warehouse**
warrm-bludded		whiggle room	
	warm-blooded		**wiggle room**
warrt	**wart**	whisle	**whistle**
wary	**wary**	wholigram	**hologram**
washdog	**watchdog**	wholistic	**holistic**
wassp	**WASP**	wholography	**holography**
wasteage	**wastage**	whores d'urve	
wastful	**wasteful**		**hors d'oeuvres**
wastline	**waistline**	whoroscope	**horoscope**
watamelon	**watermelon**	widder	**widow**
watever	**whatever**	wierd	**weird**
watsh	**watch**	wiertap	**wiretap**
watterproof	**waterproof**	wifes	**wives**
wawmharted		wijette	**widget**
	warm-hearted	wikked	**wicked**
waylayed	**waylaid**	wildurness	**wilderness**
wearhouse	**warehouse**	wilfull	**willful**
webb	**web**	wimmin	**women**
weding	**wedding**	windsheer	**windshear**
weener	**wiener**	winfall	**windfall**
weighside	**wayside**	winjammer	**windjammer**
weild	**wield****	winndows	**windows**
welch rabid	**welsh rabbit**	winse	**wince****
welhealed	**well-heeled**	winsheeld	**windshield**
wellcome	**welcome**	wiplash	**whiplash**
wellfare	**welfare**	wipperwill	**whippoorwill**
wellter	**welter**	wirkup	**workup**
welnown	**well-known**	Wisconson	**Wisconsin**
welth	**wealth**	wisedom	**wisdom**
Wensday	**Wednesday**	wisk broom	**whisk broom**
weppon	**weapon**	wisky	**whiskey**
werkfair	**workfare**	wisper	**whisper**
werkforce	**workforce**	wissful	**wistful**
werklode	**workload**	wissle	**whistle**
werkstation	**work station**	wisteria	**wisteria**
werld	**world**	wistleblower	
werld wide web			**whistleblower**
	World Wide Web	witdraw	**withdraw**
werm	**worm**	wite	**white**

Incorrect	Correct	Incorrect	Correct
wite coller	**white collar**	worp	**warp**
witewash	**whitewash**	wossel	**wassail**
withold	**withhold**	wot	**what**
withur	**wither****	wreckueum	**requiem**
wittel	**whittle**	wresle	**wrestle**
wittness	**witness**	writeing	**writing**
wiziwig	**WYSIWYG**	wumanizer	**womanizer**
wizkid	**whiz kid**	wun	**won****
wizzard	**wizard**	wund	**wound**
wolfs	**wolves**	wun-man	**one-man**
wonderous	**wondrous**	wurd	**word**
wonliner	**one-liner**	wurkaholic	**workaholic**
wonst	**once**	wurkers compenation	
won-up	**one-up**		**workers' compensation**
wooly	**woolly**	wurld	**world**
woom	**womb**	wurm	**worm**
woosted	**worsted**	wurry	**worry**
workible	**workable**	wurse	**worse**
worning	**warning**	wyre	**wire**

X, Y, Z

Incorrect	Correct	Incorrect	Correct
xlyaphone	**xylophone**	yulogy	**eulogy****
xmass	**Xmas**	yoman	**yeoman**
x-rey	**x-ray**	yondar	**yonder**
yack	**yak**	yoonyun	**union****
y'all	**you all**	yot	**yacht**
yanky	**Yankee****	your's	**yours****
yasheeva	**yeshiva**	youser-frendly	
yat	**yacht**		**user-friendly**
yawho	**yahoo**	you-turn	**U-turn**
yeest	**yeast**	yugenics	**eugenics**
yeild	**yield**	yukka	**yucca**
yeller	**yellow**	yumanatarien	
yenn	**yen****		**humanitarian**
yerself	**yourself**	yumanity	**humanity**
yestaday	**yesterday**	yumid	**humid**
yidish	**Yiddish**	yumidifer	**humidifier**
yocal	**yokel**	yumility	**humility**
yodal	**yodel**	yum kipper	**Yom Kippur**
yogee	**yogi****	yung	**young**
yoger	**yoga****	yungster	**youngster**
yogert	**yogurt** or	yunisex	**unisex****
	yoghurt	yuppity	**uppity**

Incorrect	Correct	Incorrect	Correct
yupy	**yuppy**	zeroe	**zero**
yurine	**urine**	zerography	**xerography**
yuristics	**heuristics**	zero-kuepon	**zero-coupon**
yurn	**yearn**	zillyon	**zillion**
yurocentric	**Eurocentric**	ziltsh	**zilch**
yurolojist	**urologist**	zink	**zinc****
yuth	**youth**	zippcode	**zip code**
zanee	**zany**	zithur	**zither**
zaping	**zapping**	zodeac	**zodiac**
zar	**czar**	zoftik	**zaftig or zoftig**
Zavier	**Xavier**	zoneing	**zoning**
zeel	**zeal**	zookini	**zucchini**
zeenith	**zenith**	zoolegy	**zoology**
zefir	**zephyr**	zosster	**zoster**
zein	**zine or 'zine**	zume	**zoom**
zellous	**zealous****	Zuse	**Zeus**
zennology	**zenology**	zylophone	**xylophone**
zenofobia	**xenophobia**	zyonist	**Zionist**

aberrant, deviating • **abhorrent**, detestable

aberration, deviation • **abrasion**, scrape

abject, spiritless • **object**, a material thing; to oppose

abjure, renounce • **adjure**, entreat

ablation, wearing away • **ablution**, washing off

aboard, on a vehicle • **abort**, end prematurely • **abroad**, out of country

abrasion, scrape • **aberration**, deviation

abrogate, repeal • **arrogate**, claim unjustly

abscess, sore • **abscise**, to cut • **abscissa**, math coordinate • **obsess**, to preoccupy

abstract, select, excerpt • **obstruct**, block

accede, agree • **exceed**, go beyond

accent, speech • **ascent**, rise • **assent**, agree

accept, receive • **except**, omit

access, admittance • **excess**, over a limit

accidence, word inflections • **accidents**, unfortunate events

accident, unfortunate event • **Occident**, the Far East

accomplice, crime partner • **accomplish**, achieve

acentric, not centered • **eccentric**, strange

acetic, vinegar • **aesthetic**, appreciative of beauty • **ascetic**, self-denial

acme, peak • **acne**, skin outbreak

activate, rouse • **actuate**, put in motion

acts, to perform on stage, things done • **axe**, tool

actually, really • **actuary**, insurance analyst

ad, advertisement • **add**, to increase

adapt, make fit • **adept**, expert • **adopt**, take in

addable, can be added • **edible**, can be eaten

addition, adding • **edition**, issue

adds, increases • **ads**, advertisements • **adz**, tool

adduce, quote as proof • **deduce**, draw a conclusion

adieu, farewell • **ado**, commotion

adjoin, next to • **adjourn**, put off

adjure, entreat • **abjure**, renounce

ado, commotion • **adieu**, farewell

adverse, against • **averse**, unwilling

advert, pay attention • **avert**, avoid • **overt**, obvious

advice, suggestion • **advise**, to suggest

aerie, eagle's nest • **eerie**, ghostly • **Erie**, the lake

aesthetic, appreciative of beauty • **acetic**, vinegar • **ascetic**, self-denial

afar, distant • **affair**, event • **affaire**, romance

affect, act or influence • **effect**, result of action; to bring about

affective, emotional • **effective,** impressive; actual

affluent, wealthy • **effluent,** liquid waste

Africans, people of Africa • **Afrikaans,** language • **Afrikaners,** S. African natives of Dutch descent

aggression, attack • **egression,** departure

aid, help • **aide,** assistant

aides, assistants • **aids,** helps • **AIDS,** disease

ail, to be ill • **ale,** drink

ailment, illness • **aliment,** food

air, gas • **e'er,** ever • **ere,** before • **err,** do wrong • **heir,** inheritor

aisle, passage • **I'll,** I will • **isle,** island

alimentary, nutritive • **elementary,** primary

all, every • **awl,** tool

allay, calm • **alley,** lane • **alloy,** composed of two metals • **ally,** friend

allege, accuse • **allergy,** sensitivity

allocation, share • **elocution,** speech

allow, permit • **aloe,** plant

allowed, permitted • **aloud,** speak

all ready, completely prepared • **already,** before now

all together, all in one place • **altogether,** totally

all ways, every method • **always,** every time

allude, refer to • **elude,** escape

allusion, reference to • **elusion,** evasion; escape by deception • **illusion,** false impression

allusive, referring to • **elusive,** evasive • **illusive,** deceptive

alms, charity • **arms,** body

altar, church • **alter,** change

alternate, first one, then the other • **alternative,** substitute

altitude, height • **attitude,** point of view

amateur, inexperienced • **armature,** magnet part

ambidextrous, left- and right-handed • **ambisextrous,** sex indistinguishable

amend, change • **emend,** remove errors

amiable, good-natured • **amicable,** friendly

amity, friendship • **enmity,** hostility

amoral, without a sense of moral responsibility • **immoral,** evil

amour, love • **armoire,** wardrobe • **armor,** tanks

ample, enough • **ampule,** bottle

anal, uptight • **annual,** yearly • **annul,** void

analog, electronic • **analogue,** similar

analyst, psychoanalyst • **analyze,** to dissect

anecdote, story • **antedate,** predate • **antidote,** poison cure

angel, heavenly • **angle,** mathematics

anima, feminine side • **animal,** living being

annual, yearly • **anal,** uptight • **annul,** void

anomie, disorientation • **enema,** anal cleansing • **enemy,** foe

ant, insect • **aunt,** relative

ante, before • **anti**, against • **aunty**, relative

antedate, predate • **anecdote**, story • **antidote**, poison cure

anterior, outside • **interior**, inside

antic, a caper • **antique**, anything very old

anus, opening of the alimentary canal • **heinous**, hateful

anyone, any person; people • **any one**, any of several

anyway, in any case • **any way**, one or another way

apatite, mineral • **appetite**, craving

apologia, written defense • **apology**, expression of regret

apostile, marginal note • **apostle**, disciple • **epistle**, religious letter

apposite, appropriate • **opposite**, contrary

apposition, grammatical construction • **opposition**, those opposing

appraise, to judge • **apprise**, inform

aquarium, fish tank • **Aquarius**, Zodiac sign

arc, curved line • **arch**, building • **ark**, vessel

area, portion of land • **aria**, opera selection

armature, magnet part • **amateur**, inexperienced

armoire, wardrobe • **amour**, love • **armor**, tanks

arms, body • **alms**, charity

arose, got up • **arroz**, rice • **arouse**, awaken

arraign, accuse • **arrange**, settle

arrogate, claim unjustly • **abrogate**, repeal

artist, one skilled in fine arts • **artiste**, skilled performer

artistic, relating to the arts • **autistic**, withdrawn

ascent, rise • **accent**, speech • **assent**, agreement

ascetic, self-denial • **acetic**, vinegar • **aesthetic**, appreciative of beauty

aspirant, one who seeks • **aspirate**, to draw out • **aspirin**, medication

assay, evaluate • **essay**, composition

assert, to be forceful • **assort**, to classify

assignation, appointment to meet • **assignment**, allotted task

assistance, help • **assistants**, people who help

assurance, certainty • **insurance**, protection

astray, not proper • **estray**, straying

ate, did eat • **eight**, the number

attach, bind • **attaché**, aide • **attack**, assault

attendance, act of attending • **attendants**, helpers

attitude, point of view • **altitude**, height

auger, foretell • **augur**, tool

aught, zero • **ought**, should • **out**, away; unfashionable

aunt, relative • **ant**, insect

aunty, relative • **ante**, before • **anti**, against

aural, hearing • **oral**, verbal

auricle, external ear • **oracle**, person of great wisdom

autarchy, autocratic rule • **autarky**, national economic self-sufficiency

auteur, film director • **hauteur**, haughty

autistic, withdrawn • **artistic**, relating to the arts

autograft, organ transplant • **autograph**, signature

automation, electronics • **automaton**, robot

auxiliary, subordinate • **axillary**, relating to the armpit

averse, unwilling • **adverse**, against

avert, avoid • **advert**, pay attention • **overt**, obvious

avoid, evade • **ovoid**, egg-shaped

awe, fear • **oar**, boat • **o'er**, over • **or**, alternative • **ore**, mineral

awful, terrible • **offal**, garbage

awl, tool • **all**, every

axe, tool • **acts**, performs

axes, tools • **axis**, line

axillary, relating to the armpit • **auxiliary**, subordinate

axle, wheel shaft • **excel**, to be superior

aye, yes • **eye**, see • **I**, me

B

babble, chatter • **bauble**, trifle • **bubble**, thin liquid ball

bach, to live alone • **batch**, a group or number

bad, no good • **bade**, asked

bail, security • **bale**, bundle

bait, a lure • **bate**, lessen

bald, no hair • **balled**, put in ball • **bawled**, cried

ball, round • **bawl**, cry

ballad, song, poem • **ballet**, dance • **ballot**, vote

balm, ointment • **bomb**, explosive

baloney, bunk • **bologna**, sausage

band, ring; orchestra • **banned**, barred

bands, groups • **banns**, marriage • **bans**, prohibits

banquet, feast • **banquette**, bench

banzai, Japanese cheer • **bonsai**, dwarf tree

bard, poet • **barred**, stopped

bare, naked • **bear**, carry; animal

baring, exposing • **bearing**, carriage; support

baron, noble • **barren**, empty

barred, stopped • **bard**, poet

barter, trade • **batter**, to hurt; hitter

base, foundation • **bass**, deep tone

bases, foundations; stations • **basis**, the groundwork

bastard, illegitimate • **basted**, sewed

batch, a group or number • **bach**, to live alone

bate, lessen • **bait**, lure

bath, body soaking • **bathe**, to wash body

bathos, anticlimax • **pathos**, arousing pity

bauble, trifle • **babble**, chatter • **bubble**, thin liquid ball

baud, unit of telegraph signal speed • **bawd**, a procuress

bawl, cry • **ball**, round

bawled, cried • **bald**, no hair • **balled**, put in a ball

bazaar, a fair • **bizarre**, weird

be, exist • **bee**, insect

beach, shore • **beech**, tree

bean, vegetable • **been**, past of be • **bin**, box

bear, carry; animal • **bare**, naked

bearing, carriage; support • **baring**, exposing

beat, strike • **beet**, vegetable

beatify, make happy; religious act • **beautify**, make beautiful

beau, dandy; lover • **bow**, (pron. 'oh'), with arrow

beer, drink • **bier**, coffin

belie, contradict • **belly**, stomach

bell, rings • **belle**, beauty

bellow, pumps air • **below**, under

berry, fruit • **bury**, to cover

berth, place to sleep • **birth**, born

beseech, beg • **besiege**, surround, in war

beside, at the side of • **besides**, in addition to

better, more than good • **bettor**, one who bets

biannual, twice a year • **biennial**, every two years

bib, shield tied under chin • **bibb**, part of mast

bid, request • **bide**, wait

bier, coffin • **beer**, drink

bight, bay • **bite**, to cut • **byte**, computer unit

billed, sent a bill • **build**, construct

bin, box • **bean**, vegetable • **been**, past of be

bite, to cut • **bight**, bay • **byte**, computer unit

bizarre, weird • **bazaar**, a fair

bleep, radio signal; to censor • **blip**, radar image

blew, wind; breath • **blue**, color

bloat, to make fat • **blot**, spot; fault

bloc, political group • **block**, solid piece; prevent

blotch, odd mark • **botch**, poor work

boar, swine • **bore**, drill; dull

board, lumber or climb on • **bored**, weary

boarder, roomer • **border**, edge

body, animal/human structure • **buddy**, pal

bogey, golf • **bogy**, evil • **boogie**, party; dance

bold, daring • **bowled**, did bowl

bolder, braver • **boulder**, big rock

bole, clay; tree trunk • **boll**, weevil • **bowl**, dish; game

bologna, food • **baloney**, bunk

bomb, explosive • **balm**, ointment

bonny, pretty • **bony**, big-boned

bonsai, dwarf tree • **banzai**, Japanese cheer

boom, loud sound • **boon**, blessing

boot, shoe • **bought**, purchased • **bout**, fight

bootie, baby shoe • **booty**, plunder

border, edge • **boarder**, roomer

bore, drill, dull • **boar**, swine

bored, weary • **board**, lumber; climb on

born, given birth • **borne**, carried

borough, town • **burro**, donkey • **burrow**, hole; dig

botch, poor work • **blotch**, odd mark

bough, tree • **bow**, (pron. 'ow') bend; yield

bouillon, soup • **bullion**, gold, silver

bow, (pron. 'oh') with arrow • **beau**, lover

bowl, dish; game • **bole**, clay; tree trunk • **boll**, weevil

bowled, did bowl • **bold**, daring

boy, lad • **buoy**, a float

braes, hillsides • **brays**, utters harsh sounds • **braze**, to solder

Brahman, Hindu caste; cattle • **Brahmin**, cultured person

braid, trim • **brayed**, bellowed

brake, stop • **break**, destroy

brands, marks; product types • **brans**, cereals

brash, reckless • **brass**, metal; chutzpah

breach, break; violation • **breech**, bottom

breaches, breaks • **breeches**, trousers

bread, food • **bred**, raised

breadth, expanse • **breath**, air inhaled • **breathe**, to inhale and exhale

break, destroy • **brake**, stop

breech, bottom • **breach**, break; violation

brewed, liquor • **brood**, offspring; worry

brews, makes liquor • **bruise**, wound

briar, pipe wood • **brier**, thorny bush

bridal, wedding • **bridle**, restrain; horse

Britain, country • **Briton**, person

broach, tool; discuss • **brooch**, a clasp

brows, foreheads • **browse**, read here and there

bruit, rumor • **brute**, savage

bubble, thin liquid ball • **babble**, chatter • **bauble**, trifle

buddy, pal • **body**, animal/human structure

build, construct • **billed**, sent a bill

bullion, gold, silver • **bouillon**, soup

buoy, support • **boy**, lad

burley, a thin-bodied tobacco • **burly**, large, muscular

burro, donkey • **borough**, town • **burrow**, hole; dig

bursa, body pouches • **bursar**, financial officer

bury, put in ground • **berry**, fruit

bus, vehicle • **buss**, kiss

bussed, sent by bus • **bust**, bosom

but, however • **butt**, end; object

buy, purchase • **by**, near • **bye**, sport

byte, computer unit • **bight**, bay • **bite**, to cut

C

cabal, a secret group • **cable**, wire

cacao, tree of cocoa beans • **cocoa**, chocolate

cache, hiding place • **cash**, money

caddie, golf attendant • **caddy**, tea box

calendar, time • **calender**, machine to press

call, cry out • **caul**, membrane

callous, unfeeling • **callus**, hard skin

calm, quiet • **cam**, machinery part

Calvary, crucifixion • **cavalry**, horse troops

canapé, food • **canopy**, covering

cannon, gun • **canon**, law

cant, dialect • **can't**, cannot

canvas, cloth • **canvass**, to solicit

capital, main; city • **Capitol**, the building

carat, diamond • **caret**, proofreader's mark • **carrot**, vegetable

caries, dental decay • **carries**, conveys; bears

carnal, bodily, fleshly • **channel**, waterway • **charnel**, dead bodies

carousal, orgy • **carousel**, merry-go-round

cash, money • **cache**, hiding place

cask, box • **casque**, helmet

cast, to fling • **caste**, class

caster, swivelled wheel • **castor**, secretion used in medicines

casual, easy going • **causal**, the cause of

cataclasm, breakage, disruption • **cataclysm**, great flood

caught, did catch • **court**, law

caul, membrane • **call**, cry out

causal, producing an effect • **casual**, easygoing

cause, to bring about • **caws**, the sounds made by crows

cavalry, horse troops • **Calvary**, crucifixion

cay, island • **key**, lock opener • **quay**, wharf

cease, stop • **seas**, bodies of water • **sees**, observes • **seize**, grab

cede, give up • **seed**, flower

ceiling, top • **sealing**, closing

celebrate, to honor, be festive • **celibate**, unmarried; sexually inactive

celery, vegetable • **salary**, wage

cell, prison; unit in biology • **sell**, opposite of buy

cellar, basement • **seller**, one who sells

cemetery, graveyard • **symmetry**, proportionate

censer, incense container • **censor**, moral overseer • **censure**, condemn

census, population count • **senses**, sight, touch

cents, money • **scents**, smells • **sense**, judgment; awareness

cereal, food • **serial**, in a row

cession, yielding • **session**, meeting

champagne, wine • **champaign**, a plain

channel, waterway • **carnal**, bodily, fleshly • **charnel**, dead bodies

charted, put on a chart • **chartered**, rented

chased, ran after • **chaste**, pure

chauffeur, driver • **shofar**, ram's horn

cheap, priced low • **cheep**, sound of young birds

check, money • **Czech**, nationality

chert, a rock • **shirt**, garment

chews, eats • **choose**, select

chic, stylish • **sheik**, Arab chief

Chile, country • **chili**, food • **chilly**, cold

choir, singers • **quire**, measure of paper

choler, rage • **collar**, neck band • **collard**, vegetable • **color**, hue

choral, singing • **coral**, sea life • **corral**, animal pen

chord, music • **cord**, rope • **cored**, removed the core

chow, food; dog • **ciao**, goodbye

christen, baptize • **Christian**, a believer in Christ

chute, drop • **shoot**, fire

cite, point out • **sight**, see • **site**, place

clan, family • **klan**, Ku Klux Klan

clause, contract • **claws**, sharp nails

clench, close teeth • **clinch**, to embrace; to conclude a deal

clew, ball • **clue**, hint

click, noise • **clique**, small group

climactic, refers to climax • **climatic**, refers to climate

climb, ascent • **clime**, climate

clique, small group • **click**, noise

clone, copy • **clown**, joker

close, shut • **clothes**, apparel • **cloths**, small fabrics

coal, fire • **koel**, a cuckoo • **kohl**, eye shadow

coarse, rough • **course**, class; passage

coat, garment • **cote**, shelter • **côte**, coast

cockscomb, a garden plant • **cock's comb**, comb of a cock • **coxcomb**, fop

cocoa, chocolate • **cacao**, tree of cocoa beans

cola, a drink • **kola**, a nut or tree

collage, a type of painting • **college**, higher education

collar, neck band • **choler**, rage • **collard**, vegetable • **color**, hue

collision, crash • **collusion**, fraud

cologne, fragrance • **colon**, intestine; punctuation

Colombia, a country in South America • **Columbia**, the university

colonel, officer • **kernel**, seed

coma, sleep • **comma**, punctuation

comedy, humor • **comity**, welfare • **committee**, a group with a definite purpose

comet, celestial body • **commit**, entrust

command, order • **commend**, praise

commendation, praise • **condemnation**, denunciation

complacence, self-satisfaction • **complaisance**, fulfillment of wishes of others

complacent, pleased with oneself • **complaisant**, desirous of pleasing

complement, balance • **compliment**, praise

complementary, completing • **complimentary**, free

comprehensible, understandable • **comprehensive**, inclusive

concur, agree • **conquer**, defeat

condemn, to find guilty • **contemn**, to despise

condemnation, denunciation • **commendation**, praise

confidant, a person confided in • **confident**, certain

confirmer, one who ratifies • **conformer**, one who complies with established customs

congenial, agreeable • **congenital**, dating from birth

conscience, moral sense • **conscientious**, painstaking • **conscious**, aware

conservation, preservation • **conversation**, talk

consul, diplomat • **council**, an assembly • **counsel**, advice

contact, connection • **contract**, legal agreement

contemn, to despise • **condemn**, to find guilty

contend, dispute • **content**, happy

continence, self-restraint • **countenance**, face

continual, repeated again and again • **continuous**, without a break

convection, heat transmission • **conviction**, belief; guilt

convert, changed loyalty • **covert**, secret • **covet**, desire another's property

coolie, laborer • **coolly**, in a cool manner

coral, sea life • **choral**, singing • **corral**, animal pen

cord, rope • **chord**, music • **cored**, removed the core

core, center • **corps**, army • **corpse**, dead body

corespondent, paramour in divorce proceedings • **correspondent**, one party to exchange of letters

corner, intersection • **coroner**, death investigator

corporal, of the body; a soldier • **corporeal**, material; tangible

corps, army group • **core**, center • **corpse**, dead body

cortisone, medicine • **courtesan**, a prostitute

costume, clothes • **custom**, habit

costumer, one who makes costumes • **customer**, buyer

cot, bed • **cut**, wound

cote, shelter • **coat**, garment • **côte**, coast

cough, illness • **cuff**, sleeve's end; handcuff

council, an assembly • **consul**, diplomat • **counsel**, advice

councillor, member of council • **counselor**, advisor; lawyer

countenance, face • **continence**, self-restraint

course, class; passage • **coarse**, rough

court, law • **caught**, did catch

courtesan, a prostitute • **cortisone**, medicine

courtesy, manners • **curtsy**, bow

cousin, a relative • **cozen**, to deceive

covet, desire another's property • **convert**, changed loyalty • **covert**, secret

coward, one who lacks courage • **cowered**, crouched

coxcomb, fop • **cockscomb**, a garden plant • **cock's comb**; comb of a cock

craps, dice • **crepes**, pancakes

creak, noise • **creek**, stream • **crick**, pain in the neck

cream, milk fat • **creme**, liqueur

crease, fold • **kris**, cheese; dagger

credible, believable • **creditable**, praiseworthy

crews, sailors • **cruise**, voyage

critic, one who criticizes • **critique**, criticism

crochet, a kind of knitting • **crotchet**, a quirk; a hook

croquet, a game played with mallets, balls • **croquette**, a fried cake of minced food

crudités, cold vegetables • **crudity**, vulgarity

cruise, voyage • **crews**, sailors

cue, hint; billiards • **queue**, line

cuff, sleeve's end; handcuff • **cough**, illness

culled, picked • **cult**, sect

currant, a berry • **current**, stream of water or events; contemporary

curtsy, bow • **courtesy**, manners

custom, habit • **costume**, clothes

customer, buyer • **costumer**, one who makes costumes

cygnet, a young swan • **signet**, a seal

cymbal, music • **symbol**, sign

D

daily, every day • **dally**, idle • **delay**, put off

dairy, food • **diary**, personal record

dais, platform • **dice**, craps

dam, water • **damn**, curse

days, plural of day • **daze**, confused

deacon, clergy • **decon**, deconstruction

dead, deceased • **deed**, act

dear, loved • **deer**, animal

debauch, to seduce • **debouch**, to march out

deceased, dead • **diseased**, sick

decent, good • **descent**, go down • **dissent**, disagreement

decree, law • **degree**, award from school

deduce, draw a conclusion • **adduce**, quote as proof

deer, animal • **dear**, loved one

defer, postpone • **differ**, disagree

definite, precise • **definitive**, final

defused, without a fuse • **diffused**, filtered or mixed in

degree, school award • **decree**, law

demur, to disagree • **demure**, modest

dependant, the noun: one who relies on • **dependent**, relying on another

dependence, reliance on others • **dependents**, those supported by a given person

depositary, the one receiving a deposit • **depository**, a place where anything is deposited

deposition, testimony in writing • **disposition**, temperament

depraved, evil • **deprived**, taken away

deprecate, express disapproval • **depreciate**, to lessen in value

descendant, offspring • **descendent**, falling; proceeding from an original ancestor

descent, go down • **decent**, good • **dissent**, disagreement

desecrate, act irreverently • **desiccate**, to dry out

desert, dry land • **dessert**, food

desolate, barren • **dissolute**, given to wasteful, pleasure-seeking activities

detract, to take away from • **distract**, to divert

device, a scheme; means • **devise**, invent

dew, moisture • **do**, to act • **due**, owed

diagram, sketch • **diaphragm**, part of body

diary, personal record • **dairy**, food

dice, craps • **dais**, platform

die, death • **dye**, change color

died, passed away • **diet**, food intake

differ, disagree • **defer**, postpone

diffused, filtered or mixed in • **defused**, without a fuse

dilation, widening • **dilution**, watering down

dine, eat • **dyne**, a unit of force in physics

diner, eatery • **dinner**, meal

dinghy, small boat • **dingy**, dirty

disapprove, condemn • **disprove**, prove wrong

disburse, pay out • **disperse**, break up

discomfit, to upset another • **discomfort**, uneasiness

discreet, prudent • **discrete**, separate, disconnected

discus, sport • **discuss**, to talk

diseased, sick • **deceased**, dead

disposition, temperament • **deposition**, testimony in writing

dissent, disagreement • **decent**, good • **descent**, go down

dissolute, given to wasteful, pleasure-seeking activities • **desolate**, barren

distal, away from body's center • **distill**, purify; reduce

distract, to divert • **detract**, to take away from

divers, several • **diverse**, different

do, to act • **dew**, moisture • **due**, owed

doc, short for doctor • **dock**, boat haven

doe, deer • **dough**, bread

doer, one who does • **dour**, severe • **dower**, widow's estate share

does, female deers • **doze**, nap

done, finished • **dun**, ask for payment

draft, plan • **draught**, flow of air

drier, more dry • **dryer**, machine

dual, two • **duel**, fight

dudgeon, anger; resentment • **dungeon**, cell in basement of a prison

due, owing • **dew**, moisture • **do**, act

dully, with dullness • **duly**, as is due

dye, change color • **die**, death

dyeing, changing color • **dying**, death

dyne, a unit of force in physics • **dine**, eat

E

earn, gain • **urn**, vase

eccentric, strange • **acentric**, not centered

edge, border • **etch**, draw; engrave

edible, eatable • **addible**, can be added

edition, published form or number • **addition**, anything added

e'er, ever • **air**, gas • **ere**, before • **err**, do wrong • **heir**, inheritor

eerie, ghostly • **aerie**, eagle's nest • **Erie**, the lake

effect, result; to bring about • **affect**, to cause

effective, impressive; operative • **affective**, emotional

effluent, liquid waste • **affluent**, wealthy

egression, departure • **aggression**, attack

eight, the number • **ate**, did eat

Eire, Ireland • **IRA**, Individual Retirement Account • **ire**, wrath

either, one of two • **ether**, gas

elder, n: an older person • **older**, adj. lived longer

elegy, poem; lament • **eulogy**, praise

element, part • **ailment**, illness • **aliment**, food

elementary, primary • **alimentary**, nutritive

elicit, draw out • **illicit**, illegal

eliminate, wipe out • **illuminate**, shed light on

elocution, speech • **allocation**, share

elude, evade • **allude**, refer to • **illude**, cheat

elusion, evasion; escape by deception • **allusion**, reference to • **illusion**, false impression

elusive, evasive • **allusive**, referring to • **illusive**, deceptive

emasculate, castrate • **immaculate**, pure

emend, remove errors • **amend**, change

emerge, to come out • **im-merge**, to plunge into

emersed, standing above • **im-mersed**, plunged in liquid

emigrant, leaves country • **im-migrant**, enters country

eminent, distinguished • **imma-nent**, inherent • **imminent**, impending

emit, to send out • **immit**, to send in

emollient, softening • **emolu-ment**, profit; salary; fee

empire, dominion • **umpire**, referee

enable, to make able • **unable**, not able

endogenous, from within • **in-digenous**, native

enema, anal cleansing • **ano-mie**, disorientation • **enemy**, foe

enervate, to deprive of nerve or strength • **innervate**, to invigorate

enfold, to wrap over • **unfold**, to lay open

enmity, hostility • **amity**, friendship

enroll, join • **unroll**, to display

ensure, to make sure or secure • **insure**, to obtain insur-ance; guarantee

enter, to go in • **inter**, to bury

entitled, deserving • **untitled**, lacking a title

entomology, study of insects • **etymology**, study of words

envelop, to surround • **enve-lope**, stationery

enwrap, wrap around • **un-wrap**, uncover

epic, narrative • **epoch**, era

epigraph, motto • **epitaph**, in-scription • **epithet**, curse

epistle, religious letter • **apostil**, marginal note • **apostle**, disciple

equable, not varying; even-tempered • **equitable**, fair

era, age • **error**, mistake

ere, before • **air**, gas • **e'er**, ever • **err**, do wrong • **heir**, inheritor

erect, to build • **eruct**, to belch; cast forth

Erie, the lake • **aerie**, eagle's nest • **eerie**, ghostly

erotic, sexy • **erratic**, uneven

errand, trip • **errant**, roving

error, mistake • **era**, age, pe-riod

eruption, a bursting out • **ir-ruption**, a bursting in

especial, exceptional, preemi-nent • **special**, particular, specific

essay, composition • **assay**, evaluate

estray, straying • **astray**, not proper

etch, draw; engrave • **edge**, border

etching, drawing • **itching**, tickling

ether, drug • **either**, one of two

ethnology, study of human groups • **ethology**, animal behavior

etymology, study of words • **entomology**, study of in-sects

eulogy, praise • **elegy**, lament; poem

eunuch, sexless • **unique**, sole

eunuchs, emasculated men • **unix**, computer operating system

everyone, all persons • **every one**, each one, considered separately, one after the other

everything, the entire situation, viewed as one total mass • **every thing,** each item in the given situation

ewe, sheep • **yew,** tree • **you,** person

exalt, glorify • **exult,** rejoice

exceed, go beyond • **accede,** agree

excel, to be superior • **axle,** wheel shaft

except, leave out • **accept,** agree

exceptionable, objectionable • **exceptional,** out of the ordinary

excess, too much • **access,** get to

exciting, rousing strong feelings • **exiting,** leaving

exercise, practice • **exorcise,** drive away evil spirits

exists, is real • **exits,** doors; departures

expansive, capable of stretching • **expensive,** costly

expiation, making amends • **expiration,** termination; air expulsion

expose, to uncover • **exposé,** an account of scandalous facts or shameful deeds

extant, still done • **extent,** width

eye, see • **aye,** yes • **I,** me

F

face-ism, discrimination by looks • **fascism,** dictatorial movement

faces, front parts of head • **facies,** appearance • **feces,** excrement

facet, side • **faucet,** water flow control

facility, skill • **felicity,** happiness

facts, actual occurrences • **FAQS,** frequently asked questions • **fax,** facsimile

faerie, fairies' abode • **fairy,** sprite • **ferry,** boat

fain, gladly • **feign,** pretend

faint, weak • **feint,** movement to deceive

fair, just • **fare,** pay for travel

faker, fraud • **fakir,** holy man

fantasy, a far-fetched imaginary idea • **phantasm,** ghost; illusion

farther, refers to physical distance • **father,** parent • **further,** refers to extent or degree

fascism, dictatorial movement • **face-ism,** discrimination by looks

fatal, deathly • **fateful,** of very great importance

fate, destiny • **fete,** festival

faucet, water • **facet,** side

faun, rural deity • **fawn,** servile; young deer

fays, fairies • **faze,** worry • **phase,** stage

feast, meal • **fest,** celebration

feat, act • **feet,** body

feint, pretend • **faint,** weak

felicity, happiness • **facility**, skill

ferment, yeast • **foment**, incite

ferry, boat • **faerie**, fairies' abode • **fairy**, imaginary being

fetch, get and return • **fetish**, magical object

fete, festival • **fate**, destiny

fiancé, engaged • **finance**, money

fiend, monster • **friend**, companion

file, holder • **phial**, tube

filing, putting in order • **filling**, to make full

finale, the end • **finally**, at last • **finely**, excellently

finch, bird • **flinch**, wince

find, locate • **fined**, penalty

fineness, being fine • **finesse**, subtlety, skill

fir, tree • **fur**, hair of animal

fiscal, money • **physical**, body

fisher, one who fishes • **fissure**, split

flagrant, glaring • **fragrant**, nice odor

flair, aptitude • **flare**, burn

flaunt, ostentatious display • **flout**, reject contemptuously

flaw, fault • **floor**, room surface

flea, insect • **flee**, run away

flèche, a spire • **flesh**, meat

flecks, spots • **flex**, bend

flew, did fly • **flu**, influenza • **flue**, chimney

flock, number of animals • **flog**, whip

floe, ice • **flow**, pour

florescence, flowering • **fluorescence**, giving light

florid, ornate • **fluoride**, chemical

flour, food • **flower**, plant

flout, reject contemptuously • **flaunt**, ostentatious display

foggy, blurred • **fogy**, conservative

foment, incite • **ferment**, yeast

fond, affectionate • **font**, typeface

fondling, caressing • **foundling**, deserted infant

for, in behalf of • **fore**, golf • **four**, number

forego, precede • **forgo**, do without

foreword, introduction • **forward**, move ahead

form, shape • **forum**, public discussion

formally, conventionally • **formerly**, before now

formication, prickly sensation • **fornication**, intercourse

fort, military • **forte**, strong point

forth, forward • **fourth**, number

foul, dirty, unfair • **fowl**, bird

found, located • **fount**, a spring; a source

foundling, deserted infant • **fondling**, caressing

four, number • **for**, on behalf of • **fore**, golf

fractions, math numbers • **fractious**, quarrelsome

fragrant, nice odor • **flagrant**, glaring

franc, French money • **frank**, blunt

frays, battles • **phrase**, words

freak, abnormal being • **phreak**, illegal phone user

frees, sets free • **freeze**, cold • **frieze**, cloth or ornament

friar, monk • **fryer**, fowl

friend, companion • **fiend**, monster

funeral, a ceremony for the dead • **funereal**, mournful

fur, hair of animal • **fir**, tree

furry, having fur • **fury**, anger

further, refers to extent or degree • **farther**, refers to physical distance • **father**, parent

fuss, bother • **fuzz**, sparse hair; slang for police

G

GAAP, generally accepted accounting principles • **gap**, an opening

gabble, talk • **gable**, roof • **gobble**, swallow hastily

gaff, hook • **gaffe**, mistake

gage, security • **gauge**, measure

gaggle, flock; group • **gargle**, rinse throat

gait, walk • **gate**, opening

galleon, ship • **gallon**, measure

gallstone, gall bladder mass • **goldstone**, spangled glass

gamble, bet • **gambol**, frolic

gamete, sexual cell • **gamut**, full range

gamin, a street urchin • **gammon**, a deceitful trick

gantlet, narrowing of two railroad tracks; punishment • **gauntlet**, glove

gap, an opening • **GAAP**, generally accepted accounting principles

gat, channel • **ghat**, mountain pass

gate, door • **gait**, walk

GATT, trade agreement • **get**, to obtain

gauche, naive • **gouache**, art

gauge, measure • **gage**, security

gaunt, thin • **jaunt**, trip

gauze, thin wrapping • **gays**, homosexuals • **gaze**, look

gel, colloid • **jell**, to congeal

genes, heredity • **jeans**, clothing

genius, brilliant • **genus**, subdivision

genteel, polite • **gentile**, non-Jew or non-Mormon • **gentle**, tame

German, of Germany • **germane**, relevant

gesture, movement • **jester**, clown

get, to obtain • **GATT**, trade agreement

ghoul, demon • **goal**, aim

gibe, to sneer at • **jibe**, to agree; to swing from side to side

gild, gold cover • **guild**, association

gilt, gold • **guilt**, blame

gin, liquor • **jinn**, a spirit

glacier, iceberg • **glazier**, glass maker

glitch, misfunction • **glitz**, showiness

glitterati, celebrities • **literati**, people of letters

gloom, a sad, dismal atmosphere • **glume**, grass

gluten, substance found in flour of wheat and other grains • **glutton**, one who eats to excess

glutenous, like gluten • **glutinous**, like glue • **gluttonous**, greedy

gnu, animal • **knew**, did know • **new**, not old

goal, aim • **ghoul**, demon

gobble, swallow hastily • **gabble**, talk • **gable**, roof

gofer, servant • **gopher**, animal

goldstone, spangled glass • **gallstone**, gall bladder mass

golf, game • **gulf**, bay

gorilla, ape • **guerrilla**, war

grate, bars; grind • **great**, large

grease, oil or unctuous matter

• **Greece**, a nation in Europe

grill, to broil • **grille**, a grating

grip, grasp • **gripe**, complain • **grippe**, disease

grisly, ghastly • **gristly**, containing cartilage • **grizzly**, black

gristle, cartilage • **grizzle**, grumble

groan, moan • **grown**, mature

groove, indentation • **grove**, orchard

guarantee, to secure • **guaranty**, assure debt repayment

guerrilla, warfare • **gorilla**, ape

guessed, did guess • **guest**, visitor

guild, association • **gild**, gold cover

guilt, blame • **gilt**, gold

gulf, bay • **golf**, game

gurney, stretcher • **journey**, trip

H

habitant, inhabitant • **habitat**, natural environment

hail, salute; ice • **hale**, hearty

hair, on head • **hare**, rabbit

haircut, the process of cutting hair • **haricot**, bean; stew

hall, room • **haul**, pull in

hallow, to make holy • **halo**, circle of light around head • **holler**, to shout • **hollow**, empty inside

halve, divide in two • **have**, possess

handmade, made by hand • **handmaid**, servant

handsome, attractive • **hansom**, cab

hangar, shelter • **hanger**, clothes holder

hangup, inhibition • **hang up**, to end conversation

hardly, barely • **heartily**, warmly

hardy, strong • **hearty**, vigorous

hare, rabbit • **hair**, strands on body

hart, stag • **heart**, body

hassle, trouble; bother • **hustle**, hurry; scam

hatched, gave birth • **hatchet,** chopping instrument

hatful, a filled hat • **hateful,** malicious

haul, pull in • **hall,** room

haunch, buttocks • **hunch,** conjecture

hauteur, haughty • **auteur,** film director

have, possess • **halve,** divide in two

haven, refuge • **heaven,** abode of God

hay, dried grass eaten by cattle • **hey!,** an exclamation

heal, mend • **heel,** of foot • **hell,** Hades • **he'll,** he will

hear, listen • **here,** this place

heard, did hear • **herd,** animals

hearing, ability to hear • **herring,** fish

heart, vital organ • **hart,** stag

hearty, vigorous • **hardy,** strong

heaume, helmet • **home,** a house

heaven, abode of God • **haven,** refuge

he'd, he would • **heed,** obey

heel, of foot • **heal,** mend • **hell,** Hades • **he'll,** he will

heinous, hateful • **anus,** opening of the alimentary canal

heir, inheritor • **air,** gas • **e'er,** ever • **ere,** before • **err,** do wrong

hence, from this time or place • **whence,** from which time or place • **wince,** to flinch

here, this place • **hear,** detect sound

heroin, drug • **heroine,** female hero

hew, chop • **hue,** color

hey!, an exclamation • **hay,** dried grass eaten by cattle

higher, taller • **hire,** employ

him, he • **hymn,** song

ho, exclamation • **hoe,** tool

hoard, collect • **horde,** mob

hoarse, harsh • **horse,** animal

hoary, old • **whorey,** wanton

hobby, recreation • **hubby,** husband

hockey, ice sport • **hooky,** unexcused absence

hoes, digs • **hose,** stockings

hoist, raised • **host,** person who receives guests

hole, opening • **whole,** complete

hold-up, robbery • **holed up,** taken refuge

holey, having holes • **holy,** religious • **wholly,** fully

holiday, a day of exemption from work • **holy day,** a religious feast day

holler, to shout • **hallow,** to make holy • **halo,** circle of light around head to show saintliness • **hollow,** empty inside

home, a house • **heaume,** helmet

homogeneous, of the same character, essentially alike • **homogenous,** of common origin

honk, sound of horn or geese • **hunk,** well-built male

hoop, circle • **whoop,** holler

horde, mob • **hoard,** saved treasure

horse, animal • **hoarse,** rough sound

hose, stockings; tubing • **hoes,** tools

hospitable, friendly • **hospital,** treats the sick

hostel, lodging • **hostile,** antagonistic

hour, time • **our,** belongs to us

hubby, husband • **hobby,** recreation

hue, color • **hew,** chop

human, of people • **humane,** kind

humble, modest • **umbel,** flower cluster

humerus, bone • **humorous,** funny

hunch, conjecture • **haunch,** buttocks

Hungary, the country • **hungry,** ravenous

hunk, well-built male • **honk,** sound of horn or geese

hunter, one who hunts • **junta,** coup leaders

hurdle, barrier • **hurtle,** to rush

hymn, song • **him,** he

hypercritical, over-critical • **hypocritical,** pretending to be what one is not

I

I, me • **aye,** yes • **eye,** see

idle, inactive • **idol,** statue • **idyll,** simple pastoral scene

I'll, I will • **aisle,** passage • **isle,** island

illegible, unreadable • **ineligible,** unqualified

illicit, illegal • **elicit,** draw out

illude, cheat • **allude,** refer to

illuminate, shed light on • **eliminate,** wipe out

illusion, false impression • **allusion,** reference to • **elusion,** evasion; escape by deception

illusive, deceptive • **allusive,** referring to • **elusive,** evasive

imbrue, moisten, especially with blood • **imbue,** permeate; color deeply

immanent, inherent • **imminent,** impending • **eminent,** distinguished

immerge, to plunge into • **emerge,** to come out

immersed, plunged into; absorbed • **emersed,** standing out

immigrant, enters country • **emigrant,** leaves country

imminent, about to happen • **eminent,** well-known

immit, to send in • **emit,** to send out

immoral, evil • **amoral,** without a sense of moral responsibility

immunity, exemption from duty; power to resist disease • **impunity,** exemption from punishment or harm

impassable, closed • **impassible,** incapable of being hurt • **impossible,** not possible

impostor, pretender • **imposture,** deception

imprudent, unwise • **impudent,** impertinent

impute, ascribe • **input,** to enter; to provide information

in, [prep.] on the inside • **inn**, hotel

inane, pointless • **insane**, mad

inapt, unqualified • **inept**, unskilled

incest, sex between relatives • **insects**, bugs • **insists**, demands

incidence, rate of occurrence • **incidents**, happenings

incipient, beginning to exist • **insipient**, unwise

incite, stir up • **insight**, keen understanding

indict, charge with a crime • **indite**, to compose

indigenous, native • **endogenous**, from within

indiscreet, unwise • **indiscrete**, unseparated

indivisible, can't be divided • **invisible**, can't be seen

ineligible, not qualified • **illegible**, unreadable

inept, unskilled • **inapt**, unqualified

inequity, injustice • **iniquity**, wickedness

infect, contaminate • **infest**, swarm • **invest**, to put in money

infirmary, clinic • **infirmity**, physical weakness

ingenious, original • **ingenuous**, innocent

inn, hotel • **in**, [prep.] on the inside

innervate, to invigorate • **enervate**, to deprive of strength

input, to enter; to provide information • **impute**, ascribe

insane, mad • **inane**, pointless

insert, to put in • **inset**, that which is set in

insight, keen understanding • **incite**, stir up

insipient, unwise • **incipient**, beginning to exist

insolate, to expose to the sun • **insulate**, to protect; isolate

installation, being put in place • **instillation**, inserting eye drops

insurance, protection • **assurance**, certainty

insure, guarantee; take insurance • **ensure**, to make sure or secure

intense, in an extreme degree • **intents**, purpose

inter, to bury • **enter**, to go in

intercession, petition for another • **intersession**, between semesters

interior, inside • **anterior**, outside

interjection, inserted remark • **introjection**, unconscious ideas

interment, burial • **internment**, state of being detained or held

intern, hospital assistant doctor • **inturn**, an inward turn or bend

interpellate, to question a minister or executive officer • **interpolate**, to alter or insert new matter

interstate, between states • **intestate**, without a will • **intrastate**, within state

intimate, having close relations • **intimidate**, to frighten

inturn, an inward turn or bend • **intern**, hospital assistant doctor

invisible, can't be seen • **indivisible**, can't be divided

ion, particle • **iron**, metal

IRA, Individual Retirement Account • **Eire**, Ireland • **ire**, wrath

irrelevant, not pertinent • **irreverent**, disrespectful

irruption, a bursting in • **eruption**, a bursting out

isle, island • **aisle**, passage • **I'll**, I will

itching, tickling • **etching**, drawing

its, belonging to it • **it's**, it is

I've, I have • **IV**, intravenous • **ivy**, plant

J

jab, hit lightly • **job**, employment

jam, to squeeze; a sweet spread • **jamb**, side of door

jaunt, trip • **gaunt**, thin

jealous, envious • **zealous**, enthusiastic

jeans, clothing • **genes**, heredity

jejune, childish • **jejunum**, part of small intestine

jell, to congeal • **gel**, colloid

jester, clown • **gesture**, movement

jewel, cut gem • **joule**, energy unit • **jowl**, jaw

Jewry, Jewish people • **jury**, court

Jews, people of Jewish descent • **juice**, drink

jibe, to agree; to swing from side to side • **gibe**, to sneer at

jinks, pranks • **jinx**, bad luck

jinn, a spirit • **gin**, liquor

jog, run • **jug**, liquid holder

joggle, shake lightly • **juggle**, handle several objects together

joule, energy unit • **jewel**, cut gem

journey, trip • **gurney**, stretcher

joust, to join battle • **just**, equitable

juggler, one who juggles • **jugular**, throat

junta, coup leaders • **hunter**, one who hunts

jury, court • **Jewry**, the Jewish people

just, equitable • **joust**, to join battle

jut, stick out • **jute**, fiber

K

Kaddish, Hebrew prayer for dead • **Kiddush**, prayer for wine

ken, to know • **kin**, relatives

kernel, seed • **colonel**, officer

ketch, boat • **catch**, take hold of

key, lock opener • **quay**, wharf • **cay**, island

kibbutz, Israeli commune • **kibitz**, offer advice

kid, child • **kit**, equipment • **kite**, flying toy • **kith**, relatives

kill, murder • **kiln**, oven

killed, did kill • **kilt**, Scottish skirt worn by men

kinesics, body movements • **kinetics**, caused by movement

Klan, Ku Klux Klan • **clan**, family

knave, rogue • **nave**, part of church

knead, to press • **need**, must have

kneel, to rest on the knees • **knell**, to ring, as for death

knew, did know • **gnu**, animal • **new**, not old

knight, feudal rank • **night**, opposite of day

knit, fabric • **nit**, insect

knob, protuberance • **nob**, head

knock, to strike • **nock**, notch of an arrow

knot, what you tie • **not**, denial

know, to understand • **no**, opposite of yes

knowable, can be known • **noble**, lordly; fine character • **Nobel**, prize

knows, understands • **noes**, negatives • **nose**, on face

kohl, eye shadow • **coal**, fire • **koel**, a cuckoo

kola, a nut or tree • **cola**, a drink

kris, cheese; dagger • **crease**, fold

L

lade, to load • **laid**, placed

Ladino, Sephardic language • **Latina**, Hispanic woman • **Latino**, Hispanic male

lager, beer • **logger**, tree cutter

lain, did lie • **lane**, path

lair, den • **layer**, a thickness; fold

lam, run away • **lamb**, young sheep

lama, monk • **llama**, animal

lame, can't walk • **lamé**, gold fabric

lanced, pricked • **lancet**, surgical knife

language, words and usage • **languish**, to live in misery

larva, insect • **lava**, volcano

laser, a beam of coherent light • **lazar**, a leper

lass, girl • **last**, the end one

later, afterwards • **latter**, the last one of two

lath, strip of wood • **lathe**, a machine tool

laud, praise • **lord**, a noble

law, rule • **lore**, learning

laws, rules • **loss**, amount that is lost • **lost**, past tense of lose

lay, to deposit • **lei**, a wreath

layer, thickness; fold • **lair**, den

lea, meadow • **lee**, shelter

leach, dissolve • **leech**, bloodsucker

lead, metal; to guide • **led**, did guide

leaf, tree • **leave**, depart • **lief**, gladly

leak, crack • **leek**, vegetable

lean, thin • **lien**, legal charge

least, smallest • **lest**, unless

lei, wreath • **lay**, put down

lentil, pea • **lintel**, beam

lessee, tenant • **lesser**, smaller • **lessor**, one who leases

lessen, to decrease • **lesson**, instruction

letter, written message • **litter**, garbage

levee, dike • **levy**, fine; tax

liable, obligated • **libel**, slander

liar, tells lies • **lyre**, musical instrument

libido, sexual drive • **livedo**, skin discoloration

lichen, plant • **liken**, to compare

lickerish, eager, craving • **licorice**, a flavoring

lie, falsehood • **lye**, chemical

lief, gladly • **leaf**, tree • **leave**, depart

lien, claim • **lean**, thin

lightening, making lighter; relieving • **lightning**, flash in sky

lighter, not as heavy • **liter**, liquid measure • **litter**, strewn things

limb, leg or arm • **lime**, a caustic; fruit • **limn**, draw or outline • **Lyme**, disease

linage, number of lines • **lineage**, ancestry

lineal, of descendants • **linear**, in a line

lineament, detail • **liniment**, a thin ointment

links, joins • **lynx**, animal

lintel, beam • **lentil**, pea

liqueur, sweet liquor • **liquor**, alcoholic drink

literati, people of letters • **glitterati**, celebrities

lived, did live • **livid**, enraged

llama, animal • **lama**, monk

lo!, exclamation • **low**, down; base

load, burden • **lode**, ore

loan, lending • **lone**, alone

loath, reluctant • **loathe**, despise

local, not widespread • **locale**, a place

loch, lake • **lock**, fastening

locks, fastenings • **lox**, salmon

locus, locality • **locust**, insect

lode, mineral • **load**, burden

lodge, cabin • **loge**, theater

logger, tree cutter • **lager**, beer

lone, alone • **loan**, lending

loop, closed circuit • **loupe**, magnifier

loose, not tight • **lose**, fail

loot, booty • **lute**, musical instrument

lord, noble • **laud**, praise

lore, learning • **law**, rule

loss, amount that is lost • **laws**, rules • **lost**, past tense of lose

low, down; base • **lo!**, exclamation

lox, smoked salmon • **locks**, fastenings

lumbar, part of body • **lumber**, wood

luxuriance, state of being luxurious • **luxuriant**, exceedingly fertile • **luxurious**, sumptuous

lye, chemical • **lie**, falsehood

Lyme, disease • **limb**, leg or arm • **lime**, chemical; fruit • **limn**, draw or outline

lynx, animal • **links**, joins
lyre, musical instrument • **liar**, tells lies

M

made, did make • **maid**, servant

magma, rock • **magna**, great

magnate, prominent person • **magnet**, attracts iron

mail, letters • **male**, man

main, principal • **mane**, hair of animal

maize, corn • **maze**, confusing paths

Malay, the people • **melée**, confused struggle

malt, used in brewing • **molt**, to shed

manner, method • **manor**, estate

mantel, shelf at fireplace • **mantle**, cloak

marc, refuse remaining after pressing seeds, fruits • **mark**, sign

marital, in marriage • **marshal**, official • **martial**, warlike

marriage, wedding • **mirage**, illusion

marry, wed • **merry**, gay

marshal, official • **marital**, in marriage • **martial**, warlike

mascle, a steel plate • **muscle**, body tissue • **mussel**, shellfish

mason, bricklayer • **meson**, a particle

massed, assembled • **mast**, on boat

massif, mountain • **massive**, large

mastication, chewing • **masturbation**, sexual self-stimulation

maybe, perhaps • **may be**, may happen

maze, confusing paths • **maize**, corn

mean, nasty • **mien**, bearing

meat, food • **meet**, encounter

medal, award • **meddle**, interfere • **metal**, material • **mettle**, spirit

meddler, one who interferes • **medlar**, tree

melée, confused struggle • **Malay**, the people

Mensa, genius's organization • **menses**, menstrual blood

merry, gay • **marry**, wed

meson, in physics, a particle • **mason**, bricklayer

meteor, solar particles • **métier**, one's calling

meteorology, study of atmosphere • **metrology**, system of weights and measures

mews, cat's sound; row of stables • **muse**, think

mien, bearing • **mean**, nasty

might, strength; may • **mite**, small insect; small child

mil, unit of measure • **mill**, grinding machine; factory

militate, have an effect • **mitigate**, make less severe

millenary, a thousand • **millinery,** hats

milligram, 1/1,000 of a gram • **myelogram,** spinal x-ray

mime, silent comic • **mine,** belongs to me

mince, to cut into small pieces • **mints,** places where money is made; candies

mind, brain • **mined,** dug

miner, one who mines • **minor,** below legal age; unimportant

minion, subordinate official • **minyan,** quorum

minks, animals • **minx,** pert girl

mirage, illusion • **marriage,** wedding

Miss, single woman • **Mrs.,** married woman • **Ms.,** single or married woman • **mss.,** manuscripts

missal, book for Mass • **missile,** weapon

missed, failed • **mist,** haze

misses, fails to hit • **missus,** wife

mite, small insect or child • **might,** strength; may

mitigate, make less severe • **militate,** have an effect

mnemonic, of memory • **pneumonic,** of the lungs

moat, ditch • **mote,** speck

modal, relating to mode • **model,** example

mode, manner • **mowed,** cut down

molt, to shed • **malt,** used in brewing

moor, tie up • **Moor,** the people • **more,** additional

moose, deer-like animal • **mouse,** rodent • **mousse,** pudding

moot, debatable • **mute,** silent

moral, ethical • **morale,** spirit

morays, eels • **mores,** customs

more, additional • **moor,** tie up • **Moor,** the people

morn, morning • **mourn,** grieve

morning, A.M. • **mourning,** grieving

mother, a female parent • **mudder,** a horse

motif, theme • **motive,** reason

mouse, rodent • **moose,** deer-like animal • **mousse,** pudding

mouton, sheepskin • **mutton,** meat of sheep

mowed, cut down • **mode,** manner

Mrs., married woman • **Miss,** single woman • **Ms.,** any woman • **mss.,** manuscripts

muscle, body tissue • **mascle,** a steel plate • **mussel,** shellfish

muse, think • **mews,** cat's sound; row of stables

musical, of music • **musicale,** gathering

Muslim, religion • **muslin,** cloth

mustard, spice • **mustered,** summoned

mute, silent • **moot,** debatable

myelogram, spinal x-ray • **milligram,** 1/1000 of a gram

N

NAFTA, trade agreement • **naphtha**, chemical

naught, nothing • **naughty**, mischievous

naval, navy • **navel**, body part

nave, part of church • **knave**, rogue

nay, no • **né**, original name • **née**, maiden name • **neigh**, cry of horse

need, lack • **knead**, to press

neither, nor • **nether**, below

new, not old • **gnu**, animal • **knew**, did know

news, information • **noose**, rope for hanging

nibble, bite gently • **nybble**, half a byte

niche, suitable role or position • **nick**, cut lightly

night, opposite of day • **knight**, feudal rank

nimbly, quickly • **NIMBY**, not in my backyard

nit, insect • **knit**, stitch

no, opposite of yes • **know**, to understand

nob, head • **knob**, protuberance

noble, lordly; fine character • **knowable**, can be known • **Nobel**, the prize

nock, arrow notch • **knock**, strike

nocturn, a midnight prayer • **nocturne**, musical composition

nod, head movement • **node**, small swelling • **note**, short written piece

nodule, small lump • **noodle**, pasta

noes, negatives • **knows**, understands • **nose**, on face

none, not one • **nun**, religious order

nook, secluded corner • **nuke**, to bomb

not, no • **knot**, what you tie

nougat, candy • **nugget**, lump

nozzle, spout • **nuzzle**, to snuggle

nybble, half a byte • **nibble**, bite gently

O

oar, boat • **awe**, fear • **o'er**, over • **or**, alternative • **ore**, mineral

oat, cereal • **oath**, legal pledge

obit, obituary • **orbit**, movement around a body

object, a material thing; to oppose • **abject**, spiritless

oblique, slanting; indirect • **obloquy**, shame; censure

oblivious, unaware • **obvious**, evident

obsess, to preoccupy • **abscess**, sore • **abscise**, to cut • **abscissa**, math coordinate

obstruct, block • **abstract**, select, excerpt

Occident, the Far East • **accident**, unfortunate event

ocher, pale yellow • **occur**, to happen • **okra**, vegetable

ode, poem • **owed**, did owe

of, belonging to • **off**, away from

offal, garbage • **awful**, terrible

office, work location • **orifice**, opening

oh, surprise • **ow**, cry of pain • **owe**, debt

older, refers to age only • **elder**, refers to age and wisdom gained

once, one time • **ounce**, 1/16th of a pound

one, single • **wan**, pale • **won**, did win

onion, vegetable • **union**, workers' group

op. cit., in work previously quoted • **opposite**, facing

opera, musical drama • **opry**, short for Grand Old Opry

opposite, other side • **apposite**, suitable

opposition, those opposing • **apposition**, grammatical construction

opt, choose • **upped**, increased

or, alternative • **awe**, fear • **oar**, boat • **o'er**, over • **ore**, mineral

oracle, person of great wisdom • **auricle**, ear

oral, verbal • **aural**, hearing

ordinance, law • **ordnance**, military supply

organ, part of body; musical instrument • **origin**, source

organism, living being • **orgasm**, sexual climax

oscillate, vibrate • **osculate**, kiss

ought, should • **aught**, zero • **out**, away; unfashionable

our, belongs to us • **hour**, time

overdo, overindulge • **overdue**, late

overlie, lie over • **overly**, excessively

overt, obvious • **advert**, pay attention • **avert**, avoid

ovoid, egg-shaped • **avoid**, evade

owed, did owe • **ode**, poem

P

packed, bundled • **pact**, agreement

pad, cushion; slang: to overcharge • **paid**, did pay

paddy, rice field • **pâté**, paste • **patty**, small pie

paean, hymn of joy • **peon**, peasant

pail, bucket • **pale**, enclosure; lacking color

pain, ache • **pane**, window

pair, two • **pare**, shave • **pear**, fruit

palate, taste • **palette**, artist's board • **pallet**, bed

pall, covering; gloomy effect • **Paul**, name

pall-mall, game • **pell-mell**, haste

paltry, few • **poultry**, fowl

panda, animal • **pander**, pimp

parish, diocese • **perish**, die

parity, equality • **parody**, witty imitation

parlay, bet • **parley**, talk

parole, prison • **payroll**, pay

partition, divider • **petition**, plea

passable, capable of being passed • **passible**, capable of feeling

passed, did pass • **past**, former time

pastor, clergyman • **pasture**, land for grazing

pastoral, rural • **pastorale**, music

pathos, tender • **bathos**, anti-climax

patience, forebearance • **patients**, under doctor's care

patty, small pie • **paddy**, rice field • **pâté**, paste

Paul, saint • **pall**, covering; gloomy effect

pause, delay • **paws**, touch clumsily; feet • **pores**, openings

paw, foot • **pore**, opening • **pour**, make flow

peace, no war • **piece**, portion

peak, top • **peek**, look • **pique**, anger

peaked, thin • **peeked**, looked • **piqued**, aroused

peal, bell • **peel**, strip

pear, fruit • **pair**, two • **pare**, shave

pearl, gem • **purl**, knitting

pecks, strikes; kisses • **pecs**, slang for pectoral muscles • **picks**, chooses

pedal, foot lever • **peddle**, sell

peer, look; equal • **pier**, dock

pellet, ball • **palette**, artist's board • **pallet**, bed

pell-mell, haste • **pall-mall**, game

pen, writing instrument • **pin**, thin metal piece

penal, prison • **penile**, relating to the penis

penance, religious • **pennants**, sports

pendant, ornament • **pendent**, suspended

penne, pasta • **penny**, cent

penned, written • **pent**, shut in

peon, peasant • **paean**, hymn of joy

per, for each • **purr**, cat's sound

perfect, exact • **prefect**, high official

perish, die • **parish**, diocese

persecute, to hound • **prosecute**, enforce law

personal, private • **personnel**, employees

perspective, vision • **prospective**, future

perverse, contrary • **preserve**, save

petition, plea • **partition**, divider

phantasm, ghost; illusion • **fantasy**, a far-fetched imaginary idea

phase, stage • **fays**, fairies • **faze**, worry

phial, tube • **file**, holder

philter, love potion • **filter**, purifier

phrase, words • **frays**, battles

phreak, illegal phone user • **freak**, abnormal being

physic, a remedy • **physique**, body

physical, body • **fiscal**, money

pi, Greek letter • **pie**, food

pica, printing measure • **piker**, cheapskate

picaresque, rascal • **picturesque**, colorful

picture, image • **pitcher**, vessel; baseball

pidgin, the jargon used as a language between foreigners and the Chinese • **pigeon**, a bird • **piggin**, wooden pail

piece, portion • **peace**, no war

pier, dock • **peer**, look; equal

piker, cheapskate • **pica**, printing measure

pillar, column • **pillow**, head cushion

pinnacle, peak • **pinochle**, game of cards

pious, religious • **Pius**, name of a Pope

pique, anger • **peak**, top • **peek**, look

pistil, flower • **pistol**, gun

pitcher, vessel; baseball player • **picture**, image

plague, deadly disease • **plaque**, award; tooth film

plain, simple • **plane**, smooth; airplane

plaintiff, one who sues • **plaintive**, sad

plait, braid • **plate**, dish

planed, smoothed • **planet**, heavenly body • **planned**, organized • **plant**, to put into soil

playa, desert basin • **player**, one who plays

pleas, requests • **please**, to satisfy

plod, trudge • **plot**, scheme; burial place

plum, fruit • **plumb**, line

pneumonic, of the lungs • **mnemonic**, of memory

pogrom, violent attack on Jews • **program**, plan; performance

poker, cards • **polka**, dance

pole, stick • **poll**, vote

polygamy, more than one mate at one time • **polygyny**, more than one female mate at one time

pool, swimming area; combination • **pull**, draw towards one

poplar, tree • **popular**, well-known

populace, the masses • **populous**, thickly inhabited

pore, opening • **paw**, foot • **pour**, cause to flow

pores, openings • **pause**, hesitate • **paws**, feet

porpoise, mammal • **purpose**, aim

portable, can be carried • **potable**, can be drunk

portend, foretell • **pretend**, make believe

portion, share • **potion**, dose

poultry, fowl • **paltry**, few

practice, the business of a doctor • **practise**, to repeat a performance

pray, say prayers • **prey**, victim; hunt

precede, go before • **proceed**, advance

precedence, priority of rank • **precedents**, previous decisions • **presidents**, chief officials

precedent, going before • **president**, chief official

précis, resume • **precise**, accurate

precisian, a precise person • **precision**, accuracy

prefect, high official • **perfect**, exact

prefer, choose • **proffer**, offer

premier, best; high official • **premiere**, cultural opening • **primer**, basic text

preposition, grammar • **proposition**, offer

prescribe, give directions • **proscribe**, to outlaw

prescription, something ordered • **proscription**, an imposed restriction

presence, being present • **presents**, gives; gifts

presentiment, premonition • **presentment**, presentation

preserve, save • **perverse**, contrary

president, chief official • **precedent**, going before

presidents, chief officials • **precedence**, priority of rank • **precedents**, previous decisions

pretend, make-believe • **portend**, foretell

prey, victim • **pray**, to entreat

pries, opens • **prize**, award

prince, a title of nobility • **prints**, marks made by pressure

principal, main; head • **principle**, strong belief

proceed, advance • **precede**, go before

prod, stimulate • **proud**, self-respect • **prude**, excessive propriety

prodigy, young genius • **protégé**, under care

proffer, offer • **prefer**, choose

profit, gain • **prophet**, seer

program, plan; performance • **pogrom**, violent attack on Jews

pronounce, speak, enunciate • **pronouns**, substitutes for nouns

property, possessions • **proprietary**, by one firm • **propriety**, correctness

prophecy, prediction • **prophesy**, to predict

prophylactic, disease preventive object • **prophylaxis**, preventive measures against disease, dangers

proposition, offer • **preposition**, grammar: to, of, by, etc.

proscribe, outlaw • **prescribe**, give directions

proscription, an imposed restriction • **prescription**, something ordered

prosecute, enforce law • **persecute**, to harass

prospective, future • **perspective**, vision

prostate, gland • **prostrate**, horizontal; overcome

protégé, one helped by senior • **prodigy**, young genius

pubic, region of body • **public**, people

puisne, a junior • **puny**, slight

punned, told a joke based on words • **punt**, kick; boat

pupal, development stage of larva • **pupil**, student

pure, unmixed • **purée**, food

purl, knitting • **pearl**, gem

purpose, aim • **porpoise**, mammal

pus, body fluid • **puss**, cat

put, place • **putt**, golf

Q

quack, incompetent doctor • **quark**, physical particle • **quirk**, odd behavior

quadrille, square dance • **quadrillion**, a million billions

quadruped, four-footed animal • **quadruple**, times four • **quadruplet**, one of four children born together

quality, excellence • **quantity**, amount

quarry, prey; excavation • **query**, question

quarts, 32 ounces • **quartz**, a mineral

quasi, seeming • **queasy**, ill

quaver, tremble • **quiver**, shake; arrow holder

quay, wharf • **cay**, island • **key**, lock opener

quean, female cat; an immoral person • **queen**, female sovereign

queerest, strangest • **querist**, questioner

queue, line • **cue**, hint; billiards

quiet, still • **quite**, completely; very

quietude, peace; quiet • **quietus**, death

quince, fruit • **quinsy**, throat infection • **quints**, quintuplets

quire, 24 sheets of paper • **choir**, singers

quota, number • **quote**, saying

R

rabbis, Jewish religious leaders • **rabies**, viral disease

rabbit, animal • **rabid**, intense • **rarebit**, food

raga, Indian music • **ragout**, stew • **reggae**, Caribbean music

rain, water • **reign**, rule • **rein**, guides horse

raise, lift • **rays**, light beams • **raze**, demolish

RAM, random access memory • **ROM**, read only memory

rap, knock • **wrap**, fold

rapped, knocked • **rapt**, absorbed • **wrapped**, packed

rational, having reason • **rationale**, explanation

raw, uncooked • **roar**, noise

read, book • **red**, color • **reed**, grass

real, actual • **reel**, wind in; stagger

realize, understand • **relies**, counts on

rebait, rehook • **rebate**, deduction

rebound, to spring back • **redound**, to accrue

recede, move back • **reseed**, seed again

recent, not long past • **rescind**, take back • **resend**, send again • **resent**, feel annoyance

recluse, loner • **recuse**, challenge to judge or juror

reek, smell • **wreak**, inflict • **wreck**, destroy

referee, arbitrator • **reverie**, dream

regal, royal • **regale**, feast

reign, rule • **rain**, water • **rein**, on horse

relic, souvenir of the past • **relict**, a widow

relies, counts on • **realize**, understand

replay, to play again; to view again • **reply**, respond

respectfully, with esteem • **respectively**, in the order given

rest, repose • **wrest**, pull away

retch, to vomit • **wretch**, unfortunate person

reveille, signal to awake • **revelry**, gaiety

reverend, minister • **reverent**, respectful

review, survey • **revue**, theater

rheum, watery discharge • **room**, space

rhyme, poetry • **rhythm**, meter, beat • **rime**, frost

riffle, to thumb through • **rifle**, gun

right, correct • **rite**, ceremony • **wright**, workman • **write**, put words on paper

ring, circle; bell • **wring**, squeeze

road, path • **rode**, did ride • **rowed**, pulled boat

roam, wander • **Rome**, city

roar, noise • **raw**, uncooked

robber, crook • **rubber**, elastic

roc, fabled bird • **rock**, stone; sway

roe, fish eggs • **row**, to oar

roil, to stir up • **royal**, crown

role, part • **roll**, turn around; bread

rollout, football play • **roll out**, to get out of bed

rollover, act of deferring payment • **roll over**, to defer payment

ROM, read only memory • **RAM**, random access memory

room, space • **rheum**, watery discharge

roomer, one who rooms • **rumor**, gossip

root, plant • **route**, way

rose, flower • **rosé**, wine • **rows**, lines

rote, mechanical repetition • **wrote**, did write

rough, coarse • **ruff**, collar; fish; bluster

rouse, awaken • **rows**, quarrels

row, to pull boat with oars • **roe**, fish eggs

rowed, pulled boat • **road**, path • **rode**, did ride

rude, lacking refinement • **rued**, regretted

ruin, destroy • **rune**, letter

rumor, gossip • **roomer**, one who rooms

rundown, summary • **run down**, to chase; to decline

rung, step; did ring • **wrung**, squeezed

rye, grain; alcohol • **wry**, distorted

S

Sabbat, witch's assembly • **Sabbath,** day of rest

sac, animal or plant pouch • **sack,** bag

sachet, bag • **sashay,** trip

sail, on boat • **sale,** sell at low price

sake, end; purpose • **saki,** liquor

salary, wage • **celery,** vegetable

salon, room • **saloon,** barroom

salud, Sp. for to your health • **salute,** greeting

salvage, to save from wreckage • **selvage,** the edge of woven fabric

sane, not mad • **seine,** fishing net

sanitary, hygienic • **sanitory,** conducive to health

Satan, devil • **sateen,** cotton fabric resembling satin • **satin,** fabric

satire, irony • **satyr,** a sylvan deity

sauce, liquid • **source,** origin

saver, one who saves • **savor,** taste

savior, one who saves • **Saviour,** Christ

saw, cut • **soar,** rise • **sore,** hurt

scam, crooked trick • **scan,** look over

scene, place • **seen,** viewed

scents, smells • **cents,** money • **sense,** brains

scrip, money • **script,** story

sculptor, one who carves • **sculpture,** work of sculptor

sea, water • **see,** look

sealing, closing • **ceiling,** top of room

seam, join • **seem,** appear

seamen, sailors • **semen,** male fluid

sear, burn • **seer,** prophet

seas, bodies of water • **sees,** observes • **seize,** grab

sects, people with unique views • **sex,** intimacy

seed, flower • **cede,** give up

seen, did see • **scene,** place

seine, fishing net • **sane,** not mad

sell, opposite of buy • **cell,** prison; in biology

seller, one who sells • **cellar,** basement

selvage, the edge of woven fabric • **salvage,** to save from wreckage

senior, older • **señor,** mister

sense, brains • **cents,** money • **scents,** smells

senses, sight, touch • **census,** population count

serf, slave • **surf,** sea

serge, fabric • **surge,** sudden increase

serial, in a row • **cereal,** food

session, meeting • **cession,** yielding

settler, colonist • **settlor,** one who makes a legal settlement

sew, stitch • **so,** like this • **sow,** plant

shanty, hut • **chantey,** song

sharif, Arab prince • **sheriff,** county officer

shear, clip • **sheer,** transparent

shed, hut • **she'd**, she would

sheik, Arab chief • **chic**, stylish

shirt, garment • **chert**, a rock

shoe, foot • **shoo**, send away

shofar, ram's horn • **chauffeur**, driver

shone, did shine • **shown**, did show

shoot, fire a gun • **chute**, drop

shriek, cry out • **shrike**, bird

shtick, comedy routine • **stick**, rod

sic, thus • **sick**, ill

side, next to • **sighed**, did sigh

sighs, sound • **size**, bigness

sight, see • **cite**, point out • **site**, place

sign, symbol; put name on • **sine**, mathematics

signet, a seal • **cygnet**, a young swan

singeing, burning • **singing**, song

size, bigness • **sighs**, sounds

skull, head • **scull**, boat

Slav, Eastern European • **slave**, one who has lost his freedom

slay, kill • **sleigh**, sled

sleight, trick • **slight**, small; snub

sloe, plum • **slow**, not fast

so, like this • **sew**, stitch • **sow**, plant

soar, rise • **saw**, cut • **sore**, hurt

sodality, a fellowship • **solidarity**, union

sold, did sell • **soled**, put on a sole

solder, to fuse • **soldier**, military

sole, shoe • **soul**, spirit

some, a few • **sum**, total

someone, some person • **some one**, one of several

son, child • **sun**, sky

source, origin • **sauce**, liquid

spear, weapon • **sphere**, round

special, particular, specific • **especial**, exceptional, pre-eminent

speciality, quality of being special • **specialty**, an employment limited to one kind of work

specie, coin • **species**, class

staff, employees • **staph**, bacterium

staid, sober • **stayed**, remained

stair, to climb • **stare**, look steadily

stake, post or gamble • **steak**, food

stalk, stem of plant; walk stealthily • **stork**, bird

stationary, fixed • **stationery**, paper supplies

statue, likeness • **stature**, height • **statute**, law

stayed, remained • **staid**, sober

steal, rob • **steel**, metal

step, pace • **steppe**, plain

stile, step • **style**, fashion

stodgy, uninteresting • **stogie**, cigar • **stooge**, comedian's aide

straight, direct • **strait**, body of water

stricture, binding • **structure**, form

subtile, fine • **subtitle**, movie translation • **subtle**, hard to sense

suburb, near city • **superb**, very good

succor, help • **sucker**, fool

sued, did bring legal action • **suede**, fabric • **swayed**, influenced

suit, clothes • **suite**, rooms • **sweet**, sugary

sulfa, drug • **sulphur**, mineral

sum, total • **some**, a few

summary, wrap-up • **summery**, fit for summer

sun, sky • **son**, child

sundae, ice-cream • **Sunday**, Sabbath

surf, sea • **serf**, slave

surge, sudden increase • **serge**, fabric

surplice, vestment • **surplus**, excess

symbol, sign • **cymbal**, music

symmetry, even; pleasing proportion • **cemetery**, graveyard

---

T

tableau, picture • **tabloid**, newspaper

tacked, fastened • **tact**, consideration

tacks, fasteners • **tax**, money paid government

tail, end • **tale**, story

taint, bad element • **taunt**, make fun of • **tint**, shade

talc, powder • **talk**, speak

tape, recording or measuring device • **taupe**, gray-brown

taper, candle; narrow • **tapir**, animal

tarantella, dance • **tarantula**, spider

tare, weight • **tear**, rip

taro, food • **tarot**, cards

tartar, on teeth; chemical • **Tartar**, a people • **tartare**, sauce • **Tatar**, a people

taught, did teach • **taut**, tense

tea, beverage • **tee**, golf peg

team, group • **teem**, swarm

tear, (pron. like 'ear') crying • **tier**, layer

tear, (pron. like 'air') rip • **tare**, weight

teas, drinks • **tease**, annoy

technics, technical rules • **techniques**, manners of performance

teeth, plural of tooth • **teethe**, to grow teeth

temp, temporary worker • **tempt**, induce wrongdoing

tempera, art technique • **tempura**, Japanese food

tenant, renter • **tenet**, belief

tenor, singer • **tenure**, duration

tern, bird • **turn**, rotate

terra, earth • **terror**, great fear

than, comparative: as in "greater than" • **then**, at that time

their, belongs to them • **there**, that place • **they're**, they are

therefor, for that, for it, for them, etc. • **therefore**, for this reason

thong, strap • **tong**, implement • **Tong**, Chinese gang • **tongue**, mouth

thrash, to swing or strike • **thresh**, to beat out grain

threw, tossed • **through**, penetrated; finished

throe, pang • **throw**, hurl

throne, king • **thrown**, tossed

thyme, herb • **time**, duration • **tine**, fork prong

tic, twitching • **tick**, pillow; clock

tide, ocean • **tied**, connected

tier, layer • **tear**, (pron. like 'ear') crying

timber, wood • **timbre**, tone

tinny, like tin • **tiny**, small

to, toward • **too**, also • **two**, number

tocsin, alarm • **toxin**, poison

toe, foot • **tow**, pull

toil, labor • **toile**, fabric

toiled, worked • **told**, said

toilet, bathroom • **toilette**, grooming, attire

tole, metalware • **toll**, fee; to sound

tomb, grave • **tome**, book

tong, implement • **Tong**, Chinese gang • **tongue**, mouth • **thong**, strap

topee, sun-helmet • **toupee**, hairpiece for men

topical, timely • **tropical**, hot climate

topography, maps, charts • **typography**, printing

tortious, legal term referring to tort • **tortuous**, twisting • **torturous**, painful

tot, child • **tote**, carrying bag

tour, trip • **tower**, building

toxin, poison • **tocsin**, alarm

track, path • **tract**, region

trail, path • **trial**, court

travail, toil • **travel**, journey

tray, food carrier • **trey**, three in cards or dice

treaties, agreements • **treatise**, account

troop, company of soldiers • **troupe**, company of actors

trustee, administrator • **trusty**, reliable convict

tuba, musical instrument • **tuber**, root of plant

turban, hat • **turbine**, power

turn, rotate • **tern**, bird

two, number • **to**, toward • **too**, also

typography, printing • **topography**, maps, charts

U

udder, milk gland • **utter**, speak

ultimate, final • **ultimatum**, final demand

umbel, flower cluster • **humble**, modest

umpire, referee • **empire**, dominion

unable, not able • **enable**, to make able

unaware, not aware • **unawares**, unexpectedly

underlay, a support • **underlie**, be the basis • **underline**, draw a line under

undo, reverse • **undue**, excessive

unequal, not the same • **unequaled**, unparalleled; exceptional

unexceptionable, unimpeachable • **unexceptional**, ordinary

unfold, to lay open • **enfold**, to wrap

ungird, unbind • **ungirt**, slack

unintelligent, not smart • **unintelligible**, can't be read

union, workers' organization • **onion**, vegetable

unique, sole • **eunuch**, sexless

unisex, sex not evident • **unsex**, take away sexual power

unitary, whole; relates to a unit • **Unitarian**, religious faith

universal, covering all • **universe**, cosmos; everything

Unix, computer operating system • **eunuchs**, emasculated men

unlike, not like • **unlikely**, improbable

unread, not read • **unready**, not ready

unreal, imaginary • **unreel**, unwind from a reel

unroll, to display • **enroll**, join

untidy, sloppy • **untied**, unbound

untitled, lacking a title • **entitled**, deserving

unwanted, not wanted • **unwonted**, rare

unwrap, uncover • **enwrap**, wrap around

upped, increased • **opt**, choose

urban, of a city • **urbane**, polished

urn, vase • **earn**, gain; to receive a salary

usurious, lending at exorbitant rates • **uxorious**, submits to wife

utter, speak • **udder**, milk gland

V

vacation, rest • **vocation**, job

vague, imprecise • **vogue**, fashionable

vain, proud • **vane**, weather • **vein**, blood vessel

valance, drapery • **valence**, in chemistry, degree of combining power

vale, valley • **veil**, face covering

valet, personal aide • **valley**, low area

valor, bravery • **velour**, fabric

valuable, of much worth • **voluble**, talkative

vantage, higher position • **vintage**, old

variance, conflicting • **variants**, slight differences

vary, to alter • **very**, extremely

vassal, serf • **vessel**, container; ship

vector, directed quantity; line • **victor**, winner

venal, mercenary • **venial**, pardonable

venerable, respected • **venereal**, disease

veracious, truthful • **voracious**, greedy

veracity, truth • **voracity**, hunger

verify, confirm • **versify**, write poetry

verity, truth • **vérité**, cinéma vérité: realism

verses, poetry • **versus**, against

vertebra, bone in backbone • **vertebrate**, animal with backbone

vial, glass • **vile**, loathsome • **viol**, music

vibrant, energetic • **vibrate**, move rapidly

vibrato, vibrating musical tone • **vibrator**, exerciser

vice, depravity • **vise**, clamp

victor, winner • **vector**, directed quantity; line

vigilant, alert • **vigilante**, self-appointed crimebusters

villa, estate • **viola**, string instrument • **voilà**, behold

vindicate, absolve • **vindictive**, revengeful

violate, disregard; break • **violent**, injurious; furious • **violet**, color

violation, transgression • **volition**, choice

viral, of a virus • **virile**, manly

virtual, acting in effect • **virtue**, goodness

virtuoso, exceptional performer • **virtuous**, moral

visa, travel permit • **viz.**, for example; namely

visor, sunshade • **vizier**, Muslim official

vocable, word form • **vocal**, expressive

vocation, job • **vacation**, rest

voilà, behold • **villa**, estate • **viola**, string instrument

Volga, Russian river • **vulgar**, crude, impolite

volition, choice • **violation**, transgression

voracious, greedy • **veracious**, truthful

voracity, hunger • **veracity**, truth

voyager, traveler • **voyageur**, expert guide

W

wade, walk through water • **weighed**, did weigh

wail, cry • **whale**, mammal

waist, body • **waste**, to squander

wait, stay for • **weight**, heaviness

waive, give up • **wave**, water; gesture

waiver, surrender claim • **waver**, falter

wan, pale • **one**, single • **won**, did win

wander, roam • **wonder**, speculate

wanton, sensual • **wonton**, dumpling

war, combat • **wore**, past tense of wear

ward, division • **warred**, fought

ware, goods • **wear**, clothes • **where**, which place?

wary, cautious • **weary**, tired

waste, to squander • **waist**, body

WATS, telephone • **watts**, units of electrical power • **what's**, what is

wax, sticky substance • **whacks**, hits

way, direction • **weigh**, to measure heaviness; to consider • **whey**, milk

we, us • **wee**, tiny

weak, feeble • **week**, 7 days

weal, state • **we'll**, we will • **wheel**, round body

weather, atmosphere • **whether**, if

wed, marry • **we'd**, we would • **weed**, unwanted plant

weighed, did weigh • **wade**, walk through water

weight, heaviness • **wait**, stay for

welch, cheat • **Welsh**, from Wales

wen, cyst • **when**, what time

were, past of to be • **we're**, we are • **whir**, buzzing sound • **whirl**, spin

wet, water • **whet**, appetite

whale, mammal • **wail**, cry

what's, what is • **WATS**, telephone • **watts**, units of electrical power

whence, from which place • **hence**, from this time or place • **wince**, to flinch

where, which place? • **ware**, goods • **wear**, clothes

which, what one? • **witch**, hag

Whig, political party • **wig**, hair cover

while, during • **wile**, trick

whiled, passed time away • **wield**, to hold • **wild**, uncontrolled

whine, complain • **wine**, drink

whit, smallest bit • **wit**, cleverness

whither, where • **wither**, decay

whole, complete • **hole**, opening

wholly, fully • **holey**, having holes • **holy**, religious

whoop, holler • **hoop**, circle

whore, prostitute • **who're**, who are

whorey, wanton • **hoary**, old

who's, who is • **whose**, to whom

wile, trick • **while**, during

wince, to flinch • **hence**, from this time or place • **whence**, from where

wine, drink • **whine**, complain

wit, cleverness • **whit**, smallest bit

won, did win • **wan**, pale • **one**, single

wonder, speculate • **wander**, roam

wont, habit • **won't**, will not

wonton, dumpling • **wanton**, sensual

wood, lumber • **would**, might

wore, did wear • **war**, combat

worst, least good • **wurst**, sausage

wrap, fold • **rap**, knock

wrapped, packed • **rapped**, knocked • **rapt**, absorbed

wreak, inflict • **wreck**, destroy • **reek**, smell

wrest, pull away • **rest**, repose

wretch, unfortunate person • **retch**, to vomit

wright, workman • **right**, correct • **rite**, ceremony • **write**, put words on paper

wring, squeeze • **ring**, circle; bell

wrote, did write • **rote**, mechanical repetition

wrung, squeezed • **rung,** step; did ring

wry, distorted • **rye,** grain; alcohol

Y, Z

y'all, you all • **yawl,** sailboat • **yowl,** loud cry

yang, masculine principle • **yank,** pull

Yankee, New Englander; northerner • **Yanqui,** Spanish for U.S. citizen

yawl, sailboat • **y'all,** you all • **yowl,** loud cry

yaws, tropical disease • **yours,** belonging to you

ye, religious: you • **yea,** yes

yen, desire; Japanese money • **yin,** feminine principle

yew, tree • **ewe,** sheep • **you,** person

yoga, Hindu philosophy • **yogi,** yoga practitioner

yoke, frame for animals • **yolk,** egg

yore, olden times • **your,** belongs to you • **you're,** you are

you'll, you will • **Yule,** Christmas

yours, belonging to you • **yaws,** tropical disease

yowl, loud cry • **y'all,** you all • **yawl,** sailboat

zealous, enthusiastic • **jealous,** envious

zinc, metal • **zing,** vigor

Quick List of Correct Spellings

abandon
abate
abatement
abbey
abbot
abbreviate
abdomen
abduct
aberrant**
aberration**
abet
abhor
abhorrent**
ability
abject**
abjure**
ablation**
ablaze
able
abled
ableism
ablution**
ably
aboard**
abode
abolition
aborigine
abort**
abortion
about
abrade
abrasion**
abrasive
abroad**
abrogate**
abrupt
abscess**
abscise**
abscissa**
absence
absent
absolutely
absorb
absorption

abstinence
abstract**
absurd
abuse
abyss
academic
academy
accede**
accelerate
accent**
accept**
access**
accessory
accidence**
accident**
accidentally
accidents**
acclaim
acclimate
accommo-
date
accompani-
ment
accompany
accom-
plice**
accom-
plish**
accord
according
accordion
accost
account
accountant
accredit
accredita-
tion
accrue
accumulate
accuracy
accurate
accuse
accustom
acentric**

acerb
acetic**
acetone
ache
achieve
Achilles heel
acid
acidosis
acknowledge
acknowledg-
ment
acme**
acne**
acolyte
acoustics
acquaint-
ance
acquire
acquisition
acquit
acquittal
acquitted
acre
acreage
acrobat
across
acrostic
activate**
active
activist
actor
acts**
actual
actually**
actuary**
actuate**
acumen
acupuncture
acute
ad**
adage
adamant
Adam's
apple

adapt**
add**
addable**
addenda
addict
addiction
addition**
address
adds**
adduce**
adenoma
adept**
adequate
adequately
adhere
adhesion
adieu**
adjacent
adjoin**
adjourn**
adjudication
adjure**
adjustable
adjutant
administra-
tion
administra-
tor
admirable
admiral
admissible
admission
admit
admittance
admonish
admonition
ado**
adobe
adolescence
adolescent
adopt**
adorable
adore
adrenal

155

ads**	afire	airplane	allure
adult	afraid	airwaves	allusion**
advance	Africa	aisle**	allusive**
advantage	Africans**	à la carte	all ways**
advanta-	Afrikaans**	Al-anon	ally**
geous	Afrikan-	albino	alma mater
adventitious	ers**	albumin	almanac
adverse**	Afrocentric	alchemy	almighty
advert**	aftercare	alcohol	almond
advertise	afternoon	alcoholic	almost
advertise-	afterwards	alcoholism	alms**
ment	against	al dente	aloe**
advice**	aged	ale**	alone
advisable	ageism	alert	aloof
advise**	agencies	algae	aloud**
adviser	agency	algorithm	alpha
advisory	agenda	alias	alphabet
advocate	aggrandize	alibi	alphanu-
adz**	aggravate	alien	meric
aegis	aggregate	alienation	already**
aerial	aggression**	align	also
aerie**	aggressive	aliment**	also ran
aerobic	aggrieved	alimen-	altar**
aerobics	aghast	tary**	alter**
aerodynam-	agile	alimony	alter ego
ics	agility	all**	alternate**
aeronautics	aging	allay**	alterna-
aerosol	ago	allege**	tive**
aesthetic**	agonize	allegiance	although
afar**	agony	allegro	altitude**
affable	agoraphobia	allergic	alto
affair**	agrarian	allergy**	altogether**
affaire**	agree	alleviate	altruism
affect**	agreeable	alley**	aluminum
affective**	agreed	alliance	always**
affidavit	agreeing	allocate	amalgam
affiliate	agriculture	allocation**	amal-
affinity	aground	allot	gamated
affirm	ague	allotment	amateur**
affirmative	aid**	allow**	ambassador
affix	aide**	allowance	ambiance
afflict	aides**	allowed**	ambidex-
affluence	AIDS**	alloy**	trous**
affluent**	aids**	all ready**	ambience
afford	ail**	all right	ambiguous
affront	ailment**	all to-	ambisex-
Afghan	air**	gether**	trous**
	airbag	allude**	ambition

ambulance	analogy	annuity	anywhere
ameliorate	analyses	annul**	aorta
amen	analysis	annulled	apartheid
amenable	analyst**	anoint	apartment
amend**	analytic	anomaly	apatite**
amendment	analyze**	anomie**	apex
amenorrhea	anatomy	anonymous	aphorism
American	ancestor	anorexia	aplomb
AMEX	ancestry	anorexia ner-	apnea
amiable**	anchor	vosa	apocryphal
amicable**	anchorman	another	apogee
amity**	anchovy	answer	apologia**
ammonia	ancient	ant**	apologies
ammunition	android	antacid	apologize
amnesia	anecdotal	antagonist	apology**
amniocente-	anecdote**	antarctic	apostil**
sis	anemic	Antarctica	apostle**
amoeba	anent	ante**	apostrophe
amok	anesthetic	antecede	apotheosis
among	aneurism	antecedent	appall
amoral**	aneurysm	antedate**	appalled
amorous	anew	antenna	apparatus
amount	angary	anterior**	apparel
amour**	angel**	anthrax	apparent
amp	anger	anti**	apparently
ampere	angina	anti-	appeal
ampheta-	angiocardio-	American	appear
mine	gram	antibiotic	appearance
amphithea-	angioma	antibody	appease
ter	angle**	antic**	appellate
ample**	angora	anticipate	append
amplifica-	angry	antidepres-	appendec-
tion	angst	sant	tomy
amplifier	anguish	antidote**	appendicitis
amplify	anima**	antihista-	appendix
ampule**	animal**	mine	appetite**
amputate	animus	antique**	applaud
amputation	ankh	antiseptic	apple
amputee	ankle	antitoxin	appliance
Amtrak	annex	anus**	applicant
amuse	annihilate	anxiety	application
amusement	anniversary	anxious	applicator
anabolic	annotate	any	applies
anal**	announce-	anyone**	apply
analgesic	ment	any one**	appoint
analog**	annoyance	any time	appointee
analogous	annual**	anyway**	appointment
analogue**	annually	any way**	apposite**

157

apposi- tion**	Arkansas	ascetic**	assure
appraisal	armature**	ASCII	asthma
appraise**	armful	ashamed	astigmatism
appreciable	armistice	ashen	astonish
appreciate	armoire**	ashore	astray**
apprehend	armor**	Asia	astringent
apprentice	arms**	Asian	astronaut
apprise**	arose**	asinine	astronomy
approach	around	askance	astute
appropriate	arouse**	asked	asylum
approve	arraign**	asparagus	atavism
approximate	arrange**	asphalt	ate**
apricot	arrangement	asphyxia	atheist
apron	array	aspirant**	athlete
apropos	arrears	aspirate**	athletic
apt	arrest	aspiration	atmosphere
aptitude	arrested	aspire	atom
aquarium**	arrhythmia	aspirin**	atone
Aquarius**	arrival	assail	atrium
arabesque	arrive	assailant	atrocity
arbitrary	arrogance	assassin	atrophy
arbitrate	arrogant	assassinate	attach**
arbitrator	arrogate**	assault	attaché**
arbor	arrow	assay**	attack**
arc**	arroz**	assemble	attacked
arch**	arsenic	assent**	attain
arcade	art	assert**	attempt
arch**	art deco	assertive	attend
archaic	arteriosclero- sis	assess	attend- ance**
archangel	artery	assessed	attendant
archeology	arthritis	asset	attendants**
archetype	article	assign	attention
architect	artifact	assigna- tion**	attenuate
archive	artificial	assign- ment**	attest
archives	artillery	assimilable	attic
arctic	artist**	assimilation- ist	attire
area**	artiste**	assist	attitude**
arena	artistic**	assistance**	attorney
areola	artistically	assistant	attract
argot	arts	assistants**	attribute
argue	artware	associate	attrition
argument	arty	association	auction
aria**	arugula	assort**	audacious
arise	asbestos	assume	audible
arising	ascend	assurance**	audience
aristocrat	ascent**		audio
arithmetic	ascertain		audiophile
ark**			

audit
auditorium
auger**
aught**
augur**
August
aunt**
aunty**
au pair
aura
aural**
au revoir
auricle**
austere
autarchy**
autarky**
auteur**
authentic
author
authority
authorize
autism
autistic**
autobiogra-
   phy
autofocus
autograft**
autograph**
autoim-
   munity
automatic
automati-
   cally
automa-
   tion**
automa-
   ton**
automobile
autopilot
autumn
auxiliary**
available
avalanche
avant-garde
avenue
average
averse**
aversion

avert**
aviary
aviator
avid
avocado
avoid**
avoidable
await
aware
awe**
awesome
awful**
awhile**
awkward
awl**
awry
axe**
axes**
axillary**
axis**
axle**
aye**

B
babble**
baby
babysit
bacchanal
bach**
bachelor
bacitracin
backbone
background
backlog
backstabber
backtrack
backward
bacon
bacteria
bad**
bade**
badge
bagel
baggage
bagged
bags
bail**

bailiwick
bailout
bait**
balance
balcony
bald**
bale**
balk
ball**
ballad**
balled**
ballerina
ballet**
ballistics
balloon
ballot**
ballpoint
balm**
balmy
baloney**
bamboo
banana
band**
bandage
bandana
bandit
bands**
bandwagon
banish
banister
banjos
bankrupt
bankruptcy
banned**
banner
banns**
banquet**
banquette**
bans**
banzai**
Baptist
baptize
barbarian
barbecue
barbiturate
bard**
bare**
barefaced

bargain
baring**
barley
Bar Mitzvah
barn
barometer
baron**
barracks
barracuda
barrage
barred**
barrel
barren**
barricade
barrier
barter**
basal
base**
baseball
basement
bases**
bash
basic
basically
basin
basis**
bask
basketball
Bas Mitzvah
Basque
bass**
bastard**
baste
basted**
batch**
bate**
bath**
bathe**
bathos**
baton
battalion
batten
batter**
battered
   baby
battered
   wife

159

battered	begin	beta	biography
women	beginner	betray	biology
battery	beginning	better**	bionics
bauble**	behalf	bettor**	biopsy
baud**	behavior	beverage	bipolar
baud rate	behemoth	beware	birch
bawd**	beige	bewilder	bird
bawl**	Beijing	bey	birdie
bawled**	belfry	beyond	birth**
bay	belie**	bialy	birthmark
bayou	belief	biannual**	birthmother
bazaar**	believe	bias	birthright
bazooka	belittle	bib**	birthstone
BBS	bell**	bibb**	biscuit
be**	belladonna	Bible	bisect
beach**	belle**	biceps	bisque
beacon	bellicose	bicultural	bissync
bean**	belligerent	bicuspid	bistro
beanball	bellow**	bicycle	bitch
bear**	bellwether	bid**	bite**
bearing**	belly**	bide**	bitten
bearish	below**	biennial**	bitter
beast	Beltway	bier**	bivouac
beat**	benchmark	bifocal	bivouacked
beatify**	bends	bigamy	biz
beau**	beneath	biggest	bizarre**
beautician	beneficial	bight**	blackboard
beautiful	beneficiary	bigot	blackguard
beautify**	benefit	big shot	blackhead
beauty	benefited	bigwig	blackmail
beaver	benevolent	bile	bladder
because	benign	bilingual	blameless
become	bent	bilious	blanch
becoming	benzocaine	billboard	blanket
bedbug	bequeath	billed**	blare
bedmate	berate	billet	blasé
bedspread	bereaved	billiard	blasphemy
bee**	bereft	billion	blast
beech**	beret	billionaire	blaster
been**	beriberi	bill of fare	blatant
beep	berry**	billow**	bleach
beer**	berserk	bimbo	bleak
beet**	berth**	bin**	bled
beetle	beseech**	binary	bleed
before	beside**	binoculars	bleep**
befriend	besides**	biocentrism	blessed
began	besiege**	biochemistry	blew**
beggar	bestial	biofeedback	blight

160

blind	bogosity	bossy	bravery
blintz	bogus	botch**	brawl
blip**	bogy**	bottle	brayed**
blister	boiler plate	bottleneck	brays**
blithe	boisterous	bottom	braze**
blitz	bold**	bottomless	brazen
blizzard	bolder**	botulism	breach**
bloat**	bole**	boudoir	breaches**
bloated	boll**	bough**	bread**
blob	bologna**	bought**	breadth**
bloc**	bolster	bouillon**	break**
block**	bomb**	boulder**	breakable
blockade	bombshell	boulevard	break-even
blond	BOMFOG	boundary	breakfast
blood	bone	bouquet	breakout
bloodbath	boned	bourbon	break-
blossom	bones	bourgeois	through
blot**	bonfire	bout**	breakup
blotch**	bonnet	boutique	breast
blotter	bonny**	bow**	breath**
blouse	bonsai**	bowel**	breathe**
bludgeon	bon soir	bowl**	bred**
blue**	bonus	bowled**	breech**
blue baby	bon vivant	boy**	breeches**
blueberry	bony**	boycott	breed
blueblood	boogie**	bozo	breeze
blueprint	book	bra	brethren
blues	bookkeeping	brace	brew
bluff	Boolean	bracelet	brewed**
blunder	boom**	braces	brews**
blunt	boombox	braes**	briar**
blur	boon**	braggart	bribe
blurb	boos	Brahman**	bridal**
B'nai B'rith	boot**	Brahmin**	bridegroom
B.O.	bootie**	braid**	bridge
boar**	booty**	Braille	bridle**
board**	booze	brain	brief
boarder**	border**	brainstorm	briefcase
boast	borderline	braise**	brier**
boats	bore**	brake**	brigadier
boatswain	bored**	brand-new	bright
bod	born**	brands**	brilliant
bodice-	borne**	brandy	bristle
ripper	borough**	brans**	Britain**
body**	borrow	brash**	Britannica
bodyguard	borscht	brass**	Briton**
bogey**	bosom	brassiere	brittle
bogon	bossa nova	bravado	bro'

161

broach*	bummer	by**	cam**
Broadway	bumper	bye**	camaraderie
broccoli	bundle	byline	camcorder
brochure	bungalow	bypass	camel
broke	bunion	byproduct	camellia
broken	buns	byte**	Camelot
brokerage	buoy**		cameo
bronchial	buoyant		camera
bronchitis	burden		camouflage
brooch**	bureau	**C**	campaign
brood**	burger	cabal**	camphor
brook	burglar	cabbage	campus
brothers	burglary	cabinet	Canada
brownstone	burial	cable**	canal
brows**	burlap	cacao**	canapé**
browse**	burlesque	cache**	canard
bruise**	burley**	cacophony	cancel
bruit**	burly**	cactus	cancer
brusque	burnout	caddie**	candidate
brute**	burnt	caddy**	candle
bubble**	burro**	cadenza	candor
bubo**	burrow**	cadet	canine
buck	bursa**	café	canister
bucket	bursar**	café au lait	canker
buckle	bursitis	cafeteria	cannabis
bucks	burst	caffeine	cannelloni
Buddha	bury**	cagey	cannery
buddy**	bus**	cahoots	cannibal
budge	busily	Cajan	cannon**
budget	business	Cajun	canoe
buffalo	buss**	calamity	canon**
buffer	bussed**	calcium	canopy**
buffet	bust**	calculate	cant**
buffoon	busted	calculus	can't**
bug	bustier	calendar**	cantaloupe
bugged	bustle	calender**	cantilever
bugle	busy	calf	canvas**
build**	busybody	caliber	canvass**
built	but**	calico	canyon
bulemia	butcher	California	cap
bulge	butt**	calisthenics	capable
bulldozer	button	call**	capacious
bullet	buxom	callous**	capacity
bulletin	buy**	callus**	capillary
bullion**	buy-in	calm**	capital**
bully	buy-out	calorie	capitation
bulwark	buzz	Calvary**	fee
bumblebee	buzzwords	calves	Capitol**
		calypso	

162

capitulate
capped
cappucino
caprice
capricious
capsule
captain
caption
captive
capture
carafe
caramel
carat**
caravan
carbohy-
drate
carbon
carbon diox-
ide
carbon
monoxide
carbuncle
carburetor
carcass
carcinogen
carcinoma
cardboard
cardiac
cardinal
career
careful
careworn
Caribbean
caricature
caries**
caring
carjack
carnage
carnal**
carnival
carotene
carotid
carousal**
carouse
carousel**

carpal
carriage
carried
carries**
carrot**
carrying
carte
    blanche
cartel
cartilage
carton
cartoon
cartridge
Casanova
cascade
casement
cash**
cashew
cashier
cashmere
casino
cask**
casket
casque**
casserole
cassette
cassock
cast**
castanet
caste**
caster**
castigate
castle
castor**
castrate
casual**
casualty
cataclasm**
cataclysm**
catacomb
catalog
catapult
cataract
catarrh
catastrophe
catatonic
catch
category

caterpillar
catfish
cathedral
catheter
Catholic
catlike
CAT scan
catty**
Caucasian
caucus
caught**
caul**
cauliflower
caulk
causal**
cause**
cause
célèbre
caustic
caution
cavalcade
cavalier
cavalry**
caveat
caveat emp-
tor
cavel
cavernous
cavity
caws**
cay**
CD-ROM
cease**
cedar
cede**
ceiling**
celebrate**
celebrity
celerity
celery**
celestial
celibacy
celibate**
cell**
cellar**
cello
cellophane
cellular

cellu...
celluloid
cellulose
Celtic
cement
cemetery**
censer**
censor**
censure**
census**
centennial
center
centigrade
centimeter
central
centrifugal
cents**
century
CEO
ceramics
cereal**
cerebellum
cerebral
cerebrally
ceremony
certain
certificate
cervix
cession**
cesspool
chafe
chagrin
chagrined
chain
chair
chaise
chalet
chalk
chalk talk
challenge
chameleon
chamois
cham-
pagne**
cham-
paign**
champion

		chosen	citrus
...ert**	cherub	chow**	civic
	chestnut	chowder	civil
...use	chevron	chow mein	civilization
...anukah	chews**	christen**	civil rights
...naos	chic**	Christian**	clairvoyance
chapeau	Chicago	Christmas	clairvoyant
chapel	Chicana	chrome	clamor
chaperon	chicanery	chronic	clan**
chaplain	Chicano	chronology	clandestine
character	chicken pox	chrysanthe-	clannish
charade	chief	mum	claque
charcoal	chieftain	chubby	classified
chardonnay	chiffon	chuck	classify
chariot	chignon	chummy	clause**
charisma	children	Chunnel	claws**
charitable	Chile**	chupah	cleanse
charity	chili**	church	cleanser
charlatan	chilly**	churning	clear
charnel**	chimney	chute**	clearance
charted**	Chinatown	chutzpah	cleavage
charter	chintz	ciao**	clench**
chartered**	chip	cider	clerical
chartreuse	Chippendale	cigar	clew**
chase	chiropody	cigarette	cliché
chased**	chiropractor	cinch	click**
chasm	chisel	Cincinnati	client
chassis	chivalrous	cinder	clientele
chaste**	chivalry	Cinderella	climactic**
chastity	chlamydia	cinema	climate
chat	chloral hy-	cinnamon	climatic**
château	drate	cipher	climax
chatter	chlorine	circle	climb**
chauffeur**	chloroform	circuit	clime**
chauvinism	chocolate	circular	clinch**
cheap**	choice	circumcise	clinic
cheat	choir**	circumcision	clinker
check**	choler**	circumfer-	clipper
cheddar	cholera	ence	clique**
cheep**	cholesterol	circum-	clitoris
cheese	choose**	stance	cloak
chef	chopper	circumvent	clobber
chemical	choral**	cisc chip	cloche
chemise	chord**	cistern	clock
chemist	choreogra-	citadel	cloister
chenille	phy	citation	clone**
cherish	chortle	cite**	close**
	chorus	citizen	closeout

closet
closing
closure
clothes**
cloths**
clown**
cloy
cloze**
club
clubby
clue**
clumsy
clutch
coach
coagulate
coal**
coalition
coarse**
coat**
cobbler
cobol
cocaine
cockamamie
cockpit
cockroach
cock's
  comb**
cocks-
  comb**
cocktail
cocoa**
coconut
code
codeine
coerce
coercion
coffee
coffin
cogitate
cognac
cognitive
coherent
coiffure
coincidence
coitus
coke
cola**
colander

cold
cold-
  blooded
coleslaw
colic
coliseum
colitis
collaborate
collage**
collapse
collapsible
collar**
collard**
collateral
colleague
collect
collector
college**
collegiate
collision**
colloquial
collusion**
cologne**
Colombia**
colon**
colonel**
colonic
colonnade
color**
coloratura
colossal
Colosseum
colostomy
Columbia**
column
columnist
coma**
comb
comedian
comedy**
comet**
comfortable
comic
coming
comity**
comma**
command**

commemo-
  rate
commence
commend**
commend-
  able
commenda-
  tion**
commensu-
  rate
commerce
commercial
commission
commit**
committed
committee**
commodity
common
commotion
commune
communi-
  cate
communism
communist
community
commute
commuter
compact
companion
comparable
comparative
compass
compatible
compel
compelled
compen-
  dium
compensa-
  tion
compete
competence
competent
competition
compla-
  cence**
compla-
  cent**

complai-
  sance**
compli-
  sant**
comple-
  ment**
complemen-
  tary**
complexion
compliance
complicate
compli-
  ment**
complimen-
  tary**
compose
composition
compound
comprehend
comprehensi-
  ble**
comprehen-
  sion
comprehen-
  sive**
compressed
compression
compromise
comptroller
compulsory
compute
computer
comrade
conceal
concede
conceit
conceive
concentrate
concentra-
  tion
concentric
concept
concert
concession
concierge
conciliate
concise
conclave

165

conclude
conclusion
concoct
concourse
concrete**
concur**
concurrence
concussion
condemn**
condemna-
tion**
condensa-
tion
condescend
condiment
condition
condo
condom
condomin-
ium
condone
conduct
confection-
ary
confederate
confer
conference
conferred
confess
confidant**
confidence
confident**
confinement
confirm
confirmer**
confiscate
conflagra-
tion
conformer**
Confucius
congeal
congenial**
congenital**
conglomer-
ate
congratulate
congrega-
tion

congress
congressio-
nal
congruous
conjecture
conjugal
conjugate
conjunction
conjunctivi-
tis
conjure
connect
Connecticut
connection
connoisseur
connotation
connote
connubial
conquer**
conscience**
conscien-
tious**
conscious**
consensus
consequence
conserva-
tion**
conservative
conserva-
tory
consider
considerable
consignment
consistent
console
consolidate
consonant
conspicuous
conspiracy
constable
constant
constellation
constitute
constitution
construct
construction
consul**
consult

consultant
consume
consummate
consump-
tion
contact**
contagious
contain
contaminate
contemn**
contemplate
contempo-
rary
contempt
contempti-
ble
contend**
content**
contest
conti-
nence**
continent
continual**
continually
continu-
ous**
contour
contracep-
tion
contracep-
tive
contract**
contractual
contralto
contraption
contrariwise
contrary
contrast
contretemps
contribute
contrive
control
controlled
controver-
sial
controversy
convalesce
convalescent

convec-
tion**
convenient
convent
convention
converge
conversa-
tion**
converse
convert**
convertible
convict
conviction**
convolute
convulse
cookery
cookie
cookie cutter
cookie jar
cool
coolie**
coolly**
cooperate
coordination
copious
copper
copyright
copywriter
coral**
cord**
cordial
cordless
corduroy
core**
cored**
core dump
corespond-
ent**
coriander
cornea
corned beef
corner**
cornice
corny
corona
coronary
coroner**

corporal** counterfeit cream** crotchet**
corporation countess crease** crouch
corporeal** country creation croup
corps** coup de creature croupier
corpse** grâce crèche crowd
corpuscle coup d'état credence crowded
corral** coupé credential CRT
corralled couple credible** crucial
correct coupon credit crude
correctness courage creditable** crudités**
correlate course** creditor crudity**
correlation court** credulous cruel
corre- courteous creek** cruelly
 spond courtesan** creep cruelty
correspon- courtesy** crème** cruelty free
 dent** courtmartial crème de la cruet
corridor courtroom crème cruise**
corroborate cousin** crepes** cruiser
corrugated couture crescendo crumb
corrupt cover crescent crusade
corsage coverage Cretan** crusty
corset covenant cretin** crutch
cortisone** covert** crew crypt
cosmic covet** crews** cryptic
cosmonaut coward** crick** cryptogra-
cosmopoli- cowered** cricket pher
 tan cowboy cried cryptology
Cossack cowhide criminal crystallize
costume** coxcomb** crimson Cuba
costumer** coyly cripple cubic
cot** coyote critic** cubicle
côte** cozen** critical cubism
cote** cozy criticize cuckoo
cotillion crabby critique** cudgel
cottage crack crochet** cue**
cotton crackle crocodile cuff**
couch po- cradle crone cuisine
 tato craft croquet** cul de sac
cough** crafty croquette** culinary
could cram cross-exam- culled**
couldn't cranberry ine cult**
council** crane cross- cultivate
councillor** cranium purposes culture
counsel** craps** cross- cumin
counselor** crawl reference cunning
countdown crayon crossroad cupboard
counte- creak** cross section cupidity
 nance**

167

curare	**D**	debut	defiance
curettage	dabble	decade	defibrillate
curfew	dachshund	decease	deficient
curiosity	dacron	deceased**	deficit
curious	Dada	deceit	defied
curly	daffodil	deceive	definite**
currant**	dagger	December	definitely
currency	dahlia	decency	definition
current**	daily**	decent**	definitive**
curriculum	daiquiri	deception	deflate
curry	dairy**	decibel	deflation
cursed	dais**	decided	defused**
cursor	daisy-wheel	deciduous	defy
curtain	dally**	decimal	degree**
curtsy**	dam**	decipher	dehydrate
curvaceous	damage	decision	deign
curve	damn**	declaration	deity
cusp	dandelion	decline	delay**
cuspy	dandruff	deco	delegate
custard	dangerous	décolleté	delete
custody	data	decomposed	deletion
custom**	data base	decompres-	deli
customer**	date rape	sion	deliberate
cut**	daughter	decon**	delicacy
cutting edge	dawdle	deconges-	delicatessen
cutup	dawn	tant	delicious
CYA	days**	deconstruct	delight
cybercrud	daze**	decor	delinquent
cyberculture	dazzle	decorate	delivery
cybernetics	deacon**	decrease	deluge
cyberspace	dead**	decree**	delusion
cyborg	deadline	decryption	deluxe
cybot	deadlock	dedicate	delve
cyclamate	deaf	deduce**	demagogue
cycle	deal	deductible	demean
cyclone	dealt	deed**	demeaning
cygnet**	dear**	deer**	demented
cylinder	dearth	de facto	dementia
cymbal**	death	default	praecox
cynic	debate	defeat	demi-tasse
cynosure	debauch**	defecate	democracy
cyst	debauchery	defendant	democrat
cystitis	debonair	defense	demography
cystoscopy	debouch**	defensible	demolish
cytoplasm	debris	defensive	demonstra-
czar	debt	defer**	ble
Czech**	debtor	deference	demonstrate
	debug	deferred	demur**

168

demure**
denial
dense
dental
dental dam
dentifrice
dentine
dentist
deny
deodorant
departure
dependable
dependant**
depen-
dence**
dependent**
depen-
dents**
depilatory
deplete
depo-
provera
deposit
depositary**
deposition**
deposi-
tory**
depot
depraved**
deprecate**
depreciate**
depreciation
depressant
depression
deprivation
deprive
deprived**
depths
deputy
derby
derelict
derivative
derive
derma
dermatitis
derogatory
derrick
descend

descend-
ant**
descend-
ent**
descent**
describe
description
desecrate**
desegregate
desensitize
desert**
desertion
desiccant
desiccate**
design
desktop
desolate**
despair
desperate
despicable
dessert**
destination
destroy
destruct
destruction
destructive
detached
detail
detect
detergent
deteriorate
determine
deterrent
detestable
detour
detox
detoxifica-
tion
detract**
detritus
deuce
devastate
develop
deviant
deviate
deviation
device**

devil
devious
devise**
devoid
devotion
devour
dew**
dextrous
diabetes
diagnose
diagonal
diagram**
dial
dial-a-
prayer
dialect
dialogue
diamond
dia-
phragm**
diarrhea
diary**
diaspora
dice**
dicey
dichotomy
dictionary
didn't
die**
died**
diehard
diesel
diet**
dietary
dietitian
differ**
difference
differential
difficult
diffuse
diffused**
digest
digestible
digging
digital
digitalis
dignity

digress
digs
dilapidate
dilation**
dilemma
dilettante
diligent
dilute
dilution**
dimension
diminish
diminutive
dimwit
dine**
diner**
dinette
dinghy**
dingy**
dining
dinner**
dinosaur
diocese
dioxin
diphtheria
diploma
dire
direction
dirge
dirty
disability
disabled
disadvan-
taged
disagree
disagree-
ment
disallow
disappear
disappoint
disapproba-
tion
disap-
prove**
disarray
disaster
disastrous
disburse**

169

disburse-
ment
disc
discard
discern
discharge
disciple
discipline
disclosure
disco
discomfit**
discom-
fort**
disconcert
disconsolate
discount
discourse
discourteous
discover
discreet**
discrepancy
discrete**
discretion
discretion-
ary
discriminate
discus**
discuss**
discussion
disdain
disease
diseased**
disembowel
disguise
dish
disheveled
dishonest
dishwasher
disillusion
disinfect
disinflation
disinforma-
tion
disinter
disk
diskette
dismantle
dismiss

dismissal
dismount
Disney
disparage
dispensary
disperse**
displace-
ment
display
disposable
disposal
disposi-
tion**
dispossess
dispropor-
tion
disprove**
dispute
disqualify
disreputable
disrespect
disrupt
diss
dissatisfy
dissect
disseminate
dissent**
dissident
dissimilar
dissipate
dissociate
dissolute**
dissolution
dissolve
dissonant
dissuade
distaff
distal**
distance
distasteful
distemper
distill**
distillation
distinct
distinguish
distract**
distraction

distraught
distress
distribute
district
disturb
ditto
diuretic
diva
divan
dive
diver
diverge
divers**
diverse**
diversity
divert
diverticulo-
sis
divest
divestiture
divide
dividend
divine
division
divorce
divulge
Dixie
dizzy
do**
doable
doc**
docile
dock**
doctor
doctrinaire
docudrama
document
documen-
tary
dodge
doe**
doer**
does**
dog
dogged
doggerel
doldrums

dole
dollar
dolphin
dome
domed
domestic
domicile
dominant
domineer
dominion
domino
don**
donate
done**
donkey
donor
don't
doom
door
dopamine
dork
dormant
dormitory
dosage
dose**
dossier
dot
double
double bind
double-blind
double-digit
double-
dipper
doubt
douche
dough**
doughnut
dour**
dove
dovetail
Dow
dowager
dowdy
dower**
downer**
downfall
downgrade

downpour	due**	**E**	eerie**
downside	duel**		efface
downsize	due process	eager	effect**
downstairs	dulcet	eagle	effective**
downtime	dully**	earache	effeminate
downtown	duly**	eardrum	effervescent
downzoning	dumb	earl	efficacious
dowry	dumbfound	earlier	efficiency
doze**	dummy	early	efficient
dozen	dump	earn**	effluent**
dozens	dumpy	earnest	effort
draft**	dun**	earring	effrontery
dragon	dunce	earth	eggplant
drainage	dune**	earwax	ego
drama	dungaree	easement	egocentric
draught**	dungeon**	easily	egression**
drawback	duo	east	Eiffel
drawn	duodenum	Easter	eight**
dread	duplex	easy	eighteen
dream	duplicate	eau de co-	eighth
dreary	duplicity	logne	Eire**
dredge	durable	eavesdrop	either**
dried	duration	ebony	ejaculate
drier**	duress	ebullient	eject
driftwood	during	eccentric**	elaborate
drive	dust-up	ecclesiastical	elastic
drive-by	dusty	echo	elation
drive-in	Dutch	éclair	elbow
driven	dutiful	eclampsia	elder**
driveway	duty	eclectic	elect
drizzle	dwarf	eclipse	election
droid	dweeb	ecology	electorate
droll	DWEM	economic	electricity
droop	dybbuk	economical	electrocardi-
dropping	dye**	economy	ogram
drowned	dyeing**	ecstasy	electron
drowse	dying**	ecumenical	electronic
drudgery	dynamic	eczema	electronics
druggist	dynamite	edema	elegance
drugstore	dyne**	edge**	elegant
drumstick	dysentery	edible**	elegy**
drunkenness	dysfunction	edit	element**
dryer**	dysfunc-	edition**	elemen-
dual**	tional	editor	tary**
dub	dyslexia	editorial	elephant
dubious	dyspeptic	educable	elephantiasis
dudgeon**	dystrophy	educate	elevate
		eel	elevation
		e'er**	

171

elevator	emigrant**	enervate**	entrée
eleven	eminence	enfold**	entrepreneur
elf	eminent**	enforce	entry
elicit**	emissary	enforceable	enunciate
eligible	emit**	engagement	enuresis
eliminate**	emollient**	engine	envelop**
elite	emolu-	engineer	envelope**
elitist	ment**	England	enviable
elixir	emotion	English	envious
ellipse	empathy	engrave	environment
ellipsis	emperor	enhance	envy
elliptical	emphasis	enhance-	enwrap**
elm	emphysema	ment	enzyme
el Niño	empire**	enjoyment	ephedrine
elocution**	employee	enlighten	epic**
eloquent	empower	enliven	epicine
elucidate	emptiness	en masse	epicure
elude**	empty	enmesh	epidemic
elusion**	enable**	enmity**	epidermis
elusive**	enamel	ennoble	epigraph**
elves	enamored	ennui	epilepsy
E-mail	encephalitis	enormous	episode
emanate	enchant	enough	epistle**
emasculate**	enchilada	enquire	epitaph**
emascula-	encircle	enrage	epithet**
tion	enclosure	enrich	epoch**
embalm	encode	enroll**	equable**
embark	encompass	en route	equally
embarrassed	encore	ensemble	equator
embedded	ensure**	ensign	equilibrium
embellish	encounter	ensure**	equinox
embezzle	encourage	entail	equipped
embezzler	encroach	entangle	equitable**
emblem	encrypt	enter**	equity
embolism	encryption	enterprise	equivalent
emboss	encyclopedia	entertain	era**
embrace	endear	enthrall	erase
embroider	endeavor	enthusiasm	ere**
embryo	endoge-	enthusiastic	erect**
emend**	nous**	entice	erection
emerald	endomorph	entire	ergo
emerge**	endorsement	entitled**	ergonomics
emergency	endow	entomol-	Erie**
emerging	endowment	ogy**	ERISA
emeritus	endurance	entourage	ermine
emersed**	enema**	entrance	erode
emetic	enemy**	entrap	erosion
energetic	entreat	erotic**

172

err**	ethos	examination	exonerate
errand**	etiology	example	exorbitant
errant**	etiquette	exasperate	exorcise**
erratic**	etymology**	exceed**	exotic
erroneous	Eucharist	excel**	expansion
error**	eugenics	excellent	expansive**
ersatz	eulogy**	except**	ex parte
eruct**	eunuch**	exception-	expedite
erudite	eunuchs**	able**	expedition
eruption**	euphemism	excep-	expel
erythromy-	euphoria	tional**	expelled
cin	Eurasian	excerpt	expendable
escalator	eureka	excess**	expense
escape	Eurocentric	excessive	expensive**
escarole	Eurodollar	exchange	experience
escort	Europe	excise	experiment
Eskimo	European	excitable	expert
ESOP	euthanasia	excite	expertise
esophagus	evacuate	excitement	expiation**
esoteric	evaluate	exciting**	expiration**
especial**	evaluation	exclude	expire
espionage	evaporate	exclusive	explanation
espousal	evening	excoriate	expletive
espresso	event	excrete	explicit
esquire	eventual	excruciate	exploit
essay**	eventually	excursion	explore
essence	every	exec	export
essential	everyone**	execute	expose**
establish	every one**	executive	exposé**
estate	everything**	exempt	exposure
esteem	every	exercise**	express
esteemed	thing**	exert	expressway
estimate	everywhere	exhale	exquisite
estimation	evict	exhaust	extant**
estrange-	eviction	exhibit	extempora-
ment	evidence	exhilarate	neous
estray**	evil	exhort	extend
estrogen	eviscerate	exhume	extension
et cetera	evocative	exile	extent**
etch**	evoke	Eximbank	exterminate
etching**	evolution	exist	extermina-
eternity	evolve	existence	tion
ether**	ewe**	exists**	external
Ethernet	ex	exit	extinct
ethical	exact	exiting**	extirpate
ethnocentric	exactly	exits**	extol
ethnology**	exaggerate	exodus	extoll
ethology**	exalt**	exomorph	extort

173

extortion
extra
extract
extracurricu-
    lar
extraordi-
    nary
extrapolate
extrasensory
extrater-
    ritorial
extravagant
extreme
extricate
extrovert
exult**
eye**
eyebrow
eyelash
eyesight
eyestrain
eyewitness
ezine

F
fable
fabric
fabricate
fabulous
façade
face
face-ism**
faceless
face-lift
face-off
faces**
facesaving
facet**
facetious
facial
facies**
facile
facilitate
facility**
facing
facsimile
fact

faction
factious
factor
factory
facts**
factual
faculty
fad
fade
faerie**
Fahrenheit
fail
faille
failsafe
failure
fain**
faint**
fair**
fairly
fairy**
faith
faker**
fakir**
falcon
fall
fallacious
fallacy
fallback
fallible
fallopian
    tube
false
falsehood
falsetto
falsies
falsify
falter
fame
familiar
familiarize
family
famine
famished
famous
fanatic
fanciful
fancy
fantasize

fantastic
fantasy**
FAQS**
far
farce
fare**
farfetched
farm
farmer
faro
farsighted
farther**
fascinate
fascism**
fascist
fashion
fashionable
fasten
fastidious
fatal**
fatality
fate**
fateful**
father**
fathom
fatigue
fatten
fatty
fatuous
faucet**
fault
faun**
faux pas
favorable
favorite
fawn**
fax**
fays**
faze**
fear
feasibility
feasible
feast**
feat**
feather
feature
February
feces**

federal
Federales
fedora
Fed, the
feebly
feed
feedback
feeder
feeling
feet**
feeze**
feign**
feint**
feisty
felicitate
felicity**
feline
fellow
felony
felt
female
feminine
feminism
femur
fence
fender
ferment**
ferocious
ferret
ferry**
fertile
fertilize
fervor
fest**
fester
festival
fetal**
fetch**
fete**
fetish**
fetter
fettle
fetus
feud
feudal
fever
few
fiancé**

174

fiasco
fiberglass
fiber-optic
fibrillation
fibroid
fibrous
fickle
fiction
fictitious
fiddle
fidelity
fidget
field
fiend**
fierce
fiery
fiesta
FIFO
fifth
fight
figurative
figure
figurehead
file**
filet
filial
filibuster
filigree
filing**
Filipino
filling**
film
filter
filthy
finagle
final
finale**
finalize
finally**
finance**
financial
finch**
find**
fined**
finely**
fineness**
finesse**
finest**

finger
fingerprint
fingertip
finite
fir**
firebug
firefighter
firetrap
firing
firm
first
first aid
first-rate
fiscal**
fisher**
fishnet
fission
fissure**
fitting
fix
fixation
fjord
flabbergast
flabber-
    gasted
flaccid
flagellation
flagging
flagrant**
flagship
flail
flair**
flake
flaky
flambé
flamboyant
flame
flamenco
flammable
flap
flapper
flare**
flatfoot
flatten
flatter
flattery
flatulent
flaunt**

flavor
flaw**
flea**
fleabag
fleche**
flecks**
fledgling
flee**
fleece
fleet
flesh**
flew**
flex**
flexible
flextime
flicker
flicks
flies
flight
flimsy
flinch**
flip
flippant
flirt
flirtatious
float
flock**
floe**
flog**
flood
floor**
floppy
flores-
    cence**
florid**
Florida
florist
flounce
flounder
flour**
flourish
flout**
flow**
flowchart
flower**
flown
flu**
flub

fluctuate
fluctuation
flue**
fluent
fluid
fluke
fluores-
    cence**
fluorescent
fluoride**
fluorine
fluoroscope
flurry
flute
flutter
flux
fly
foam
fob
focal
focus
foe
foggy**
fogy**
foible
fold
foliage
folio
folk
folks
follicle
follow
folly
foment**
fond**
fondle
fondling**
fondue
font**
football
footloose
for**
forbid
force
forceful
forceps
forcible
ford

fore** forecast forecastle foreclose foreclosure forego** foregone forehead foreign foreman foremost forensic foreperson foresee foresight foreskin forest forestall forever foreword** forfeit forge forgery forget forgive forgo** fork forklift form** formal formalde- hyde formalism formally** format former formerly** formica- tion** formidable formula fornica- tion** forsake forsythia fort** forte** forth**

forthright forties fortitude fortuitous fortunately fortune forty forum** forward** fossil foster fought foul** found** foundation foundling** fount** fountain four** fourteen fourth** fowl** fox foxy fracas fractions** fractious** fracture fragile fragment fragrance fragrant** frail frame frame-up framework franc** franchise frank** frankfurter fraternal fraud fraudulent fraught frays** freak** freckle Freddie Mac

free agent freebie freedom freelance freeload frees** freeway freeze** freeze-dry freight frenetic frenzy frequency freshen Freud Freudian friar** fricassee friction Friday friend** friendship frieze** fright frill fringe fritter frivolous frock frolic frontal front-end frontiersman frontispiece frown frozen frugal fruitful fryer** fuchsia fudge fugitive fugue fulfill fulfillment fullback full-time

fumble fume function functional fundamental fundamental- ist funeral** funereal** fungus funnel funny fur** furious furlough furnish furniture furor furry** further** furthermore fury** fuselage fuss** futile future fuzz**

G

GAAP** gabardine gabble** gable** gadfly gadget Gaelic gaff** gaffe** gage** gaggle** gait** galaxy gale gall gallant gallbladder galleon**

gallery	gauze**	geology	girlfriend
galley	gavel	geometry	girlie
gallon**	gawk	geriatrics	giveaway
gallop	gays**	German**	giveback
gallows	gaze**	germane**	gizmo
gallstone**	gazelle	germicide	glacial
galvanize	gazette	gerontology	glacier**
gamble**	gear	gerrymander	glamorous
gambol**	geezer	gerund	glamour
game	gefilte fish	gestalt	glance
gamete**	Geiger	gestation	glare
gamin**	counter	gesture**	glass ceiling
gamma	geisha	gesundheit	glaucoma
gamma glob-	gel**	get**	glaze
ulin	gelatine	getaway	glazier**
gammon**	gelding	geyser	gleam
gamut**	gellato	ghastly	glider
gamy	gem	ghat**	glimmer
gander	gendarme	ghetto	glimpse
gangrene	gender	ghost	glitch**
gantlet**	genealogy	ghoul**	glitter
gap**	generally	giant	glitterati**
garage	generate	gibe**	glitz**
garbage	generation	giddy	global
garden	generator	gig	gloom**
gardener	generic	gigabit	glorify
gargle**	generous	gigabyte	glossary
garish	genes**	gigahertz	glossies
garlic	genesis	gigantic	glossy
garnishee	genetic	gigantism	glottis
garret	genial	giggle	glucose
garrulous	genital**	GIGO	glue
garter	genitalia	gigolo	glume**
gas	genius**	gild**	gluten**
gaseous	geniuses	gilt**	glutenous**
gasket	genocide	gimmick	glutinous**
gasoline	genotype	gin**	glutton**
gastritis	genre	ginger	glutton-
gat**	genteel**	gingham	ous**
gate**	gentile**	gingiva	glycerin
gatekeeper	gentle**	gingivitis	gnarled
GATT**	gentleman	Ginnie Mae	gnash
gauche**	gently	Ginny Maes	gnat
gaudy	genuflect	giraffe	gnaw
gauge**	genuine	gird	gneiss
gaunt**	genus**	girder	gnocci
gauntlet**	geodesic	girdle	gnome
gauss	geography	girl	

gnosis	grabber	gregarious	grudge
gnu**	graceful	gremlin	gruesome
goad	gracious	grenade	grumpy
goal**	grade	greyhound	grunge
goat	gradual	gridiron	G-string
goatee	graduate	gridlock	guacamole
gobble**	graduation	grief	guarantee**
goblet	graffiti	grievance	guaranty**
gocart	grain	grieve	guard
goddess	gram	grievous	guardian
godless	grammar	grill**	guerrilla**
gofer**	Grammy	grille**	guess
goggles	granddaugh-	grimace	guessed**
go-go	ter	grime	guest**
goiter	grandeur	grin	guidance
goldbrick	grandfather	grind	guide
golden para-	grand mal	gringo	guild**
chute	grand-	grip**	guile
goldstone**	mother	gripe**	guileless
golf**	granny	grippe**	guillotine
gonad	grantsman-	grisly**	guilt**
gondola	ship	grist	guilty
gone	granule	gristle**	guinea
gonorrhea	grapefruit	gristly**	guise
goodlooking	graph	grit	guitar
goodwill	graphic	grits	gulag
goof	graphics	grizzle**	gulf**
goofy	graphology	grizzly**	gullible
goose	grasp	groan**	gunner
gopher**	grate**	grocery	gurgle
gore	grateful	groin	gurney**
gorge	gratis	groom	guru
gorgeous	gratitude	groove**	gusto
gorilla**	gratuitous	groovy	Gutenberg
gospel	gratuity	grope	guts
gossamer	grave	gross	gutter
gossip	gravel	grotesque	guttural
gotten	gravity	grouch	gymnasium
gouache**	grease**	ground	gymnast
gouge	great**	groundwork	gymnastics
goulash	Greece**	group	gynecology
gourd	greedy	groupie	gynophobia
gourmet	green	grove**	gyp
government	greenhouse	grovel	gypsum
governor	greenmail	grown**	gypsy
gown	greet	grown-up	gyrate
grab	greeting	growth	gyroscope

H

habeas corpus
habilitate
habit
habitant**
habitat**
habitual
habituate
hacienda
hack
hacker
hackneyed
haddock
haggard
haggle
hail**
Hail Mary
hair**
haircut**
hairdo
hairdresser
hairy
Haiti
halcyon
hale**
half
halfway
halitosis
hall**
hallelujah
hallmark
hallow**
Halloween
hallucinate
hallucination
hallucinogen
halo**
halve**
halves
hamburger
hamlet
hammer
hammer toe
hamstring
handbag
handbook

handcuffs
handful
handicap
handicraft
handiwork
handkerchief
handle
handmade**
handmaid**
hand-me-down
handsome**
handwriting
hangar**
hanger**
hangover
hang-up**
hang up**
hansom**
Hanukah
happen
happily
harangue
harass
harassment
harbor
hardboiled
hard disk
hardening
hardly**
hardship
hardware
hardy**
hare**
harebrained
Hare Krishna
harelip
harem
haricot**
harlequin
harmless
harmonic
harmonica
harmonious
harness
harp**

harpy**
harridan
harried
harsh
hart**
harvest
has-been
hashish
Hasidim
hassle**
hasten
hatch
hatched**
hatchet**
hate
hateful**
hatful**
hatred
haughty
haul**
haunch**
haunt
haute couture
hauteur**
have**
haven**
havoc
Hawaii
hay**
hazard
hazel
hazy
head**
headache
headdress
headhunter
headlight
headline
head-on
headquarters
heady
heal**
healer
health
heap
hear**

heard**
hearing**
hearsay
hearse
heart**
hearth
heartily**
hearty**
heat
heathen
heatstroke
heaume**
heave
heaven**
heavy
heavyweight
Hebrew
heckle
hectic
he'd**
hedge
hedonist
heed**
heel**
hegemony
heifer
height
Heimlich maneuver
heinous**
heir**
heir apparent
heiress
heirloom
heist
helicopter
hell**
he'll**
heller**
hellion
hellish
hello
helm
helmet
helpful
helpless
hem

179

hematoma
hemisphere
hemoglobin
hemophilia
hemorrhage
hemorrhoids
hence**
henceforth
henna
heparin
hepatitis
herald
herb
herbaceous
herd**
here**
hereafter
hereby
hereditary
heredity
hereon
heresy
heretofore
heritage
hermaphro-
dite
hermitage
hernia
hero
heroes
heroic
heroin**
heroine**
heroism
herpes
herring**
hers
hesitate
heteroge-
neous
heterosexual
heuristics
hew**
hexagon
hey!**
hi**
hiatus
hibernate

hiccough
hiccup
hickory
hidden
hideous
hie**
hierarchical
file
hierarchy
hieroglyphic
high
highball
highbrow
high density
higher**
higher-up
high fidelity
high fre-
quency
high-handed
high-level
highness
high resolu-
tion
high-rise
high school
high-strung
high-tech
highway
hijack
hilarious
him**
himself
hindrance
hindsight
Hindu
hinge
hiphop
Hippocratic
oath
hippopota-
mus
hippy
hire**
hireling
hirsute
Hispanic
histamine

history
hitch
HIV
HMO
ho**
hoard**
hoarse**
hoary**
hoax
hobble
hobby**
Hobson's
choice
hockey**
hodgepodge
hoe**
hoes**
hoi polloi
hoist**
holdings
holdout
hold-up
hole**
holed up**
holey**
holiday**
holiness
holistic
hollandaise
holler**
hollow**
holocaust
hologram
holography
holy**
holy day**
homage
home**
homeboy
homeless
homely
homemaker
homesick
homestead
homework
homicide
homogene-
ous**

homoge-
nous**
homonym
homophobia
homosexual
honcho
honest
honey
honeydew
honeymoon
honk**
honor
honorable
honorary
hood
hoof
hook
hookworm
hooky**
hoop**
hoot
hope
hopeful
hopeless
hoping
horde**
horizon
horizontal
hormone
hornet
horny
horoscope
horrendous
horrible
horrified
horror
hors
d'oeuvres
horse**
horsepower
horseshoe
horsy
horticulture
hose**
hosiery
hospice
hospitable**
hospital**

hospitality	humility	hypertext	ignition
host**	humming	hyperther-	ignominious
hostage	humongous	mia	ignominy
hostel**	humor	hyphen	ignorant
hostile**	humorous**	hypnosis	ignore
hotbed	hump	hypnotist	iguana
hotdog	hunch**	hypocrisy	ikon
hotel	hundred	hypocrite	ileitis
hotelier	Hungary**	hypocriti-	Iliad
hotheaded	hunger	cal**	I'll**
hothouse	hungry**	hypodermic	illegal
hound	hunk**	hypoglyce-	illegible**
hour**	hunter**	mia	illegitimate
hourglass	hunting	hypotenuse	illicit**
hour hand	hurdle**	hypothesis	Illinois
house-	hurl	hypothetical	illiterate
breaker	hurray	hysterec-	illness
household	hurricane	tomy	illogical
housekeeper	hurry	hysteria	illtempered
houses	hurt	hysterical	illude**
housewife	hurtle**		illuminate**
housing	husband		illusion**
hovel	hussy	**I**	illusive**
hover	hustle**	**I****	illustrate
however	hustler	iatrogenic	illustrious
howl	hybrid	ibuprofen	image
hub	hydrangea	iceberg	imagery
hubbub	hydrant	ichthyology	imagination
hubby**	hydraulic	icing	imagine
hubcap	hydrochloric	icon	imbalance
hubris	acid	iconoclast	imbecile
huckleberry	hydrofoil	icy	imbibe
huckster	hydrogen	id	imbroglio
HUD	hydro-	idea	imbrue**
huddle	phobia	ideal	imbue**
hue**	hyena	identical	imitation
huge	hygiene	identify	immaculate
human**	hymen	ideology	immanent**
humane**	hymn**	idiom	immaterial
humanitar-	hymnal	idiosyncrasy	immature
ian	hyper	idiot	immeasura-
humanities	hyperactive	idle**	ble
humanity	hyperbole	idol**	immediate
humble**	hypercriti-	idolater	immediately
humerus**	cal**	idyll**	immemora-
humid	hypersensi-	idyllic	ble
humidifier	tive	iffy	immense
humiliate	hypertension	ignite	immensely

181

immerge** impious inaccurate incompara-
immerse implacable inadequate ble
immersed** implant inadmissible incompati-
immigrant** implausible inadvertent ble
immigration implement inalienable incompetent
imminent** implicit inane** incompre-
immit** implore inappropri- hensible
immobile imply ate inconceiv-
immodest impolite inapt** able
immolate import inarticulate inconclusive
immoral** importance inasmuch as incongruous
immortal** imposition inaudible inconsolable
immune impossibility inaugurate inconspicu-
immunity** impossible** inauspicious ous
impact impostor** incalculable incontinent
impair imposture** incandescent inconvenient
impale impotence incapable incorporate
impartial impotent incapacitate incorrigible
impassa- impractical incarcerate incorrupt-
ble** impregnable incarnate ible
impasse impregnate incendiary increase
impassible** impresario incense incredible
impassioned impress incentive incredulous
impatient impression incessant increment
impeach impression- incest** incriminate
impeccable ism incidence** incriminator
impecunious imprinting incident incubator
impede imprison incidentally incumbent
impediment improbable incidents** incurable
impel impromptu incinerator incurred
impenetra- improper incipient** incurring
ble impropriety incise indebted
impenitent improve- incision indecent
imperative ment incisive indecisive
impercepti- improvident incisor indefensible
ble improvise incite** indelible
imperfect imprudent** inclement indemnity
imperial impudent** inclination indent
imperialism impugn incline indenture
impersonal impulse inclined independent
impersonate impulsive include indescrib-
impertinent impunity** inclusive able
imperturb- impurity** incognito index
able impute** incoherent Indian
impetigo in** income indicative
impetus inability incom- indict**
impiety in absentia municado indictment
impinge inaccessible indifferent

182

indigenous** infallible infringe inquisitive
indigent infamous infuriate in rem
indigestible infancy infuse insane**
indigestion infant infusion insanity
indignant infantile ingenious** inscription
indigo infantry ingenuous** inscrutable
indiscreet** infarction ingestion insect
indiscrete** infect** ingrate insecticide
indiscriminate infection ingratiate insects**
indispensable infectious ingredient insecure
indisposed infer inhabit inseminate
indistinguishable inference inhabitant inseparable
indite** inferior inhale insert**
individually inferiority inherit insertion
indivisible** infertility inhibition inset**
indoctrinate infest** inhospitable inside
indolent infidel inhuman insidious
indomitable infidelity iniquity** insight**
indoors infiltrate initial insignia
induce infinite initialize insignificant
inducement infinitely initiate insincere
induction infinitive initiation insipid
inductive infinity initiative insipient**
indulge infirm inject insist
industrial infirmary** injection insistent
industry infirmity** injunction insists**
inebriate inflammable injury insolate**
inedible inflammation injustice insolent
ineffable inflate in-law insoluble
ineffective inflation inlay insolvent
inefficient inflection inn** insomnia
ineligible** inflexible innate inspection
inept** influence ineffective inspiration
inequality influenza inner instability
inequity** influx innervate** installation**
inert infomercial innocence installment
inertia informal innocuous instance
inescapable informant innovate instantaneous
inevitable information innuendo instead
inexcusable informercial innuendoes instigate
inexorable infraction innumerable instill
inexpensive infrared inoculate instillation**
inexperienced infrastructure inordinate instinct
infrequent input** institute
inquest institution
inquire
inquiry

institutional-
ization
instruct
instruction
instrument
insubordi-
nate
insufferable
insulate**
insulin
insult
insurance**
insure**
insurgent
intangible
integral
integrate
integration
integrity
integument
intellectual
intelligence
intemperate
intense**
intensify
intention
intents**
inter**
interactive
intercede
intercept
interces-
sion**
intercom
intercourse
interdepen-
dent
interdict
interdiscipli-
nary
interest
interesting
interface
interfere
interference
interferon
interior**

interjec-
tion**
interlude
intermarry
intermediary
intermediate
interment**
intermittent
intern**
internal
international
Internet
intern-
ment**
interpel-
late**
interper-
sonal
interpo-
late**
interpret
interracial
interrogate
interrupt
intersect
interses-
sion**
interstate**
interval
intervene
intervention
interview
intestate**
intestine
intimacy
intimate**
intimidate**
intolerance
intolerant
intoxicate
intractable
intramural
intransigent
intrastate**
intrauterine
intravenous
intricacy

intrigue
intrinsic
introduce
introjec-
tion**
introspec-
tion
introvert
intrude
intruder
intrusion
intuition
inturn**
Inuit
invade
invalid
invaluable
invariably
invasion
invective
inveigh
inveigle
inventor
inventory
invertebrate
invest**
investigate
investigation
investment
inveterate
invidious
invigorate
invisible**
invitation
in vitro
invoice
invoke
involuntary
involve
invulnerable
inward
iodine
ion**
ipecac
IRA**
irascible
ire**

iridescence
iridescent
iris
irk
iron**
irony
irradiation
irrational
irreconcila-
ble
irredeemable
irredentist
irrefutable
irregular
irrelevance
irrelevant**
irresistible
irresponsible
irreverent**
irrevocable
irrigate
irritable
irruption**
Islam
island
isle**
isolate
isometric
isotope
Israel
issuance
issue
isthmus
Italian
Italy
itch
itching**
item
itemize
itinerary
its**
it's**
IUD
IV**
I've**
ivory
ivy**

184

J

jab**
jack
jackal
jackass
jacket
jackknife
jackpot
jacuzzi
jade
jag
jagged
jaguar
jail
jailbreak
jalopy
jam**
Jamaica
jamb**
jambalaya
jamboree
jangle
janitor
January
Japanese
jargon
jasmine
jaundice
jaunt**
java
javelin
jaws
Jaycee
jaywalk
jazz
jazzy
jealous**
jeans**
jeep
jeer
Jeffersonian
jejune**
jejunum**
Jekyll and
   Hyde
jell**
jellies
jelly

jeopardy
jeremiad
jerk
jersey
Jerusalem
jester**
Jesuit
jet
jet lag
jetsam
jet set
jettison
jetty
jewel**
jewels
jewelry
jewels
Jewish
Jewry**
Jews**
jib**
jibe**
jiffy
jiffybag
jig
jigger
jiggle
jigsaw
jihad
jimmy
jingle
jingo
jinks**
jinn**
jinx**
jitney
jitters
jive
job**
jobber
jockey
jockstrap
jocular
jocund
jodphurs
jog**
joggle**
joi de vivre

join
joinder
joint
joist
joke
joker
jolly
jolt
jostle
jotting
joule**
jounce
journal
journalist
journey**
joust**
jovial
jowl**
joyful
joyous
joyride
jubilant
jubilee
Judaica
Judaism
Judas
judge
judgment
judicial
judiciary
judo
jug**
juggernaut
juggle**
juggler**
jugular**
juice**
juicy
jujitsu
juju
jukebox
julep
July
jumble
jump
junction
juncture
June

jungle
junior
junk
junk bond
junket
junkie
junky
junta**
jurisdiction
jurist
jury**
just**
justice
justify
jut**
jute**
juvenile
juxtapose

K

Kaddish**
kaffee-
   klatsch
Kafkaesque
kale
kaleidoscope
kamikazi
kangaroo
kapok
Kaposi's sar-
   coma
kaput
karate
karma
kayak
kayo
kazoo
kebob
keel
keen
keep
keeper
keg
kelp
ken**
Kennedy
kennel

185

Keogh plan	kindly	knot**	lair**
kept	kindness	knotted	laissez-faire
kerchief	kindred	know**	lam**
kernel**	kinescope	knowable**	lama**
kerosene	kinesics**	knowledge	lamb**
ketch**	kinetic	knows**	lambaste
ketchup	kinetics**	knuckle	lambskin
ketone	kingdom	K.O.	lame**
ketosis	kingpin	Koel**	lamé**
kettle	kiosk	kohl**	lame duck
kewpie	kipper	kola**	lamentable
key**	kirsch	kosher	lamentation
keyboard	kissed	kris**	laminate
Keynesian	kit**	kummel	LAN
keynote	kitchen	kwashiorkor	lance
keypunch	kite**		lanced**
keystone	kith**		lancet**
khaki	kitten	**L**	landlady
kibble	kiwi	lab	landlocked
kibbutz**	Klan**	label	landlord
kibitz**	kleenex	labor	landmark
kibitzer	kleptomania	laboratory	landscape
kibosh	kludge	labyrinth	lane**
kickback	klutzy	lace	language**
kickoff	knack	lacerate	languish**
kid**	knapsack	laceration	languor
Kiddush**	knave**	lachrymose	lanolin
kidnap	knead**	lackadaisical	lantern
kidney	knee	lackey	laparoscope
kielbasa	kneecap	laconic	lapel
kill**	kneed**	lacquer	lapse
killed**	kneel**	lactation	larceny
killer	knell**	lactose	large
killjoy	knew**	lacuna	largesse
kiln**	knickknack	ladder	larva**
kilo	knife	lade**	laryngitis
kilobaud	knight**	ladies	larynx
kilobyte	knight er-	Ladino**	lascivious
kilocycle	rant	ladle	laser**
kilogram	knish	laetrile	lass**
kilohertz	knit**	lag	lassitude
kilometer	knitting	lager**	lasso
kilowatt	knives	laggard	last**
kilt**	knob**	lagging	latch
kimono	knock**	lagniappe	latchkey kid
kin**	knock-knee	lagoon	late
kindergarten	knockoffs	laid**	lately
kindle	knoll	lain**	latent

186

later**
lateral
latest
latex
lath**
lathe**
Latin
Latina**
Latino**
latitude
latter**
latticework
laud**
laudable
laudanum
laughable
laughter
launch
launder
laundry
laurel
lava**
lavaliere
lavatory
lavender
lavish
law**
lawn
laws**
lawsuit
lawyer
lax
laxative
lay**
layaway
layer**
layoff
lazar**
laziness
l'chaim
L-dopa
lea**
leach**
lead**
leader
leaf**
league
leak**

leakage
lean**
leaped
learn
lease
leased**
least**
leather
leave**
leaven
leaves
lechery
lecithin
lecture
led**
ledger
lee**
leech**
leek**
left
left-handed
leftovers
legacy
legal
legalize
legend
legerdemain
legible
legion
legionnaires'
    disease
legislature
legitimate
lei**
leisure
leisurely
leitmotiv
lemon
lemonade
length
lenient
lens
lent
lentil**
leopard
leprechaun
leprosy
lesbian

lese majesty
lesion
lessee**
lessen**
lesser**
lesson**
lessor**
lest**
lethal
lethargy
let's
letter**
lettered
letterhead
lettuce
letup
leukemia
levee**
level
leveler
lever
leverage
levitation
levy**
lewd
lexicon
liability
liable**
liaison
liar**
libel**
liberal
liberalism
libertarian
liberty
libidinous
libido
libido**
LIBOR
library
libretto
license
licentious
lichen**
lickerish**
licorice**
lie**
lief**

liege
lien**
lieu
lieutenant
lifeboat
lifeguard
lifetime
liftoff
ligament
ligature
light
lightening**
lighter**
lighthearted
lightning**
light pen
lightweight
likely
liken**
likeness
likewise
lilac
lily
limb**
limber
limbic
limbo
lime**
limelight
limit
limn**
limousine
limps
linage**
linchpin
Lincoln
lineage**
lineal**
lineament**
linear**
lineman
linen
lineup
linger
lingerie
linguine
linguist
liniment**

linkage	loathsome	loot**	lumpectomy
linked	lobby	loquacious	lunacy
links**	lobe	lord**	lunar
linoleum	lobotomy	lore**	lunatic
lint	lobster	lorgnette	luncheon
lintel**	lobster shift	lose**	luncheonette
lion	local**	loser	lung
lipstick	locale**	loss**	lupus
lip-sync	localize	lost**	lurch
liquefy	locate	lotion	lure
liqueur**	location	lottery	lurk
liquid	loch**	lotto	luscious
liquidate	lock**	loud	luster
liquor**	locket	loudspeaker	lustrous
lissome	lockjaw	lounge	lute**
list	lockout	loupe**	luxuriance**
listen	locks**	lousy	luxuriant**
litany	locomotive	lout	luxurious**
liter**	locus**	louver	luxury
literacy	locust**	Louvre	lydocaine
literal	lode**	lovable	lye**
literary	lodge**	love	lying
literati**	loft	lovely	Lyme**
literature	lofty	loving	Lyme dis-
lithium	logarithm	low**	ease
litigious	loge**	lowball	lymph
litmus	logger**	lowbrow	lymphoma
litter**	logic	low-cal	lynx**
litterbug	logo	lox**	lyre**
little	log-off	loyal	lyric
liturgical	log-on	lozenge	lysergic acid
lived**	loiter	luau	
livedo**	loload	lubricate	
livelihood	lone**	lucid	**M**
lively	loneliness	luck	macabre
livery	lonely	lucrative	macadam
lives	lonesome	lucre	macaroni
livestock	longevity	ludicrous	macaroon
livid**	longhand	lues**	mace
lizard	longitude	luftmensch	machete
llama**	long-winded	luge	Machiavel-
lo!**	loofah	luggage	lian
load**	lookism	lukewarm	machinery
loafer	lookout	lullaby	machismo
loan**	loony	lulu	macho
loanshark	loop**	lumbar**	mackerel
loath**	loophole	lumber**	mackintosh
loathe**	loose**	luminescent	macro

macrobiotic	malaprop-	mankind	Marxism
mad	ism	manned	Mary**
madame	malaria	mannequin	Maryland
made**	Malay**	manner**	mascara
mademoi-	male**	manor**	mascle**
selle	malediction	mansion	masculine
Madonna	malfeasance	mantel**	masochism
madras	malforma-	mantelpiece	masochist
maelstrom	tion	mantle**	mason**
maestro	malice	manual	masonry
Mafia	malicious	manufacture	masquerade
magazine	malign	manure	Massachu-
maggot	malignant	manuscript	setts
magic	malinger	many	massacre
magistrate	malleable	maple	massage
magma**	malnutrition	maraschino	massed**
magna**	malocclu-	marathon	masseur
magnani-	sion	marauder	masseuse
mous	malpractice	marble	massif**
magnate**	malt**	marc**	massive**
magnesium	mambo	Mardi Gras	mast**
magnet**	mammal	margarine	mastectomy
magnificence	mammary	margin	master
magnitude	mammo-	marijuana	mastermind
maharajah	gram	marine	masterpiece
mahogany	mammoth	marital**	masticate
maid**	manacle	maritime	mastica-
maidenly	manageable	mark**	tion**
mail**	manager	markdown	mastoid
mailbox	mañana	market	masturbate
mailman	mandatory	markup	masturba-
maim	mandible	marmalade	tion**
main**	mane**	maroon	material
mainframe	maneuver	marquis	maternal
mainland	manganese	marquise	maternity
mainstream	mange	Marrano	mathematics
maintain	manger	marriage**	matinée
maintenance	mangle	marriage-	matriarch
maitre d'	mania	able	matriculate
maize**	maniac	married	matrimony
majesty	manic de-	marrow	matrix
major	pressive	marry**	matronly
majority	manicotti	marsala	matter
makeup	manicure	marshal**	mattress
making	manifesto	martial**	maturation
maladjusted	manifold	martini	mature
malady	manipula-	martyr	matza
malaise	tive	marvelous	matzoh

maudlin	megabyte	meringue	microorgan-
mausoleum	megaloma-	merit	ism
maven	nia	meritocracy	microphone
maverick	megillah	merrily	microproces-
maxi	melancholy	merry**	sor
maximum	mélange	mesa	microscope
maybe**	melanin	mescaline	microsur-
may be**	melanoma	mesmerize	gery
mayonnaise	melée**	meson**	microwave
mayor	mellow	messenger	midday
maze**	melodious	messing	middle
mazeltov	melodrama	messy	midnight
mazuma	melon	metabolism	midst**
mea culpa	meltdown	metal**	midterm
meadow	member	metallic	midwife
meager	membrane	metamor-	mien**
mean**	memento	phosis	might**
meanness	memoir	metaphor	mighty**
meant	memorable	metaphysics	migraine
measles	memoran-	metastasis	migrate
measure	dum	meteor**	mike
meat**	memorial	meteoro-	mil**
meat market	memory	logy**	mile**
mecca	menace	meth	mileage
Mecca	ménage à	methadone	milieu
mechanic	trois	methamphet-	military
mechanize	menagerie	amine	militate**
meclizine	menial	method	militia
medal**	meningitis	Methodist	mill**
medallion	menopause	meticulous	millenary**
meddle**	menorah	métier**	millennium
meddler**	Mensa**	metric	milligram**
media	mensch	metro	millimeter
mediate	menses**	metrology**	millinery**
mediation	menstruate	metropoli-	millionaire
Medicaid	menstrua-	tan	mime**
Medicare	tion	mettle**	mimosa
medicine	mental	mews**	mince**
medieval	mention	Mexican	mind**
mediocre	menu	Mexico	mine**
mediocrity	mercenary	mezzanine	mined**
meditate	merchandise	miasma	miner**
Mediterra-	merchant	Michigan	mineral
nean	mercury	micro	mingle
medium	mercy	microbi-	mini
medlar**	merely	ology	miniature
medley	merge	microchip	minicom-
meet**	merger	microfilm	puter

minimize
minimum
minion**
miniseries
minister
minks**
Minnesota
minor**
minority
minoxidil
mints**
minus
minuscule
minute
minutia
minx**
minyan**
miracle
mirage**
Mirandize
mirror
mirth
misanthrope
misappropri-
ate
miscarriage
miscast
miscella-
neous
mischief
mischievous
misconcep-
tion
misconduct
misde-
meanor
miser
miserable
misery
misfit
misfortune
misgiving
mishap
mislaid
misogyny
Miss**
missal**
missed**

misses**
missile**
missing
mission
missionary
Mississippi
Missouri
misspell
misstate
misstep
missus**
mist**
mistake
mister
mistress
mistrial
misunder-
stand
mite**
mitigate**
mitomycin
C
mitosis
mitten
mixture
mnemonic
moan
moat**
mob
mobbed
mobile
mobilize
moccasin
mocha
mockery
mockup
modal**
modality
mode**
model**
modem
moderate
modern
modernism
modest
modifier
modulate

modus ope-
randi
mogul
moisture
molar
molasses
mole
molecule
molestation
mollify
molt**
momentous
momentum
mommy
track
monarch
monastery
Monday
monetary
money
monitor
monk
monkey
mono-
chrome
monogamist
monolith
monologue
monopoly
monorail
monotone
monotonous
monsieur
monster
monstrous
montage
month
monument
moor**
Moor**
moose**
moot**
mope
moral**
morale**
morality
morass
morays**

morbid
morbidity
more**
moreover
mores**
morgue
moribund
Mormon
morn**
morning**
Morocco
moron
morphine
morsel
mortal**
mortality
mortally
mortar
mortgage
mortify
mortuary
mosaic
mosh
mosque
mosquito
mossy
most
mote**
mother**
motif**
motion
motivate
motive**
motor
motorcycle
mottled
motto
mountain
mourn**
mournful
mourning**
mouse**
mousse**
mouthpiece
mouthwash
mouton**
movement
movie

mowed** muscular naïveté nectarine
moxie dystrophy naked née**
mozzarella muse** nameless need**
Mrs.** museum nanny needle
Ms** mushroom nanosecond needy
mss.** music naphtha nefarious
mucilage musical** naphtha** negate
mucous musicale** narcissist negative
mucus Muslim** narcissistic neglect
mudder** muslin** narcolepsy negligee
muddy mussel** narcotics negligence
muff mustache narration negotiate
muffin mustard** narrative Negro
mug muster narrow Negroes
mugger mustered** narrowband neigh**
Muhamma- mustn't narrow- neighbor
dan mutant minded neighbor-
mulatto mutation nasal hood
mulish mute** nascent neither**
mullah mutiny NASDAQ nemesis
mul- mutton** nastiness neo
ligatawny mutual nasturtium neologism
multicul- muumuu national neonatal
tural muzzle native nephew
multimedia myasthenia nativity nephritis
multimillion- gravis natty nepotism
aire myelo- naturally nerd
multina- gram** nature nerve
tional myeloma naturopathy nervous
multiple scle- myopia naught** nestle
rosis myopic naughty** nether**
multiplex myrtle nausea network
multiplier mysterious nauseous neural
multiply mystery naval** neuralgia
multitasking mystic nave** neuritis
multitude mysticism navel** neurologist
mumble mystify navigable neuron
mundane myth navy neurosis
muni mythical nay** neurotic
municipal né** neuter
mural Neanderthal neutral
murder **N** nearsighted neutralize
murderer nab neat neutron
murky nadir nebulous new**
murmur NAFTA** necessary news**
Murphy's nagged necessity newscaster
Law nail necrology newspaper
muscle** naïve necromancy newspeak

192

newt
next
nexus
Niagara
nibble**
nice
nicely
niche**
nick**
nickel
nickname
nicotine
niece
Nielsen's
night**
nightclub
nightfall
nightmare
nihilism
nil
nimble
nimbly**
NIMBY**
nineteen
ninety
ninth
nipple
nirvana
nit**
nitrogen
no**
nob**
Nobel**
noble**
noblesse
    oblige
nock**
nocturn**
nocturnal
nocturne**
nod**
node**
nodule**
noes**
no-fault
no-frills
no-hitter
noise

no-knock
noload
nomad
nom de
    plume
nominal
nominate
nonchalant
noncom
nondeduct-
    ible
none**
nonentity
nonexempt
nonfat
nonpareil
nonplus
nonprofit
nonsectarian
nonsense
non sequitur
nonsizist
nonsupport
non-U
nonviolence
noodle**
nook**
noose**
norm
normal
norming
north
northerly
nose**
nosebleed
nosegay
no-show
nostalgic
nostril
nosy
not**
notable
notary
notation
notch
note**
notebook
noteworthy

nothing
notice
noticeable
notify
notion
notorious
nougat**
noun
nourish
nouveau
    riche
novel
November
novice
Novocaine
nowhere
noxious
nozzle**
nubile
nuclear
nucleus
nudge
nudist
nudity
nugget**
nuisance
nuke**
nullification
numb
number
numeral
numeric
numerical
numerous
numskull
nun**
nunnery
nuptial
nurse
nursemaid
nursery
nurture
nutrition
nutty
nuzzle**
nybble**
nymph

nymphoma-
    niac
NYSE

O

oaf**
oar**
oasis
oat**
oath**
obbligato
obdurate
obedience
obeisance
obese
obesity
obey
obfuscate
obit**
obiter dic-
    tum
obituary
object**
objection
objection-
    able
objective
objet d'art
obligation
obligatory
oblige
oblique**
obliterate
oblivious**
oblong
obloquy**
obnoxious
oboe
obscene
obscuran-
    tism
obscure
obsequies
obsequious
observance
observation
observatory

observe
obsess**
obsession
obsolescent
obsolete
obstacle
obstetrician
obstinate
obstreperous
obstruct**
obstruction
obtain
obtrusive
obtuse
obverse
obviate
obvious**
occasion
occasional
Occident**
occlusion
occult
occupancy
occupant
occupation
occupied
occur**
occurred
occurrence
ocean
oceanogra-
  phy
ocher**
o'clock
octal
octane
octave
October
octogenar-
  ian
octopus
ocular
oculist
odd
odd lot
ode**
odious
odometer

odor
odorous
odyssey
OECD
Oedipus
Oedipus
  complex
OEM
oenophile
o'er**
oeuvre
of**
off**
offal**
offbeat
offense
offer
offering
offhand
office**
officer
official
officious
off-line
offload
off-price
off-putting
offset
offshore
offspring
off-the-
  record
off year
often
ogle
ogre
oh**
ohm
oil
ointment
okra**
old
old-boy
  network
older**
old-
  fashioned

old-girl
  network
old-line
old-timer
olé
olfactory
oligarchy
oligopoly
olive
Olympic
om
ombudsman
omelet
ominous
omission
omit
omnibus
omnipotent
omnipresent
omniscient
omnivorous
once**
oncogene
oncologist
oncology
one**
one-liner
one-man
onerous
oneself
one-sided
one-up
ongoing
onion**
on-line
onlooker
only
onoma-
  topoeia
onshore
onslaught
ontogeny**
ontology**
onus
oocyte
ooze
opaque
op. cit.**

OPEC
op-ed
open-ended
opener
opening
open-
  minded
openness
opera**
operant
operate
operative
operator
operetta
ophthal-
  mologist
ophthalmol-
  ogy
opiate
opinion
opium
opponent
opportune
opportunist
opportunity
oppose
opposite**
opposi-
  tion**
oppress
oppressor
opprobrium
opry**
opt**
optic
optical
optician
optimism
optimum
option
optional
optometrist
opulent
opus
or**
oracle**
oral**
orange

orator
orbit**
orchard
orchestra
orchid
ordain
ordeal
order
orderly
ordinance**
ordinary
ordination
ordnance**
ore**
organ**
organic
organism**
organist**
organization
organize
orgasm**
orgy
orient
oriental
orientation
orifice**
origin**
original
ornament
ornate
ornery
ornithologist
orphan
orthodontist
orthodox
orthopedist
Oscar
oscillate**
oscilloscope
osculate**
osculatory
OSHA
osmosis
ossify
ostensible
ostentatious
osteopath
osteoporosis

ostracize
ostrich
OTC
other
otherwise
otter**
ottoman
ouch
ought**
ounce**
our**
ours
ourselves
oust
out**
outage
outboard
outbreak
outcast
outclass
outcome
outcry
outdated
outdo
outdoor
outer
outfield
outfit
outgoing
outing
outlaw
outlay
outlet
outline
outlook
out-of-date
outpatient
outpouring
output
outrageous
outreach
outsider
outspoken
outstanding
outward
outwit
oval

ovary
over
overall
overbearing
overbite
overboard
overcome
overcompen-
sate
overdo**
overdue**
overexpo-
sure
overhead
overkill
overlie**
overlook
overly**
overnight
overrate
overreach
override
overrule
overrun
overseer
overt**
over-the-
counter
overthrow
overtime
overture
overview
overwhelm
overwrought
overzealous
ovoid**
ovulate
ovulation
ow**
owe**
owed**
own**
oxen
oxygen
oxymoron
oyster
ozone

P

pacemaker
Pacific
pacification
pacifist
pacify
package
packed**
pact**
pad**
paddy**
padlock
padre
paean**
paella
pageant
paginate
pagoda
paid
pail**
pain**
painstaking
painter
pair**
paisley
pajama
Pakistan
palace
palatable
palate**
palatial
pale**
paleon-
tology
Palestine
palette**
palindrome
palisade
pall**
pallbearer
pallet**
palliative
pall-mall**
pallor
palm
palmistry
palomino
palpable

palpitate
palsy
paltry**
pamphlet
pan**
panacea
panache
panatella
pancake
pancreas
panda**
pandemic
pandemonium
pander**
pane**
panel
panhandle
panicky
panjandrum
panoply
panorama
pansy
pantheism
pantomime
pap
papacy
paparazzi
papaverine
paperback
papier-
  mâché
papilloma
paprika
parable
parabola
parachute
parade
paradigm
paradise
paradox
paraffin
paragraph
parakeet
paraldehyde
parallel
paralysis
paralyze

paramecium
parameter
paramount
paranoia
paraphernalia
paraphrase
paraplegic
paraprofessional
parapsychology
parasite
paratha
parathion
paratrooper
parcel
parcheesi
pardon
pare**
parent
parenthesis
paresis
parfait
parietal
pari-mutuel
pari passu
parish**
parity**
parking
parking
  meter
Parkinson's
parlay**
parley**
parliament
parlor
Parmesan
parochial
parody**
parole**
parquet
parrot
parse
parson
parthenogenesis
partial

participate
participle
particle
particular
particulars
parties
partisan
partition**
partner
parturition
party
passable**
passage
passé
passed**
passenger
passible**
passion
passive
Passover
passport
password
past**
pasta
pastel
pasteurize
pastille
pastime
pasting
pastor**
pastoral**
pastorale**
pastrami
pastry
pasture**
patchwork
pâté**
pâté de foie
  gras
patella
patent
paternal
pathetic
pathing
pathology
pathos**
patience**
patient

patients**
patina
patio
patriarch
patrimony
patriot
patriotism
patrol
patron
patronage
patronize
pattern
patty**
paucity
Paul**
pause**
pavement
pavilion
paving
paw**
paws**
payback
paycheck
payee
payload
payment
payoff
payola
payout
payroll**
PC
peace**
peach
peak**
peaked**
peal**
peanut
pear**
pearl**
peasant
pecan
peccadillo
pecks**
pecs**
pectoral
peculiar
pecuniary
pedagogue

196

pedal** | Pennsyl-vania | perjury | petite
pedant | penny** | perks | petition**
peddle** | penology | permanent | petit mal
pederast | pension | permeate | petrify
pedestal | pent** | permissible | petroleum
pedestrian | Pentagon | permit | petticoat
pediatrics | pentagram | permutation | petty
pediculosis | pentameter | pernicious | petulant
pedigree | Pentateuch | peroxide | pew
pedophilia | pentathlon | perp | phallocracy
peek** | Pentecostal | perpendicu-lar | phallus
peeked** | pentobarbi-tal | perpetrate | phantasm**
peel** | pent-up | perpetrator | phantom
peephole | penurious | perpetual | phantom limb
peer** | peon** | perpetuity | Pharaoh
peerless | people | perplex | pharmaceuti-cal
peevish | pepper | perquisite | pharmacy
pegged | peptic | persecute** | pharyngitis
peignoir | per** | persevere | pharynx
pellagra | per annum | persistence | phase**
pellet** | perceive | person | phenobarbital
pell-mell | percent | personal** | phenomenal
pelvis | perception | personality | phenome-non
pen** | perch | persona non grata | phial**
penal** | percolator | personnel** | philanderer
penalty | percussion | perspec-tive** | philan-thropy
penance** | per diem | perspica-cious | philately
penchant | peremptory | perspiration | philhar-monic
pencil | perennial | perspire | Philippines
pendant** | perfect** | persuade | philosophy
pendent** | perfecta | pertain | philter**
pendulum | perfidious | pertinent | phlebitis
penetrate | perforate | perturb | phlegm
penetration | perform | peruse | phobia
penguin | perfume | pervade | Phoenix
penicillin | perfunctory | perverse** | phonetic
penile** | perhaps | perversion | phonics
peninsula | peril | pervert | phonograph
penis | perimeter | peso | phony
penitent | period | pessary | phosphate
penitentiary | periodontal | pessimist | phosphores-cence
penknife | peripheral | pesticide |
penmanship | periphery | petal |
pennant | periscope | |
penne** | perish** | |
penned** | peritonitis | |
penniless | | |

197

phosphorus
photo
photogenic
photograph
photography-
phy
photosynthe-
sis
phrase**
phreak**
phrenetic**
phrenology
physic**
physical**
physically
physician
physics
physiog-
nomy
physiology
physiother-
apy
physique**
pi**
pianist
piano
piazza
pica**
picaresque**
picayune
piccolo
picket
pickle
pickpocket
picks**
pickup
picnic
picture
pictur-
esque**
pidgin**
pie**
piece**
piecemeal
piecework
pied-à-terre
pier**
pierce

piety
pigeon**
piggin**
piggyback
pigment
piker**
pilfer
pilgrim
piling
pillage
pillar**
pillbox
pillory
pillow**
pilot
pimento
pimple
pin**
pince-nez
pincers
pineapple
pink eye
pinnacle**
pinochle**
pinpoint
pinstripe
pinup
pioneer
pious**
pipeline
piping
piquant
pique**
piqued**
pirouette
pistachio
pistil**
pistol**
piston
pitch
pitcher**
pitfall
pitiful
pittance
pituitary
pity
Pius**
pivot

pixel
pizza
placard
placate
placebo
placement
placenta
placid
plagiarism
plague**
plaid
plain**
plaintiff**
plaintive**
plait**
plane**
planed**
planet**
planetarium
planned**
plant**
plantation
plaque**
plasma
plaster
plastered
plastic
plate**
plateau
platelet
platform
platinum
platitude
Platonic
platoon
platter
plaudit
plausible
playa**
playback
player**
playoff
playwright
plaza
plaza**
plea
plead

pleas**
pleasant
please**
pleasure
pleat
plebe
plebeian
plebiscite
pledge
plenary
plentiful
plenty
plethora
pleurisy
pliable
pliers
plight
plod**
plodding
plop
plot**
plow
ploy
pluck
plug
plum**
plumb**
plumber
plunder
plural
pluralism
plus
plutonium
ply
plywood
PMS
pneumatic
pneumonia
pneu-
monic**
pocket
pocketbook
podiatry
podium
poem
poet
poetry
pogrom**

198

poignant
poinsettia
pointless
poise
poison
poison pill
poker**
polar
Polaris
polarize
Polaroid
pole**
polemic
police
policy
polio
poli-sci
polish
polite
politically
   correct
politics
polity
polka**
poll**
pollen
pollute
pollution
Pollyanna
poltergeist
polycentric
polyester
polyethylene
polygamy**
polyglot
polygon
polygraph
polygyny**
polymer
polyp
polyun-
   saturated
pomade
pompadour
pompous
poncho
Pontiff
pontiff

ponytail
pool**
poolside
poop
pooped
poplar**
populace**
popular**
population
populist
populous**
porcelain
pore**
pores**
pornogra-
   phy
porous
porpoise**
porridge
portable**
portal
portend**
porter
portfolio
porthole
portico
portion**
portrait
portray
poseur
position
positive
positron
posse
possess
possession
possible
postage
postal
postcard
posterior
posterity
posthumous
postman
postmaster
postmortem
post office
postpaid

postpone
posture
potable**
potassium
potato
potent
potential
pothole
potion**
potpourri
pottery
pouch
poultice
poultry**
pounce
pound
pour**
pout
poverty
powder
power
practical
practice**
practise**
pragmatic
prairie
praise
pray**
prayer
preach
preacher
preamble
preamplifier
precarious
precaution
precede**
prece-
   dence**
precedent**
precedents**
precept
precinct
precious
precipice
precipitate
précis**
precise**
precisian**

precision**
preclude
precocious
predator
predecessor
predicament
predicate
predict
predictable
prednisone
predominant
preemie
preeminent
preempt
prefabricate
preface
prefect**
prefer**
preference
preferred
pregnant
prejudice
preliminary
prelude
premarital
premature
premen-
   strual
premier**
premiere**
premise
premium
premonition
preoccupa-
   tion
preparation
prepare
preponder-
   ant
preposi-
   tion**
preposterous
prepubes-
   cent
prepuce
prerogative
presage
Presbyterian

prescient
prescribe**
prescription**
presence**
present
presentation
presentiment**
presentment**
presents**
preserve**
preside
president**
presidents**
pressure
prestige
presume
presumption
pretend**
prettify
pretty
pretzel
prevail
prevalent
prevaricate
prevention
preview
previous
prey**
priapism
priceless
prickly
pries**
priest
prima donna
prima facie
primal
  scream
primarily
primary
primate
primitive
prime
primer**
primeval
primitive

prince**
princess
principal**
principle**
prints**
priority
prism
prison
privacy
private
privatization
privatize
privilege
privy
prize**
pro
proactive
probable
probate
probation
probe
probity
problem
pro bono
procaine
procedure
proceed**
process
procession
processor
pro-choice
proclaim
procrastinate
procreate
proctologist
proctor
proctoscope
procure
prod**
prodigious
prodigy**
produce
product
production
productivity
profess
profession

professor
proffer**
proficient
profile
profit**
profligate
profound
profuse
progenitor
progeny
progesterone
prognosis
prognosticate
program**
programmer
progress
prohibit
project
projection
prole
pro-life
proliferate
prolific
prologue
prom
promenade
prominent
promiscuous
promise
promissory
prompt
pronounce**
pronouns**
pronto
pronunciation
propaganda
propagate
propel
propensity
proper
property**
prophecy
prophecy**
prophesy**
prophet**

prophylactic**
prophylaxis**
propitious
proponent
proportion
proposal
propose
proposition**
proprietary**
proprietor
propriety**
propulsion
prosaic
proscribe**
proscription**
prosecute**
prospect
prospective**
prospectus
prostate**
prosthesis
prostitute
prostrate**
protagonist
protect
protégé**
protein
protest
Protestant
protocol
proton
protoplasm
prototype
protrude
proud**
prove
proverb
provide
providence
province
provincial
provision

proviso
provoke
provost
proximity
proxy
prude**
prudence
prurient
pruritis
pry
psalm
pseudo
pseudonym
psittacosis
psoriasis
psyche
psychedelic
psychiatrist
psychic
psycho
psychoanaly-
sis
psychobabb-
le
psychology
psychosis
psychoso-
matic
psychother-
apy
psycopath
ptarmigan
pterodactyl
pterosaur
ptomaine
pub
puberty
pubes
pubescent
pubic**
public**
publication
publicity
pudding
pudgy
pueblo
puerile
Puerto Rico

pugnacious
puisne**
pulchritude
pull**
pullet
pulley
pulmonary
pulp
pulpit
pulsar
pulse
pulverize
pummel
pumper-
nickel
pumpkin
punctilious
punctual
punctuate
puncture
pungent
punish
punitive
punk
punks
punned**
punt**
puny**
pupal**
pupil**
puppet
purchase
pure**
purée
purgatory
purge
Purim
purl**
purloin
purple
purport
purpose**
purr**
purse
purser
pursue
pursuit
purview

pus**
push-up
pusillani-
mous
puss**
pussyfoot
put**
putative
putrefy
putrid
putsch
putt**
puzzle
pyelitis
pyorrhea
pyramid
pyre
pyromaniac
pyrotechnics
Pyrrhic vic-
tory

Q

quack**
quad
quadrangle
quadrant
quadratic
quadrille**
quadril-
lion**
quadripar-
tite
quadriplegic
quadro-
phonic
quadru-
ped**
quadruple**
quadrup-
let**
quaff
quake
Quaker
qualify

quality**
qualm
quantity**
quantum
quarantine
quark**
quarrel
quarreled
quarry**
quarter
quarterback
quarterly
quartet
quarts**
quartz**
quasar
quasi**
quatrain
quaver**
quay**
quean**
queasy**
queen**
queer
queerest**
quench
querist**
QUERTY
query**
question
question-
naire
queue**
quibble
quiche
quick
quicksand
quid
quid pro
quo
quiet**
quietude**
quietus**
quill
quince**
quinella
quinine

quinsy** radiologist rapt** real estate
quintet radish rapture realism
quints** radium rarebit** reality
quintuplet radius rarefy realize**
quire** radix rarely really
quirk** radon rarity realm
quit** raffia raspberry Realtor
quite** raffle ratable ream
quiver** raft ratchet reap
quixotic raga** rate reappear
quiz raged rather reason
quizzed ragged ratify reasonable
quizzes raglan rating reassure
quizzical ragout** ratio rebait**
quorum railing ratiocination rebate**
quota** railroad ration rebel
quotation rain** rational** rebellion
quote** rainbow rationale** rebirthing
quotidian raincoat rationalize rebound**
quotient rainmaker rattle rebuff
rainy rattlesnake rebuke
raise** rattrap rebuttal
R raisin ratty recalcitrate
rabbi raison d'être raucous recall
rabbis** rakish raunchy recapitulate
rabbit** rally ravage recapture
rabble RAM** ravel recede**
rabid** Ramadan raven receipt
rabies** ramble ravenous receivable
raccoon ramification ravish receive
race rampage ravishing receiver
racetrack rampant raw** recent**
racial rancid rayon reception
racism random rays** receptionist
racist range raze** receptor
racket ranking razor recertify
racketeer rankle reach recess
raconteur ransack react recession
racy ransom reaction recessive
radar rap** reactionary recidivism
radial rapacious reactor recipe
radiant rape read** recipient
radiation rapist reader reciprocal
radiator rapped** readily reciprocity
radical rappel read-only recital
radio rapport ready recitation
radioactivity rapproche- reaffirm reckless
radioisotope ment real** reckon

202

reclamation
recline
recluse**
recognize
recollect
recombinant
  DNA
recommend
recompense
reconcile
reconnais-
  sance
reconnoiter
reconstruct
record
recorder
recoup
recovery
recreation
recrimina-
  tory
recruit
rectal
rectangle
rectify
rectum
recuperate
recurrence
recuse**
recycle
red**
redden
redecorate
redeem
redemption
red-handed
redhead
red herring
redirect
redline
redound**
redress
red tape
reduce
reducible
redundant
reed**

reek**
reel**
reelection
reenact
reenforce
reentry
reestablish
reevaluate
reexamine
refer
referee**
reference
referendum
refined
refinement
reflection
reflex
reform
reformation
refraction
refrain
refresher
refrigerator
refuel
refuge
refugee
refund
refurbish
refusal
refuse
refute
regal**
regale**
regard
regardless
regatta
regency
reggae**
regime
regiment
region
register
registrar
registration
regression
regrettable
regular
regulate

regurgitate
rehabilitate
rehearsal
rehearse
reign**
rein**
reincarna-
  tion
reindeer
reinforce-
  ment
reinvent
reissue
REIT
reiterate
reject
rejoice
rejuvenate
relapse
relater**
relation
relative
relator**
relax
release
relegate
relent
relentless
relevant
reliable
reliant
relic**
relict**
relied
relief
relies**
relieve
religious
relinquish
relish
relocate
reluctance
rely
REM
remain
remark
remarkable
rematch

remedial
remedy
remember
reminisce
remission
remit
remittance
remnant
remonstrate
remorse
remorseful
remote
removable
removal
remunerate
renaissance
renascence
rendezvous
renegade
renege
renew
renounce
renovate
renown
rental
reorder
reorganize
repair
reparable
reparation
repartee
repatriate
repeal
repeat
repel
repellent
repent
repercus
repert
repert
repe
rep
r
r

reply**	resistance	retro	rhinoceros
report	resistible	retroactive	rhizome
reporter	resolution	retrofit	rhododen-
repose	resolve	retrogres-	dron
repository	resonance	sion	rhubarb
repossess	resort	retrospect	rhumba
reprehensi-	resource	retroussé	rhyme**
ble	respectable	retrovirus	rhythm**
represent	respect-	return	ribald
repressed	fully**	reunion	ribbon
reprieve	respec-	reunite	rich
reprimand	tively**	revaluation	rickety
reprisal	respirator	reveal	rickshaw
reprise	respite	reveille**	ricochet
reproach	response	revelation	ricotta
reprobate	responsible	revelry**	riddance
reproduce	rest**	revenge	riddle
reproductive	restaurant	revenue	ridge
reprove	restitution	revere	ridiculous
reptile	restoration	reverend**	riffle**
republic	restrain	reverent**	rifle**
Republican	restrict	reverie**	rig
repudiate	restriction	reversible	right**
repugnant	restrictive	revert	righteous
repulsive	restructure	review**	rightful
reputable	result	revise	right-to-
request	resume	revision	work
requiem	resumption	revisionism	rigid
require	resurrection	revival	rigmarole
requisite	resuscitate	revocation	rigor
requittal	retail	revoke	rigorous
⸱lable	retain	revolt	rime**
d**	retaliate	revolution	ring**
	retard	revolve	ringer
	retch**	revolver	ringworm
	retention	revue**	rinse
	⸱icent	revulsion	rinsing
		reward	riot
		rewind	riotous
		rewrite	ripe
		rhapsody	ripen
		rheostat	rip-off
		rhetoric	ripple
		rheum**	risc chip
		rheumatism	rise
		rhinestone	rising
		rhinitis	risqué
			rite**

sion
ure
ory
tion
itive
acement
play**
plish
eplenish
replete

ritual
rival
rivet
road**
roadblock
roam**
roar**
roaring
roast
robber**
robbery
robin
robot
roc**
rock**
rock and roll
Rockefeller
rocket
rococo
rode**
rodent
rodeo
roe**
Roentgen
rogue
roguish
roil**
role**
roleplay
roll**
rollout
roll out**
rollover**
roll over**
ROM**
Roman
romance
Rome**
roofs
room**
roomer**
roommate
Roosevelt
root**
Rorschach
rosary
rose**
rosé**

Rosh Ha-
  shanah
rosin
rosy
rotary
rotate
rote**
rotten
roué
rouge
rough**
roughneck
roulette
rouse**
route**
routine
roving
row**
rowdy
rowed**
rows**
royal**
royally
rubber**
rubbish
rubeola
rudder
rude**
rue
rued**
ruff**
ruffian
ruin**
ruler
rumble
rummage
rummy
rumor**
runaway
rundown**
run down**
run-down
rune**
rung**
runner
running
rupture
rural

rushes
russet
Russia
rustbelt
rustic
rustle
rusty
Rwanda
rye**

S
Sabbat**
Sabbath**
sabbatical
sabotage
saboteur
sac**
saccharin
sachet**
sack**
sacrament
sacred
sacrifice
sacrilegious
sadist
safari
safe
safety
saffron
sage
said
sail**
saint
sake**
saki**
salacious
salad
salami
salary**
sale**
salesperson
saliva
salmon
salmonella
salon**
saloon**
salsa

salud**
salutation
salute**
salvage**
salvation
salve
Samaritan
samba
sample
samurai
sanctimoni-
  ous
sanction
sanctity
sandbag
sandlot
sandstone
sandwich
sane**
sanguine
sanitary**
sanitation
sanitory**
sanity
santeria
saphire
sapphire
sarcastic
sarge**
sarsaparilla
sashay**
sassy
Satan**
Satanism
sateen**
satellite
satin**
satire**
satisfaction
satisfactory
saturated
Saturday
satyr**
sauce**
saucy
Saudi Ara-
  bia
sauerkraut

sausage
sauté
savage
saver**
saving
savior**
Saviour**
savor**
savvy
saw**
sawed-off
saxophone
says
scab
scalable
scam**
scan**
scandal
scanner
scapegoat
scar
scarce
scarcely
scarcity
scare
scarf
scavenger
scenario
scene**
scenery
scenic
scents**
schedule
schematic
scheme
schism
schlock
schmuck
schnaps
scholar
scholastic
school
schoolmate
schooner
sciatica
science
sci-fi
scintillate

scissors
sclerosis
scofflaw
scone
scope
scotch
scout
scrabble
scratch
scream
screw
scrip**
script**
Scripture
scroll
scrub
scrupulous
SCSI port
scuba
scull**
sculptor**
sculpture**
scum
scurrilous
scuttle
scythe
sea**
seal
sealing**
seam**
seamen**
sear**
search
seas**
season
seatbelt
secede
secession
second
second-rate
secret
secretary
secretive
sects**
secular
secure
securities
security

sedan
sedative
sedentary
Seder
seduce
see**
seed**
seedy
seeing
seem**
seen**
seer**
sees**
segregate
segue
seine**
seismic
seismograph
seize**
seizure
seldom
select
self-
    discipline
self-esteem
self-help
selfish
sell**
seller**
seltzer
selvage**
selves
semantics
semen**
semester
semiauto-
    matic
seminar
seminary
Semitic
senator
senior**
señor**
sense**
senseless
senses**
sensitive
sensitivity

sensor
sentence
sentiment
separate
Sephardim
September
sequel
sequence
serendipity
serf**
serge**
sergeant
serial**
series
serif
serious
sermon
service
serviceable
sesame
session**
settee
settler**
settlor**
seventh
several
severe
sew**
sex**
sexcapade
sexism
sexy
shack
shake**
shalom
shampoo
shamus
shanty**
shareware
sharif**
shear**
sheath
shed**
she'd**
sheer**
sheik**
shelter
shelves

206

shepherd
sherbet
sheriff**
shield
shillelagh
shining
shipment
shipped
shirk**
shirt**
shish kebab
shmear
shock
shoe**
shoestring
shofar**
shone**
shoo**
shoot**
short
shorthand
shot
should
shoulders
shouldn't
shove
shown**
shriek**
shrike**
shrine
shrubbery
shtick**
shun
shutdown
shutout
shuttle
si**
sibil
sibling
sic**
sick**
sickle
sickly
side**
sidearm
sidebar
sideline
sidetrack

SIDS
siege
sieve
sighed**
sighs**
sight**
sign**
signature
signet**
significant
silence
silhouette
silicon
silicone
silver
silverware
similar
SIMM
simulate
sin
since
sincere
sincerely
sine**
sinecure
singeing**
singing**
single
sinus
sis
sisterhood
site**
situation
sixth
size**
sizzle
skateboard
skein
skeleton
skeptical
skew
skiff
skillful
skull**
slack
slacks
slain
slaughter

Slav**
slave**
slavery
slay**
sleigh**
sleight**
slight**
slim
slippery
sloe**
slope
slow**
slowdown
sluggish
smother
smudge
smug
snack
snafu
snapshot
snarl
snorkel
snort
snowbird
snowmobile
so**
soaps
soar**
social
socialist
society
sociology
sociopath
sodality**
sodium
sofa
soften
software
solace
solar
sold**
solder**
soldier**
sole**
soled**
solemn
solenoid

solicit
solidarity**
solo
solution
some**
somebody
someone**
some one**
son**
sonata
soon
soothe
sophisticate
sophomore
sore**
sorrow
sorry
sought
soul**
sound
source**
southern
souvenir
sovereign
sovereignty
sow**
spaghetti
Spanish
sparrow
spasm
spastic
spat
speaker
speaker-
phone
spear**
special**
speciality**
specialty
specie**
species**
specify
specimen
specious
spectacle
spectacular
spectator
spectrum

speculate
speech
speed
speller
sperm
sphere**
sphinx
spiffy
spin
spinoff
spiral
spirit
spiritual
splash
sponsor
spoof
spooler
sportscast
sportswear
spotlight
spousal
spouse
spree
spryly
spumoni
spur
spurious
spy
squad
squalid
square
squash
squat
squeeze
Sri Lanka
stab
stability
staff**
staid**
stair**
stake**
stakeout
stale
stalk**
stamp
stampede
standard
standby

stanza
staph**
staphylococ-
  cus
starboard
stare**
stark
starship
startup
statement
static
stating
stationary**
stationery**
statistic
stats
statue**
stature**
status
status quo
statute**
stayed**
steak**
steal**
stealth
stealthy
steel**
stein
stench
step**
steppe**
stereo
stereotype
sterilize
stick**
stiff
stigma
stile**
stiletto
stimulus
stipend
stipulate
stock
stockbroker
stocks
stodgy**
stogie**
stomach

stooge**
stopped
storage
stork**
story
straddle
straight**
strait**
strait jacket
strategic
streaker
strength
strenuous
stretch
strictly
stricture**
strife
strike-
  breaker
striptease
strobe
stroke
structure**
strudel
struggle
stubble
study
studying
stuff
stupid
stupor
style**
stylus
suave
sublimate
sublime
subliminal
submarine
subordinate
suborn
subpoena
subscription
subsistence
subtile**
subtitle**
subtle**
subtract
suburb**

suburban
subversive
succeed
success
successor
succinct
succor**
succumb
sucker**
sued**
suede**
sufficient
suffix
suffrage
sugar
suggest
suggestion
suit**
suite**
suitor
sulfa**
sulfur**
sulphur**
sum**
summary**
summery**
summit
summons
sumptuous
sun**
sundae**
Sunday**
super
superb**
supercom-
  puter
superfluous
superintend-
  ent
superior
superman
supernatural
supersede
superstitious
supervise
supplies
supply
support

suppose	syndication	tantrum	technical
suppress	synergetics	tape**	technics**
sure	synonym	taper**	technique
surf**	synopsis	tapeworm	techniques**
surface	syntax	tapir**	technology
surfeit	synthetic	tarantella**	tedious
surfing	syringe	tarantula**	tee**
surge**	syrup	tardy	teem**
surgeon	system	tare**	teenager
surgery		target	teeter
surgical		tariff	teeth**
surmise	**T**	tarnish	teethe**
surplice**	tab	taro**	telecast
surplus**	taberbacle	tarot**	telecommun-
surpress	tableau**	tartar**	ication
surprise	tablespoon	tartare**	telecompute
surrogate	tablet	Tarter**	telegram
surround	tabloid**	tasteless	telemarket-
surveillance	taboo	tasting	ing
survey	tabulate	Tater**	telephone
survival	tacit	tatter**	telescope
survive	tacked**	tattered	telethon
suspect	tackle	tattle	television
suspend	tacks**	tattoo	telex
suspicion	taco	taught**	telltale
swayed**	tact**	taunt**	temerity
swear	tactics	taupe**	temp**
sweatshirt	tactile	taut**	tempera**
sweatshop	taffeta	tavern	tempera-
sweeps	tail**	tawdry	ment
sweepstakes	taillight	tax**	temperance
sweet**	tailor	taxable	temperature
sweetheart	taint**	tax lien	template
swirl	take-out	taxpayer	temporal
sword	takeover	T-bills	lobe
swordfish	taking	t-cell	temporarily
sycophant	talc**	tea**	temporary
syllable	tale**	teach	tempt**
syllabus	talent	team**	temptation
sylph	talk**	teammate	tempura**
symbol**	Talmud	teamster	tenable
symmetrical	tamale	teamwork	tenacious
symmetry**	tamper	tear**	tenacity
sympathy	tampon	tearful	tenant**
symphony	tandoori	teas**	tendency
symptom	tangent	tease**	tendentious
synagogue	tangible	teaspoon	tenderfoot
syndicate	tantalize		

tender-
  hearted
tendinitis
tendon
tenement
tenet**
tenor**
tension
tentacle
tentative
tenuous
tenure**
tepee
tepid
tequila
terabyte
teriyaki
terminal
terminate
termite
terms
tern**
terra**
terrace
terra cotta
terrain
terrestrial
terrible
terribly
terrific
terrify
territorial
territory
terror**
terrorist
terse
tersely
tertiary
testament
testicle
testify
testimony
testis
testosterone
test tube
test-tube
  baby
tetanus

tête-à-tête
tetracycline
text
textbook
textile
texture
thalamus
thalidomide
than**
Thanksgiv-
  ing
theater
theft
their**
theirs
theme
themselves
then**
thence**
theology
theorem
theoretical
theory
therapeutic
there**
thereafter
thereby
therefor**
therefore**
thermometer
thermonu-
  clear
thermostat
thesaurus
these
thesis
they're**
thick-
  skinned
thief
thieves
thimble
thinkpad
thin-skinned
thirsty
thirteen
thirty

thong**
thorax
thorough
thorough-
  fare
though
thought
thoughtful
thousand
thrash**
thread
threat
thresh**
threshold
threw**
thrifty
thrilling
thriving
throat
throe**
thrombosis
throne**
through**
throw**
thrown**
thug
thumb
thumbtack
thunder
thunder-
  storm
Thursday
thwart
thyme**
thymus
thyroid
tiara
Tibet
tibia
tic**
tick**
tickle
tide**
tidings
tied**
tie-in
tier**
tiff

tight
tightfisted
tightrope
till
timber**
timbre**
time**
timetable
timid
timing
timorous
timpani
tincture
tine**
tingle
tinnitus
tinny**
tinsel
tint**
tiny**
tip-off
tirade
tissue
titan
tithe
titillate
title
titular
to**
toady
tobacco
toboggan
tocsin**
today
toddler
toe**
toehold
toga
together
toggle key
toil**
toile**
toiled**
toilet**
toilette**
token
tokenism
told**

210

tole**
tolerant
toll**
tolled**
tomato
tomb**
tomboy
tombstone
tome**
tomography
tomorrow
tong**
Tong**
tongue**
tonic
tonight
tonnage
tonsil
tonsillec-
tomy
too**
tooth
toothpaste
toothpick
topee**
topic
topical**
topogra-
phy**
Torah
toreador
torment
tornado
torpedo
torpor
torque
torrent
torrid
torso
tortious**
tortuous**
torture
torturous**
tot**
totaling
totalitarian
tote**
totem

touchdown
touché
tough
toupee**
tour**
tourist
tourniquet
tow**
tower**
toxic
toxin**
tracer
trachea
track**
trackball
tract**
traction
trade-in
trademark
trade name
tradition
traffic
tragedy
trail**
train
traitor
trajectory
tranquilizer
transaction
transcend
transcript
transcription
transfer
transference
transfusion
transient
transistor
transit
transition
translate
translator
transmit
transparent
transplant
transport
transposi-
tion
transsexual

transvestite
trauma
traumatic
travail**
travel**
travesty
tray**
treacherous
treachery
treason
treasure
treasurer
treasury
treaties**
treatise**
treaty
trek
trekkie
tremendous
tremor
trespass
trey**
triad
triage
trial**
triangle
tribe
tributary
triceps
tricycle
tried
tries
trigger
trilogy
trim
trimester
trio
triplicate
triumph
trivial
troll
troop**
tropical**
trouble
troupe**
trousers
trousseau
truly

trumpet
trustee**
trusty**
truthfully
tryst
tsetse
tuba**
tubal
tuber**
tuberculosis
Tuesday
tuition
tulip
tumescence
tummler
tummy
tumor
tumult
tunnel
turban**
turbine**
turbojet
turf
turkey
turmoil
turn**
turnaround
turncoat
turndown
turnip
turnover
turnpike
turntable
turpentine
turpitude
turquoise
tush
tutti frutti
tutu
tweak
tweezer
twelfth
twilight
twitch
two**
tycoon
tying
tympani

211

type	uncomfort-	unexception-	university
typewriter	able	able**	Unix**
typhoid	uncommon	unexcep-	unkempt
typhus	uncondi-	tional**	unknowable
typical	tional	unfair	unknown
typist	unconscious	unfavorable	unlawful
typogra-	uncontrolla-	unfinished	unlicensed
phy**	ble	unfit	unlike**
tyrannical	unconven-	unfold**	unlikely**
tyranny	tional	unforgetta-	unload
tyrant	uncouth	ble	unmistak-
	unctuous	unfortunate	able
	undeniable	unfriendly	unnamed
U	underdog	unfurl	unnatural
ubiquitous	undergo	ungainly	unnecessary
udder**	undergrad	ungird**	unobtrusive
ufology	undergradu-	ungirt**	unoccupied
Ukraine	ate	ungodly	unorganized
ukulele	under-	ungrateful	unparalleled
ulcer	ground	unguarded	unpleasant
ulterior	under-	unhealthy	unpopular
ultimate**	handed	unholy	unprece-
ultimatum**	underlay**	unicorn	dented
ultrasound	underlie**	uniform	unpreju-
ultraviolet	underline**	unify	diced
umbilical	under-	unilateral	unprincipled
umbrage	privileged	unimpeach-	unread**
umbrella	understand	able	unready**
umpire**	undertaker	uninhibited	unreal**
unable**	underwear	unintelli-	unreel**
unaccept-	underworld	gent**	unroll**
able	underwriter	unintelligi-	unruly
unaccus-	undesirable	ble**	unscrupu-
tomed	undo**	union**	lous
unadul-	undoubtedly	unique**	unsex**
terated	undress	unisex**	untidy**
un-	undue**	unison	untied**
American	unduly	unit	until
unanimous	undying	Unitarian**	untitled**
unappealing	unearned	unitary**	unveil
unattached	unearth	United Na-	unwanted**
unavoidable	uneasy	tions	unwonted**
unaware**	unemployed	United	unwrap**
unawares**	unequal**	States	upgrade
unbelievable	unequaled**	unity	upped**
uncertain	unequivocal	universal**	uppers
uncle	unerring	universally	uppity
unclouded		universe**	upright

uproar
uproot
upticks
uptight
uranium
urb
urban**
urbane**
urbs
urchin
urea
urge
urgency
urinal
urinalysis
urine
urn**
urologist
usable
usage
used to
useful
Usenet
user-friendly
using
usually
usurious**
usury
uterus
utility
utopia
utter**
u-turn
uxorious**

V

vacancy
vacant
vacation**
vaccination
vaccine
vacillate
vacuous
vacuum
vagina
vaginitis
vague**
vain**

valance**
vale**
valedictory
valence**
valentine
valet**
valid
validate
Valium
valley**
valor**
valuable**
valve
vampire
van**
vandal
vane**
vanguard
vanilla
vanish
vanity
vanquish
vantage**
vapid
vapor
variable
variance**
variants**
varicose
variety
various
varnish
vary**
vase
vasectomy
vaseline
vassal**
Vatican
vaudeville
VD
veal**
vector**
veer
vegetable
vegetarian
veggie
vegie
vehement

vehicle
veil**
vein**
velcro
vellum
velocity
velour**
velvet
venal**
vendor
veneer
venerable**
veneration
venereal**
venom
venomous
venous
ventilate
ventilation
ventricle
ventriloquist
venture
venue
veracious**
veracity**
verb
verbal
verbally
verdict
verifiable
verification
verify**
verité**
verity**
vermin
Vermont
vermouth
vernacular
Versailles
versatile
verse
verses**
versify**
version
versus**

vertebra**
vertebral
vertebrate**
vertical
vertigo
very**
vessel**
vest
vested
vestibule
vestige
veterans
veterinary
veto
vetoes
vex
viable
viaduct
vial**
vibrant**
vibrate**
vibrato**
vibrator**
vicar
vicarious
vice**
vicinity
vicious
victim
victor**
victory
victuals
video
videocas-
sette
vie
Vienna
Viet Nam
view
viewfinder
viewpoint
vigil
vigilance
vigilant**
vigilante**
vignette
vigor
vigorous

vile**	vitiate	waiver**	weak**
vilify	viva	waken	weal**
villa**	vivid	wallet	wealth
village	vixen	wallop	weapon
villain	viz.**	walnut	wear**
vindicate**	vizier**	waltz	weary**
vindictive**	vocable**	wan**	weather
vinegar	vocabulary	wander**	web
vintage**	vocal**	wane	wed**
vintner	vocation**	wannabee	we'd**
vinyl	vociferous	wanton**	wedding
viol**	vodka	war**	Wednesday
viola**	vogue**	warble	wee**
violate**	voice	ward**	weed**
violation**	voice mail	warden	week**
violent**	voilà**	ware**	weigh**
violet**	volatile	warehouse	weighed**
violin	Volga**	warm-	weight**
violinist	volition**	blooded	weightism
viper	voluble**	warm-	weird
viral**	volume	hearted	welch**
virgin	voluntary	warning	welcome
virile**	voluptuous	warp	welfare
virility	vomit	warrant	we'll**
virtual**	voodoo	warranty	well-heeled
virtual real-	voracious**	warred**	well-known
ity	voracity**	warrior	Welsh**
virtue**	voucher	wart	welsh rabbit
virtuoso**	vowel	wary**	welter
virtuous**	voyageur	WASP	wen**
virulence	voyeur	wassail	were**
virulent	vulgar**	wastage	we're**
virus	vulnerable**	waste**	western
visa**	vulture	wasteful	wet**
visage	vulva	watch	wetware
viscera	vying	watchdog	whacks**
viscid		watermelon	whale**
viscous		waterproof	whaler
vise**	**W**	WATS**	what
visible	wade**	watts**	whatever
vision	wafer	wave**	what's**
visionary	wage	waver**	wheel**
visor**	wagon	wax**	when**
vista	wail**	way**	whence**
visual	waist**	waylaid	where**
vital	waistline	waylay	whereof
vitally	wait**	wayside	whet**
vitamin	waive**	we**	whether**

whey** \
which** \
Whig** \
while** \
whiled** \
whine** \
whiplash \
whipper-
snapper \
whippoor-
will \
whir** \
whirl** \
whisk
broom \
whiskey \
whisper \
whistle \
whistle-
blower \
whit** \
white \
white collar \
whitewash \
whither** \
whittle \
whiz kid \
who \
whole** \
whole-
hearted \
wholesale \
wholesome \
wholly** \
whoop** \
whore** \
who're** \
whores** \
whorey** \
who's** \
whose** \
wicked \
widget \
widow \
wield** \
wiener \
wig** \
wiggle room

wild** \
wilderness \
wile** \
willful \
wince** \
windfall \
windjammer \
windows \
windshear \
windshield \
wine** \
wintry \
wire \
wiretap \
Wisconsin \
wisdom \
wisteria \
wistful \
wit** \
witch** \
withdraw \
wither** \
withhold \
witness \
wives \
wizard \
wolves \
womanizer \
womb \
women \
won** \
wonder** \
wondrous \
wont** \
won't** \
wonton** \
wood** \
woolly \
word** \
wore** \
workable \
workers'
compensa-
tion \
workfare \
workforce \
workload \
workoholic

work station \
workup \
world \
World Wide
Web \
worm \
worry \
worse \
worship \
worst** \
worsted \
worth \
would** \
wound \
wraith \
wrangle \
wrangler \
wrap** \
wrapped** \
wrath \
wreak** \
wreath \
wreck** \
wrest** \
wrestle \
wretch** \
wriggle \
wright** \
wring** \
wrinkle \
wrist \
writ \
write** \
write-in \
write-off \
write-protect \
writer \
writhe \
writing \
written \
wrong \
wrote** \
wroth \
wrought \
wrung** \
wry** \
wurst** \
WYSIWYG

X \
Xavier \
xenophobia \
xerography \
Xmas \
x-ray \
xylophone

Y \
yacht \
yahoo \
yak \
y'all** \
yang** \
yank** \
Yankee** \
yanqui** \
yawl** \
yaws** \
ye** \
yea** \
yearn \
yearned \
yeast \
yellow \
yen** \
yeoman \
yeshiva \
yesterday \
yew** \
Yiddish \
yield \
yin** \
yodel \
yoga** \
yogi** \
yogurt \
yoghurt \
yokel \
yoke** \
yolk** \
Yom Kip-
pur \
yonder \
yore**

you**	yucca	zenith	zing**
you all	Yule**	zenology	Zionist
you'll**	yuppy	zephyr	zip code
young		zero	zither
youngster		zero-coupon	zodiac
your**	**Z**	Zeus	zoftig
you're**	zaftig	zilch	zoning
yours**	zany	zillion	zoology
yourself	zapping	zinc**	zoom
youth	zeal	zine	zoster
yowl**	zealous**	'zine	zucchini